NATIVE AMERICAN MYTHS AND LEGENDS

NATIVE AMERICAN MYTHS AND LEGENDS

EDITORIAL CONSULTANT
COLIN F. TAYLOR Ph.D

SMITHMARK

This edition published in 1994 by SMITHMARK Publishers Inc., 16 East 32nd Street, New York, NY 10016.

SMITHMARK books are available for bulk purchase for sales promotion and premium use. For details write or call the manager of special sales, SMITHMARK Publishers Inc., 16 East 32nd Street, New York, NY 10016; (212) 532-6600.

Produced by Salamander Books Ltd
129-137 York Way
London N7 9LG
United Kingdom

ISBN 0-8317-6290-X

Printed in Italy

10 9 8 7 6 5 4

Library of Congress Cataloging-in-Publication Data

Native American myths and legends / editorial consultant, Colin F. Taylor.
   p.   cm.
  Includes bibliographical references p.   and index.
  ISBN 0-8317-6290-X : $15.98 (est.)
  1. Indian mythology – North America. 2. Indians of North America –
  Legends. 3. Indians of North America – Religion. I. Taylor, Colin F.
E98.R3N37 1994
299'.793 – dc20   94-8904
                                                    CIP

CREDITS
Project Editor: Christopher Westhorp
Designer: John Heritage
Map: Janos Marffy (© Salamander Books Ltd)
Filmset: SX Composing Ltd, England
Color reproduction: Scantrans PTE Ltd, Singapore

Page 1: A *Goomokwey* mask in alder and cedar, carved in the Bella Coola style but painted in Kwakiutl manner. The eagle figure is clearly Kwakiutl, as are the projections which probably represent starfish.

Page 2: Transferring the Medicine Shield by Howard Terpning. This wonderful and dramatic painting reconstructs a Blackfeet ritual. The shield in question is a medicine object and symbol of protection being sold to another. The buyer is painted in a ferocious manner, while the seller is passing the shield through the smoke four times and using it to ward off imaginary attacks. Having demonstrated their power and the shield's strength the exchange can be made and the energy of the tribe enhanced.

Page 5: Raven stealing the Moon by Robert Davidson, Haida, British Columbia. The traditional home of the Haida people is the Queen Charlotte Islands where fish and shellfish comprise the main diet. The Haida consider that animals possess souls and regard them as special types of people with particular abilities and intelligence. At the center of many Haida myths is Raven, considered to be a lecherous and gluttonous trickster-performer not to be trusted. The painting shows Raven stealing the Moon and bringing darkness to the Earth.

CONTRIBUTING AUTHORS

Colin Taylor Ph.D (Introduction, The Plains, and Editorial Consultant) is the author of many papers and a number of books on Native American subjects, including Smithmark's highly successful *The Native Americans*. He is currently preparing a definitive volume on the Plains Indians.

Gary Carden (The Southeast) is a writer, storyteller, and folklorist from Sylva, North Carolina. Praised as an entrancer of his audiences, he is steeped in the Native American and folk history of his region and has received The Economic Development Office's Peacepipe Award for outstanding contribution to grant writing for Native Americans.

Dr. Natalie Tobert (The Southwest) is Assistant Keeper of Ethnography at the Horniman Museum in London, curator of the American Indian collections. She received her doctorate in ethno-archaeology, was a contributor to Smithmark's highly successful *The Native Americans*, and has had several articles published on craft technology and architecture.

Fiona Pitt (The Southwest) is a research assistant at the Horniman Museum, having formerly been Senior Archaeologist at the Museum of London. She studied archaeology and has written support materials for exhibitions and prepared a number of handbooks on using the various collections.

Dr. Mick Gidley (Plateau and Basin) is a Reader in American Studies at the University of Exeter. His books include *With One Sky Above Us*; *Kopet*, on Chief Joseph; *Representing Others: White Views of Indigenous Peoples*; and a forthcoming selection from and study of the work of Edward S. Curtis.

Ruth M. Gidley (Plateau and Basin) is a graduate in English and American Studies.

Craig D. Bates (California) is Curator of Ethnography at Yosemite National Park in California. He has worked with California's Native Americans over many years and has published numerous books about their culture and beliefs.

Carol Sheehan (The Northwest Coast) has a degree in anthropology from the University of British Columbia and a doctorate in the same from the University of Toronto. She is now a freelance writer and consultant, having worked until recently as a lecturer at the University of Calgary in Alberta, and having previously been the Assistant Curator of Ethnology at the Glenbow Museum. She is the author of *Pipes That Won't Smoke; Coals That Won't Burn*, has contributed to a number of other books, and written many articles and papers on ethnographic subjects.

Marion Wood (The Subarctic and The Arctic) has written a number of books on Native American subjects, including *Ancient America: Cultural Atlas for Young People* and *Spirits, Heroes and Hunters in North American Indian Mythology*.

Cath Oberholtzer (The Northeast) is based in Ontario where she teaches university courses in anthropology as well as native art and architecture of the Americas. Her specific interest is the Cree of the eastern Subarctic, with whom she has done fieldwork, as well as the more general one of native cultures in the Northeast and Subarctic regions.

CONTENTS

INTRODUCTION

IN COMMON WITH MYTHOLOGY throughout the world, North American Indian myths are of considerable interest since they not only indicate the literary perception of the group, often embodying a fantastic story of things and personages, but also give insights into the way human thought interprets experience, be it customs, art, or natural phenomena. The complex tales which purport to explain such things as earthquakes, meteors, the aurora borealis, and even why the chipmunk has stripes on its back or the otter has a flat nose, require the ingredients of impossible events or attributes which common sense must clearly reject and thus the myth emerges.

These stories were often told during the long winter nights, when people were gathered around the fire; old people – particularly those who were recognized as effective raconteurs – being invited to narrate the tales. Audience participation was desired. Typical was that described for the Crow Indians where the listeners were expected to answer 'yes' after every sentence or two. When no one replied it 'was a sign that all had fallen asleep and the story-teller broke off his narrative, possibly to resume it the following night.'[1]

The fundamental nature of North American Indian mythology is intertwined with religion and can be separated into two major groups – that which concerns the tribe or clan, and that which relates to the individual. However, most important was the belief in the existence of a higher power, far superior to the natural qualities of Man – and it had mysterious potency. The power was variously referred to as *Wakanda* (Siouans), *Manitou* (Algonquians), *Orenda* (Iroquoians), *Sulia* (Salishans), and *Naualak* and *Tamanoas* by the Kwakiutl and Chinook respectively of the Northwest Coast. This power could be invoked and gained by participants in the tribal ceremonials which, not infrequently, acted out mythical events. Alternatively, an individual might attempt to address the sacred being during a dream or vision and hence acquire some of its magical power.

If we consider the mythology of the North American Indian in the broadest outlines, there emerge some distinctive characteristics from most of the cultural areas. For the Arctic and Subarctic, there appears to be considerable emphasis on hero-tales associated with humans and a limited number of traditions which attempt to account for the origin and development of animals, and even when these do occur there is a strong link to the human setting, which integrates what would otherwise be disparate tales. In contrast, the Northwest Coast people put great emphasis on the characteristics and peculiarities of many different animals, and their transformer myths attempt to account for the

While cloth turbans were a costume feature of the Southeastern tribes once fabric was available from traders, the more exotic materials present in this Creek or Seminole turban (below, made of flamingo and eagle feathers) suggest a more ancient style, and one which might be evoking associations with the animal and spiritual world.

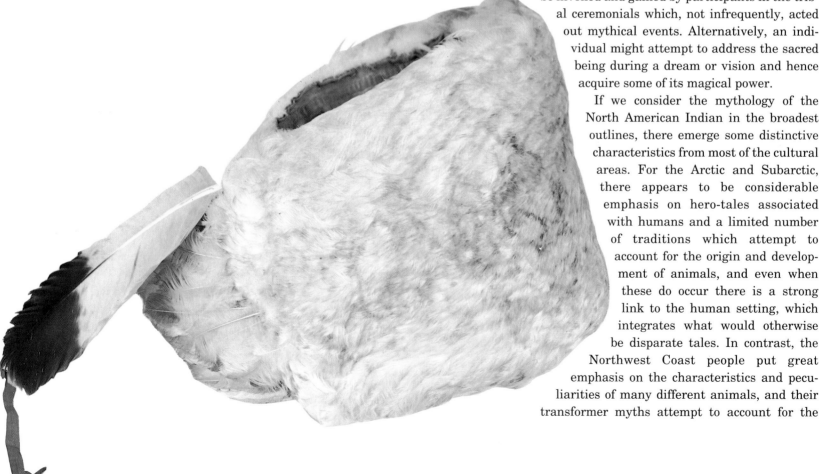

origin of much of their artwork; their mythology thus emerges as composed of innumerable diverse elements, generally disconnected from one another.

Animal tales also abound in the Plateau and Basin area, and in this respect there is common ground with the Northwest Coast as well as the Plains region – although those which account for the conditions of the world, often with outlandish contradictions, seem less emphasized both on the Plains and Northwest Coast. An interesting feature in the southern Californian cultural area, is the repetition of myths relating to creation by man's will-power, which, although found elsewhere, is far less emphasized in other regions. There are frequent references to the human spirit, to the relation of life and death, to the soul, and also to the emergence of a brother and sister from an original void.[2]

A definite tendency toward systematization of mythology within the framework of complex ritual and ceremonial is a characteristic of the Plains, Northeast, Southwest, and possibly, if we consider their prehistory, the Southeast also. Ceremonial which pivoted on the sacred mythology was paramount to these cultures and thus, in

This superbly detailed painting (above) of the Apache Mountain Spirit dancers brilliantly captures the drama of the ceremony which is such a feature of Apache culture. Note the shaman (back, center) who is supervising the proceedings.

Even the bravest warriors stood in awe of the mighty thunder powers. When Omens Turn Bad by Frank McCarthy captures the moment when a Comanche war chief turns back his raiding party after encountering the bad omen he had dreamt of.

this respect, mythology dictated a fundamental pattern of conduct which, on several counts, led to a degree of regimentation of the tribe, although there was some variation in emphasis. For example, in the Southwest the keynote of mythological concepts of the Pueblos was embedded in the explanation of the origin of societies and clans, while, in contrast, the Pawnee (Plains) inspiration for much of their ritual came from contemplation of the heavens.[3]

A very common theme which runs through all

North American mythological tales relating to genesis is the recognition of several regions or groups of worlds which are the habitat of the myth, with one in each of the four directions and in the above-, below-, and mid-world, which in some myths may then correspond to the seven primary colors. The world itself was regarded as a humanized being in both form and person, a living substance which bestowed life on all who fed on her. Thus, plants and trees, as well as animals and humans, received life substance from the

concept of continuous war between the Sky and Underwater powers. Thus, almost universally, Thunderbird was considered to be a bird of enormous size which produced thunder by the flapping of its wings and lightning by its flashing eyes. On the Northwest Coast, a Thunderbird was considered to be catching whales during a thunderstorm, perhaps using its wings as a bow to shoot arrows, the rebound after shooting making the thunder.[4] On the Plains, the thunderstorm signified a contest between the Thunderbird and a huge underwater monster – referred to as *Unktéhi* by the Sioux and greatly feared. Similar themes occur in western Great Lakes mythology; among some of the eastern Algonquian tribes and the Iroquois, however, the Thunderbird might be replaced by the Thunder People who were human in form and mind, and unfailing friends of mankind.

Perhaps the most frequently mentioned creature, particularly in the origin myths, is Coyote, who generally makes claim to the status of First Creator. Tension, however, exists between him and an original culture hero who in some areas was referred to as Old Man Above, in others as

Nimpkish Village in 1909 (above), one of the 30 or so autonomous groups that made up the Kwakiutl people. These carved posts for the houses came into common usage in the 1870s. The carvings represent crest figures and mythical beings associated with the owner's ancestors and clan. The eagle on top here is the paternal crest; below it is the maternal crest of a grizzly bear crushing a rival chief's skull.

earth and hence were like primal beings, bestowed with both volition and mind. Since the earth was the giver of life, it was regarded with affection and referred to as Mother, although under some circumstances she might be regarded as a cannibal and wicked as she could also take life and devour dead bodies.

The formation of the Earth from mud scooped up from the depths of a primal lake by a diving animal is a recurring theme found throughout the North American culture areas; so, too, is the

Our Father or Lone Man. Together, Coyote and Lone Man discover the world and prepare it for the people and animals that will ultimately populate it. Having achieved this, Lone Man becomes intent on destroying Coyote because of his unhealthy desires, boisterous evil, and unreliable ways – even though at times these are moderated by benevolence and foresight. In such struggles for supremacy, Lone Man may be assisted by another powerful spirit, such as the Conqueror in Maidu mythology (California) who has the power

to destroy evil beings and monsters but who himself is ultimately dangerous to mankind. In the ensuing struggles, Lone Man invariably emerges as the winner and Coyote concedes him to be the older and hence the more powerful of the two. Lone Man is then generally described as taking an altruistic stance toward Coyote who then, in subsequent myths, appears in many guises, often as a trickster-transformer, and is credited as one who was responsible for many cultural and natural conditions. Coyote firmly emerges as one whose behavior explains ill fortune and bad manners while at times he engages in acts that turn out to be to mankind's advantage; more frequently he is the trickster who imposes unfortunate hardships and causes death in what would otherwise be a perfect world. Thus, as a mythical figure, Coyote often becomes more important in mankind's everyday activities than Lone Man.

For convenience of analysis, the myths have been divided into six topics, repeated for each chapter. These topics or themes are Origin Myths; All-Powerful Spirits; Hero Creatures and Monsters; Holy Places, Sacred Sites; Revered Animals; and Rituals and Ceremonies. As we move from one region to another, it will become apparent that there is considerable variation in emphasis – holy places and sites appear less important in the Arctic and Subarctic regions when compared with The Plains, for example; and, in turn, while the people of the Plains cultural area put considerable emphasis on revered animals, they were relatively unimportant in the mythology of the Southwest.

What does emerge, however, is that, broadly speaking, the myths reflect the atmosphere of each cultural area; constant references to the sea or underwater spirits being characteristic of the Arctic while on the Plains the flavor is that of the warpath and buffalo hunt. What we may thus conclude is that, in common with the rest of mankind, American Indian mythology is an attempt to explain the world in which the people lived, and there was often room for bizarre and imaginative thought.

The mythology discussed in this volume embraces the nine major cultural areas of North America (above). The boundaries are, of course, fluid rather than rigid and the map thus serves to delineate them approximately. They are: Southeast (**1**), Southwest (**2**), Plains (**3**), Plateau and Basin (**4**), California (**5**), Northwest Coast (**6**), Subarctic (**7**), Arctic (**8**), and Northeast (**9**).

THE SOUTHEAST

> *'The Southeastern Indians are the victims of a
> virtual amnesia in our historical consciousness.
> And this amnesia has afflicted Southerners as much
> as it has people in other parts of the United States.'*
>
> CHARLES HUDSON, 1976[1]

THE CULTURE OF THE Southeastern Native American is like a great shattered bowl. Historians and anthropologists assemble the broken shards, knowing they will never be able to recreate the original, but sometimes their efforts produce discernable themes and patterns which provide a momentary insight into the diversity and harmony that once existed. Charles Hudson, author of *The Southeastern Tribes*, noted that our lack of knowledge about the region's original inhabitants is due largely to the fact that many of them were killed, their societies disrupted, and their cultures greatly changed before educated people thought them worth studying.[2]

There is evidence that this social and cultural breakdown was beginning even before De Soto's exploration of the region in 1540. De Soto found villages that had been abandoned, emptied by epidemics. The majority of the Southeastern tribes ceased to exist during the next 200 years. The wars and forced migrations of the 18th century obliterated hundreds of tribes, and others found themselves shuttled to and fro, often decimated to the point that they were forced to take refuge with a neighboring tribe. Such assimilations were completed with remarkable ease: Waxsaws and Cheraws joined the Cherokees, Choctaws mingled with Creeks, and Creeks with Seminoles. Historians noted that even though the tribes spoke different languages, the world view was essentially the same.

The mythical cosmology of America's Southeastern tribes is markedly consistent. Their myths describe a three-tiered world: the Upper, which contains deities and spirits; the Middle, which is the abode of Native Americans, along with most of the animals; and the Lower, which is inhabited by evil spirits and abnormal life forms. Mortals are thus trapped between the good and the bad, aspiring upward but frequently falling victim to the dark forces lying in wait.

All life forms are defined by their proximity to the opposing worlds. Birds are powerful forces of good, while snakes and turtles live close to the Lower World. In an earlier time, gigantic hawks and eagles lived in the Middle World with mankind, and plants and animals had the power of speech; however, when mankind became deceitful, the great birds returned to the Upper World. Finding themselves victims of mankind's greed and violence, the animals withdrew and refused to communicate. Thus, the plant and animal life that now lives on the Earth are poor imitations of the divine forms which once thrived.

To the tribes of the Southeast the Earth is a great island floating in a boundless sea. Four cords hanging from the great crystal sky vault (located between the Upper and Middle worlds) are attached to each of the cardinal directions. Their mythology states that 'no one remembers who suspended the island,' but many of the creation stories end on a fatalistic note. In time, the cords will weaken and fall, the island will sink, and the dark waters will bring death to all life.[3]

Brightly dressed with patchwork and ribbons, these Cow Creek Seminole women (left) are wearing native elaborations of the white fashions of the period (about 1917). More typically native in origin is the scroll-like beadwork design of a Yuchi woman's belt (right and far left), this particular example representing storm clouds breaking up. The Seminole were one of the so-called Five Civilized Tribes, with the Cherokee, Chickasaw, Choctaw, and Creek. At one time the Seminole were called Lower Creek, but those still residing in Florida today call themselves *Ikaniuksalgi*, or 'peninsula people.' The Cherokee are one of the largest of all Native American groups and the drum seen here (above left) is an example of one of their ceremonial water drums. It has several inches of water at the bottom to give the drum voice greater power.

'In the thinking of the Indians, however, the Master of Breath had given them the Earth not to enslave them but to free them to enjoy it. They were Adam, not Jacob.'

FLORETTE HENRI, 1986[4]

Before the time of Man, there were only two worlds: the Upper and the Lower. Eventually, the great birds, animals, and insects that lived in the Upper World came to feel that there was not enough room, and their dissatisfaction caused them to look for another home. Water Beetle offered to explore the Lower World which was a great ocean. Diving beneath the water, Water Beetle found soft mud on the bottom. Returning with the mud, Water Beetle began to build a great mound which became the island of the Middle World.[5] (To the Cherokee it was Water Beetle, to the Creek and Yuchi it was Crayfish.)

The animals of the Upper World refused to inhabit the island until the soft mud became dry.

Great Buzzard was sent to hasten the drying by flapping his wings over the island. Sometimes he flew so low, his great wings struck the soft mud, creating valleys and great mountain peaks which would one day become the home of the Cherokee.

When the animals descended to live on the Earth, the land was in darkness, so the Sun was brought from the Upper World to provide light. The animals had trouble determining the distance between the Sun and the land and only found the right position after seven attempts.[6] Each day, the great stone vault of the sky rises twice: once to allow the Sun to enter, and again at nightfall when the Sun departs.

The Coming of Fire

The nights, however, were cold and the Moon gave neither warmth nor light. The animals appealed to their relatives in the Upper World for help and fire came in a great flash of lightning. The animals saw it strike a hollow sycamore tree on an island far out in the great water. Who should go and bring back the fire? The animals conferred and Raven offered to go. The smoke and heat blackened his feathers, but he returned without the fire; so it was too with the Screech Owl, the Hooting Owl, the Black Racer, and the Black Snake. Each was marked by the fire, but

The spider was particularly important in Southeastern cultures. These gorgets (below) are from the Dallas Phase of the Mississippian period (c.1450). Some 3-4in (7.5-10cm) in diameter, they refer to the myth of the water spider which first brought fire to mankind.

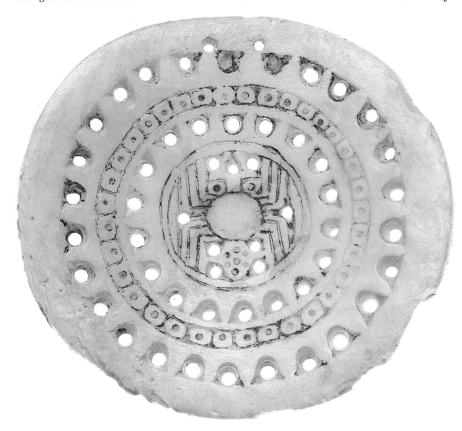

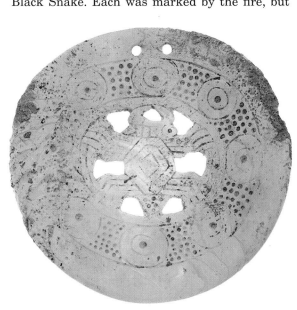

they failed to grasp a burning ember. Then, the little Water Spider offered to go, and she succeeded where the others had failed, for she wove a tusti bowl and placed it on her back to carry the fire.[7] Variations of this Cherokee story exist throughout the Southeast with a different assortment of animals attempting to retrieve the fire.

Creation of Mankind

Myths dealing with the creation of the human race are rare in Southeastern mythology. Some stories simply conclude that no one knows where they (people) came from. However, a fragmented Cherokee myth says that a being which they called Someone Powerful created the first man and woman from the mud of the Lower World. Hence, humanity is a mixture of Darkness (Evil) and Divine Spirit (Good). When the first man and woman awoke, Someone Powerful told them to walk around the island on which they lived. With the completion of each circuit, the couple discovered a new gift: corn, beans, a dwelling, etc. At first, the acquisition of food was effortless and life was good. Then Someone Powerful told the man to strike the woman with a fish. He did so, and seven days later she gave birth. Every seven days, another child was born which became an adult in seven days. In a short time, this world

(Middle World) became crowded, so Someone Powerful decided that the woman would bear one child each year, and that becoming an adult would take much longer. It has been so ever since then.[8]

The creation myths of the Creek and Choctaw, however, seem to have been influenced by the mythology of western tribes. In both cultures, the human race emerges from a great hole in the ground. Their flesh is pale and damp and they bask in the sunlight until their skin darkens. Then they begin migrating eastward in separate groups, thus accounting for the different tribes. The Cherokees, according to this, become lost and wander to the north; the Creeks and Chickasaws travel to the east and south; only the Choctaws remain near their origin.

A variant notes that the tribes migrated because 'the Earth began to swallow them.' However, their migration is fruitless since the Earth develops arms that reach for hundreds of miles. The Choctaws are safe because they cluster about the devouring giant's feet where he cannot reach. It is noteworthy, however, that in all creation myths, the Native American is created from the damp mud of the Lower World and warmed by the divine Sun, thus becoming a composite of the two opposing worlds.[9]

The Flood

Like all preliterate culture throughout the world, the Southeast has numerous deluge stories. In the majority, a man and his wife become aware of the approaching flood due to some form of supernatural warning. Variations include an avenging spirit from the Upper World (Caddo), a prophetic frog repaying a kindness done him by a human (Alabama), and a speaking dog (Cherokee). Usually, the man and his wife are told to build a raft, make a great earthen jar, or climb inside a huge hollow reed. As the waters subside, various birds are sent to find land (usually the woodpecker or dove) and the couple undertake the task of re-populating the earth, frequently with supernatural assistance.

This shell gorget (left) from Tennessee would have been worn suspended around the neck. The circle and cross motifs have several symbolic meanings: they represent both the world and the four cardinal directions, but the circle is also symbolic of the Sun – a principal deity – and the cross represents the sacred fire.

ALL-POWERFUL SPIRITS

The pipe or calumet was important to many tribal cultures. This Cherokee example (below) was collected by Lewis and Clark in 1804-06. It is decorated with a fan of golden eagle feathers dyed red and embellished with porcupine quills, woodpecker beaks, and tufts of red horsehair hanging down. The bowl is of carved catlinite stone and it is probable that the pipe was received from a more northerly tribe as a token of peace and to attest contracts and treaties which could not then be violated without incurring the wrath of the gods – for whom the creatures on this pipe were spiritual messengers.

'All these tribes (Southeastern) paid their religious devoir to Loak Ishto-hoola-aba, *"the great, beneficent, supreme, holy Spirit of Fire," who resides, they think, above the clouds, and on Earth among unpolluted people. He is with them the sole author of warmth, light, and of all animal and vegetable life.'*

JAMES ADAIR, 1775[10]

Although the world of the Southeastern tribes contains an awesome variety of supernatural beings, there is no doubt that those which appear with the greatest regularity are the Little People and the Immortals. The Cherokees call them the *Yunwi Tsunsdi* and the *Nunnehi*, and both supernatural beings appear in the myths of the Choctaws, Creeks, and Catawbas, although with different names.

The Little People

The Little People bear a marked resemblance to the Irish Leprechauns, or 'wee folk.' They are

mischievous, given to pranks, and delight in the company of children. However, when angered they can be most terrifying and deadly. Like the Cherokees, the Catawbas have numerous stories about children stolen by the 'little wild people,' and all Southeastern cultures have stories that attribute magical powers to them. According to the Cherokees, they are about two-and-a-half feet tall and have long hair. Although usually described as unclothed, some stories describe their 'white clothing.' One Cherokee myth describes an annual festival of little folk who meet in the spring on a great flat mountain-top, and their white clothing makes the mountain appear to be covered with snow.[11]

Invariably, to see them is an omen of approaching death. A number of Southeastern myths tell of Cherokees who have become lost in a mountainous wilderness; discovered by the Little People, they are escorted to villages where they have a number of magical encounters. Snakes become belts, and necklaces and terrapins are transformed into seats. Food appears magically, but if the Cherokees attempt to carry it home it turns to dust and ashes. Frequently, after leading their lost visitors within sight of their home, the Little People caution them not to tell where they have been until three weeks have elapsed. Often, the lost Cherokee ignores the warning and dies shortly afterward.

The Little People sometimes train children to be medicine men. The Choctaws call the Little People *Kwanoka'sha* and relate a story in which a stolen child (usually a sickly one) is conducted to a cave in which three spirits test the child's worthiness to be a healer. The child is offered a choice of three things: a knife, poisonous herbs, and 'herbs of good medicine.' Selection of the knife indicates a cruel nature; if the poisonous herbs are selected, the child lacks discernment and cannot cure others; if the good herbs are selected, the child is trained for three days and told never to repeat what has been learned and not to use the new-found healing powers until attaining adulthood.

The Immortals

Although occurring in many Southeastern cultures, the Immortals are most fully described by the Cherokees. Usually invisible, they disregard natural law and live where they wish: beneath the waters of lakes, in the sky, or beneath the earth. A mound called Nikwasi near Franklin, North Carolina, was allegedly built over one of their towns.[12] 'Clear smoke' from their townhouse rises from a rock fissure in nearby Tuckaseigee, and a number of regional stories deal with the curative powers of the warm vapor. The Cherokees describe these *Nunnehi* as gourd-headed, hairless, and tall. Since they love to dance, the *Nunnehi* frequently disguise themselves as women and attend Cherokee festivals. There are a number of comical stories dealing with men who become enamored of the disguised *Nunnehi* and attempt to follow them home. The *Nunnehi* walk into a lake or a rock cliff leaving their bewildered suitor behind.

The *Nunnehi* are benevolent spirits who are saddened by the suffering incurred by the mortal Cherokees and, occasionally, they offer assistance. A well-known story relates how the *Nunnehi* once attempted to move the Cherokees to their own world where they would never sicken or grow old. (A variation of this myth warns the Cherokees about the coming of the white man and urges them to join the *Nunnehi* in a world beyond the white man's reach.) These stories relate how the *Nunnehi* came to all the Cherokee villages and told the inhabitants to fast for seven days and seven nights. The *Nunnehi* returned on the seventh night and led all those who had fasted to a nearby mountain (now called Pilot Knob) where the villagers passed through the solid rock and into the realm of the *Nunnehi*.[13] Since the majority of the Cherokees had not kept faith with the *Nunnehi* and had not completed the fast, they remained behind. Since that time, the Cherokees have waited in vain for the *Nunnehi* to return.

The forked eye design on this shell mask (above, left) is believed to be derived from the distinctive eye markings of raptorial birds. The zig-zag lines are probably lightning symbols which refer to the Thunderbird and the Thunder Beings. Bird-power is also a feature of the other gorget (right) from the same area which shows a human figure wearing a feather cape and an antler headdress, and having talons on his hands. Such imagery may relate to the *Tlanuwa*, or Great Hawk.

'They all believe that this world is round, and that there are two spirits; the one good, the other bad: the good one they reckon to be the Author and Maker of every thing, and say that it is he that gives them the Fruits of the Earth, and has taught them to hunt, fish, and be wise enough to overpower the Beasts of the Wilderness.'

JOHN LARSON, 1700[14]

To the Southeastern Indian, his world (Middle World) was often the battleground for the endless war between the divinities above and the evil forces beneath the earth. Symbolically, this war was depicted by the hawk and the serpent. Although mortals felt a kinship with creatures of the Upper World, they frequently found themselves to be the victims of both hawks and serpents. The Alabama, Natchez, and Cherokee tell stories of the *Tlanuwa*, or Great Hawk; and the Cherokee, Creek, and Coasati of the *Uktena*, or Great Serpent.

The Great Hawk

The *Tlanuwa* built nests on mountain peaks near villages and great rivers. The gigantic birds preyed on children, carrying them back to feed their young. A popular story tells of a young man who was carried to the nest of the Great Hawk, but managed to escape by riding one of the half-grown chicks into a tree-top.

A variant on this particular theme has a grandmother who rescues her grandchild from the nest and hurls the young birds into the river where they are consumed by the water serpent, the *Uktena*. (In one variant she magically 'creates' the serpent by dropping a rope into the river.) The returning parents find the nest empty and see the *Uktena* consuming their young. Enraged, both birds attack the serpent, dragging it from the water, and while one Great Hawk holds it aloft its mate slashes the serpent into pieces. (This story is used to explain how a series of unusual rock formations in the Tennessee River came into being. They were created by pieces of the *Uktena* falling into the river.)

These two shells (right), some 6in (15cm) in diameter, illustrate a curled rattlesnake, a creature that is associated with the Lower World and continuously at war with land animals and birds. It is a monster composite form of the rattlesnake – the *Uktena* – which figures prominently in Cherokee myths.

Having lost their brood, the birds ascended to the Upper World and never returned.

The Great Serpent

The *Uktena* permeates Southeastern mythology. There are minor variations in his appearance: in Cherokee mythology he is horned with a great flashing jewel in his head and seven bands of color around his neck; in some versions the serpent has 'antlers like a stag,' or is winged, making it possible for him to function in water, on land, or in the air. Among the Creek, Yuchi, and Hitchiti the serpent becomes a 'tie-snake' and preys on children and fishermen.

Strangely enough, the shaman who finally destroyed the *Uktena* was not a Cherokee but a Shawano – a hated enemy of the Cherokees. In exchange for his life, *Aganunitsi* (Grandhog's Mother) promised the Cherokees that he would kill the serpent and bring the magic crystal embedded in its skull back to the Cherokees where it would heal the sick, make the rivers teem with fish, and cause the corn to grow. The shaman was as good as his word. Shooting an arrow through the seventh band of color encircling the *Uktena's* head, *Aganunitsi* pierced the serpent's heart. Then, he called all the birds in the world to come and feed on the snake's flesh for seven days. Finding the magic stone among the *Uktena's* bones, he returned to the Cherokee village. As promised, the 'flashing crystal' brought prosperity to the Cherokees, but the shaman was less fortunate. Because a drop of the serpent's blood struck him, a red-eyed snake grew from his head. He became a slave to it and the magic stone, killing to feed them.

The extensive number of stories about the Great Serpent, and the frequent references by early travelers in the Southeast to the widespread belief in his existence, suggest that the *Uktena* had acquired something akin to totem status. He is incised on conch shells, pots, and gorgets. Similar carvings among Florida tribes depict a serpent with a cougar's head, and the corresponding myths about the Great Water Cougar are variations of the *Uktena* myths. When Sir Alexander Cumming visited the Southeast in 1730, he encountered frequent references to the 'healing crystal' that had once been in the *Uktena's* head and talked to medicine men who claimed to possess it. Medicine men among the Seminole, Creek, Choctaw, and Cherokee tribes *still* speak of the healing crystal which can

prophecy, cure disease, and end barrenness in women. Throughout the Southeast there is considerable mystery associated with the 'healing crystal.' Tribal shamans believe that the stone will lose its power if non-Indians know where it is located. In some traditions, the crystal must be fed fresh blood every seventh day or it becomes an avenging spirit, searching in the night for the medicine man who has neglected to feed it.

A mask representing the 'Angry' Indian in the midwinter Booger Dance. In this Cherokee dance some subjects are Europeans, identified as a people who brought sickness and oppression. The dance was to drive their evil away.

'Is there a human being who does not revere his homeland, even though he may not return? . . . In the language of my people . . . there is a word for land: Eloheh. *This same word also means history, culture, and religion. We cannot separate our place on Earth from our lives on the earth nor from our vision nor our meaning as a people . . .'*

JIMMIE DURHAM (CHEROKEE)[15]

For the tribes of the Southeast, the homes of deities and mythical creatures were numerous and familiar. Each deep pool, rounded hill, and rocky mountain crest carried a story. Deeply incised scars on boulders in a river bore mute witness to a mythical battle, and warm air rising from a fissure in the earth denoted the presence of a *Nunnehi* town beneath the ground. The mountains, valleys, and streams of eastern Tennessee, northern Georgia, and western North Carolina are teeming with dozens of significant places.

A characteristic of the early Southeastern Indians was the construction of gigantic mounds for ritual or burials, undoubtedly an influence from Central and South America due to the migrations which took place from there more than 2,000 years ago and which enriched the Archaic cultures of the Southeast. As a result, man-made or natural formations – such as Pilot Knob, Tennessee (right) – were of particular significance to the later historic tribes, and the Cherokee and Creek have many myths associated with them referring to powers who dwell at the sites and can assist in warfare and hunting.

The Nikwasi Mound

According to Cherokee tradition, the Nikwasi Mound near Franklin, North Carolina, is one of many sacred sites associated with the *Nunnehi* (Immortals). In ancient times, the Cherokee came here to ask the *Nunnehi* for assistance in warfare. If their prayers were answered, the *Nunnehi* would emerge from beneath the ground with magic weapons and join the Cherokee in battle. James Mooney, the noted authority on Cherokee culture and myth, recounted the story of such a battle. According to oral tradition, the Cherokees of Nikwasi were attacked by a superior force. When defeat seemed certain, a mighty force of *Nunnehi* streamed from the mound and became invisible as they rushed to the attack. The bows and tomahawks floated across the battlefield, and the terrified enemy force fled. However, the spears and arrows of the *Nunnehi* pursued them, swerving around rocks and trees. When the enemy force was reduced to six warriors, they fled to the head of the Tuckaseigee River, turned round, and in despair

pleaded for their lives. The Cherokees named the place *Dayulsunyi* (Where They Cried). The *Nunnehi* spared the six warriors and returned to vanish into the mound.

Because of the ancient traditions associated with the mound, the Cherokees frequently choose the site for important tribal meetings. Local legends recount stories of hunting parties who have camped near it only to be awakened in the night by the sounds of drumming and chanting.

Mounds and Effigies

The temple mounds near Cartersville, Georgia, are among the most impressive in the Southeast. Containing some of the finest examples of Southeastern art, the Etowah Mounds undoubtedly functioned as a ceremonial center. Gorgets, necklaces, and carved statuary recovered from this site contain representations of falcons, eagles, and snakes which suggest associations with Southeastern mythology.

Numerous sites along the Tuckaseigee River are associated with the *Uktena*, and each bears a name specifying its significance. A rock ledge was a sleeping place, and misshapen rocks still bear the scars of the *Uktena's* battle with the *Tlanuwa*. Cohutta Mountains, Georgia, was not only the place where the *Uktena* was finally killed, but is also the location of an ancient 855ft long (261m) rock wall which many historians feel is a replica of the mythical serpent. One of the most impressive serpent effigies is in southern Ohio. Built atop a steep bluff, this earthen structure represents the body of a snake which undulates for 737ft (225m). The body of the snake is about 20ft (6m) wide and 4-5ft (1.2-1.5m) in height with a coiled tail and a carefully detailed head.

Several rock bluffs along the Tennessee River are identified as nesting sites for the *Tlanuwa*, the most noteworthy being the one near Chattanooga, Tennessee. An effigy mound in Georgia (Rock Eagle) consists of rocks which have been piled in the shape of a great bird, perhaps an eagle.

Thunder Beings and Daktu

Whiteside Mountain in Jackson County, North Carolina, is associated with the Cherokee Thunder Gods and the monster Spearfinger, the witch who constructed a stone bridge on its summit which she traditionally crossed in order to prey on Cherokee villages.[16] Deep pools in the French Broad in North Carolina and Toco Creek, in Monroe County, Tennessee, are associated with the *Daktu*, the giant fish that used its tail to slap Cherokee hunters into the water where the fish swallowed them. There are variations of this story throughout the Southeast which involve a hero who cuts his way out of the *Daktu's* stomach with a mussel shell.

A family of Thunder Beings, similar to those that lived on Whiteside Mountain, occupied a home behind Tallulah Falls in Rabun County, Georgia, from where they produced terrifying sounds when fishermen came too near.

The Great Smoky Mountains of North Carolina are the home of the Cherokee, a tribe linguistically related to the Iroquois. The heavy vegetation of this area exudes an unusual amount of oil and water vapor which produces an almost perpetual smoke haze – hence the name. The area is replete with sacred sites, many of them associated with the Thunder Beings.

REVERED ANIMALS

'When the animals and plants were first made they were told to watch and keep awake for seven nights . . . on the seventh night, of all the animals only the owl, the panther, and one or two more were still awake. To these were given the power to see and to go about in the dark, and to make prey of the birds and animals which must sleep at night . . .'

JAMES MOONEY, 1900[17]

Birds were often associated with particular powers. In common with many tribes, the Cherokee considered Eagle to be a great and powerful spirit, and they held an Eagle Dance, in which carved masks (above) were worn to honor its strength and courage. Feathered capes or mantles were normally worn in such dances too. Owl was another respected figure, and has been carved in effigy on this ceramic bottle (right), together with an incised rattlesnake motif around its lower half. The figures can be related to a Seminole tale telling of a competition between the horned owl and rattlesnake as to whom could go longer without eating.

The fragments of oral tradition that have survived stress the ancient bond which exists between Man and animals. Tradition and custom indicated that the harmonious balance between the two could only be retained through mutual respect. Man must hunt and kill animals in order to survive; and animals accepted their inevitable death provided that their sacrifice was properly acknowledged. Many of the early settlers commented on the 'curious custom' they sometimes observed among the Southeastern Indians: hunters who had slain a deer or bear would kneel by the dying animal and ask its forgiveness. 'My family is hungry,' the Indian would say. 'I regret taking your life, but I must feed them.'

Bear, the Brother

The Cherokees and Creeks have an old story about a time in the dim past when their people were almost destroyed by a famine. After repeated treks into the forests, the elders called a great meeting in the townhouse. 'This may be the end of us,' said the elders, 'for we can find no food.' In the Cherokee version, the people gathered in their clan towns to discuss the famine. In recent times there are seven clans, but at this ancient time there were eight.[18] It was the members of the eighth clan that came to the elders with a solution: 'We have decided to die that our brothers may live,' they said. Then, they turned and walked into the forest. Several days later they returned, but they were almost unrecognizable.

Long, black hair grew all over their bodies – they had become bears. The starving villagers shot them and ate them.

One hunter, finding a family of bears in the woods, felt that he could not kill them. 'You are my brothers,' he said. 'It is not right that I should kill you.' The bears approached and spoke to him. 'It is meant that you should kill us,' they said. 'Our bodies will nourish you, and our souls will not die, but will return to the Upper World where they will be clothed in flesh again so that we may return and give you our flesh.' And so it was that hunters would kneel by the slain bear and say, 'Thank you, my brother.'

Among the Alabama, the sacrificial bear is white, and although there is no famine, the close bond between the hunter and the hunted is always stressed.

Success in hunting is due not to skill but to the power of the animal which grants the hunter the ability to find and kill the animal. If a hunter is unmindful of an animal's sacrifice and fails to show proper respect, the animal's spirit will send sickness and disease to him.

The Corn Maiden

In the plant world the close tie with mankind is even more pronounced. The Southeastern Indians believed that for every sickness or disease visited on them by the animal world, there was a corresponding plant or herb that would cure them. In addition, there are numerous stories about food plants that illustrate the same kinship. The following is an extract from the story of *Selu*, the Corn Maiden.

Selu, the first woman, gave birth to two sons. They were mischievous boys who were always hungry. 'We are hungry and there is nothing to eat,' said the boys. Finally, *Selu* told her sons that she would go in search of food. She left with a basket, and in a short time returned. The basket was filled with corn. She made a bread and baked it and the sons were delighted. Each day, she left the house and returned with corn. 'I won-der where she is getting that corn,' said her sons. 'Let us follow her and see.' And so, the two boys followed their mother, and when they saw her enter a little cabin they peered between the logs. Inside, they saw *Selu* place the basket on the ground. Then, she shook herself violently and the basket filled up with corn.

Returning home, the sons said nothing until she had baked the bread and they had eaten it. 'We saw you, mother,' they said. 'We know where you got the corn.' *Selu* smiled sadly. ' I am sorry that you spied on your mother,' she said. 'Now that you know the secret, I must die. After my death, you must drag my body through the field. And after I am gone, corn will grow in the field. From this time on, you must work for your bread.' Then, she lay down and passed away.

There are numerous variations of the *Selu* myth. The Cherokee and Creek sometimes amend it with a version that requires the sons to kill and dismember their mother, scattering bits of her body in the field. The sons are told that they should not be reluctant to kill her since her body will produce food for everyone. In the Choctaw version, corn is brought by a crow after the waters of the Great Flood have subsided.

Various myths from the Southeastern tribes relate the turkey to warfare, and the Shawnee, Creek and Yuchi war whoop was in imitation of a turkey's gobble. Magical properties were ascribed to the bird, its feathers being used by shamans at an early period for both fans and capes. The image of aggression is reflected in the confrontational stance taken by the turkeys on the gorget (above left). In contrast to that destructive image is that of the frog, alternating with human heads, on an early Mississippian Period ceramic jar (above right). This may be related to their belief system which referred to the phenomena of metamorphosis and emergence from water.

RITUALS AND CEREMONIES

Members of the elite class of Etowah, northern Georgia, are prepared for ceremony (below). Shell and pearl, feather capes, headdresses, and elaborate body painting complete the transformation of men into spiritual leaders evoking awe and respect.

'There was no disease in the world before the time of Stone Coat . . . Death originated through him.'

FRANK SPECK, 1951[19]

One of the most popular legends among the Southeastern tribes was the story of Stone Man. This monster is a classic example of the supernatural beings described by the historian, Frank G. Speck: '. . . Monsters clad in stone, bone, metal, or scales are very characteristic of the region. The monster is usually a cannibal, and is finally slain by persons or beings who have learned the secret of its only vulnerable spot.' In addition, the Stone Man legend gives an explanation as to where the ceremonies, dances, and rituals of the Southeast came from: they were gifts from Stone Man.

Stone Man

According to the Cherokee, Stone Man's body was covered with slabs of rock, but the Yamasee claim that he had made himself a great coat out of small pieces of flint after seeing a hunter kill a deer with a flint-tipped arrow. In his hand he carried a magic staff which enabled him to cross ravines. When he pitched his staff into the air, it became a stone bridge, and when he was safely on the other side the bridge vanished and the staff returned to his hand. Stone Man also used the staff to find human livers – his favorite food. Stone Man was a shape-changer, and would frequently travel into villages disguised as an old woman.

In an effort to defend themselves against Stone Man, the villagers asked their shaman to help them. The shaman told the villagers that Stone Man could be destroyed by 'moon-sick' (menstruating) women. When Stone Man was seen approaching the village, the elders sent seven such women to lay by the path. As Stone Man passed each successive woman, he grew weaker; and at the seventh, he fell to the earth, vomiting blood. The women rushed forward with seven basswood stakes and, pulling aside the stone covering, drove the stakes through his body.

When Stone Man did not die, the villagers built a great fire on top of him. Stone Man told his captors that he did not fear death since he knew his spirit would survive. Further, he said that he bore them no ill-will, and would teach them songs and rituals which would aid them in hunting,

planting, and war. Then, Stone Man began to sing and the villagers memorized his songs. He muttered magic incantations that would cure sickness and the villagers learned them all. Finally, when his voice no longer rose from the fire, the villagers raked the ashes and found a lump of red 'wadi' paint which they used afterward to paint their faces when they spoke the words and performed the ceremonies that Stone Man had given them.

Purification

Many ceremonies, songs, and ritual dances deal with purification and cleansing. Others celebrate the balance and harmony between mankind, animals, and plants. The complex tobacco rituals recorded by James Mooney concern cleansing, divination, and conjuring. The Green Corn Dance, one of 12 seasonal celebrations of thanksgiving, involved ritual cleansing of homes and public buildings, and extended to physical and mental purification.

Perhaps the most well-known Southeastern purification ritual is the Black Drink Ceremony. Among the Cherokee, Creek, and Choctaw, the drink was brewed from a species of holly and acted both as a stimulant and a diuretic. Consuming large amounts invariably produced vomiting and perspiration.[20]

Going to Water denotes a Southeastern purification ritual which was most commonly conducted prior to traditional ballgames. Performed in conjunction with the scratching of each player with a ritual comb with seven rattlesnake teeth, the ceremony was performed in sacred streams. Each player received over 300 scratches on his body, and then waded into a stream at a point that allowed him to face the east. As the player washed the blood from his body, the shaman asked that the player be granted strength, agility, and quick thinking.

Although no longer performed, historians generally consider such rituals to be remnants of a vast and complex system that existed prior to the coming of the white man. Then, the Southeastern tribes perceived everything in terms of balance.[21] The sole purpose of a ceremony was to restore or maintain balance. Everything was in opposition: Upper World and Lower World, north and south, man and woman. Charles Hudson states:

'The aboriginal Southeastern Indians would have understood traditional Chinese cosmology with its opposed Yang and Yin forces far better than they would have understood our own . . . philosophy that man should conquer nature by tampering with it in a thousand new and unheard ways.'[22]

A pre-ballgame dance (above) performed by the Eastern Cherokee men and women on the Qualla Reservation, western North Carolina, in 1888. As with the related Choctaw, the playing of the ballgame was both a contest of magic power as well as a contest of skill, and the events of the evening before the game included ritualized dancing by both men and women. In this scene, the line of women will move in a uniform step, chanting to the higher powers to solicit favor in deciding the game, and encouraging the players to exert every power to win.

THE SOUTHWEST

'A long time ago people used to say that if you remembered the stories that were passed down, they would make you strong. Even just a little portion of the stories would keep you and your children strong so you could face whatever is in the future.'

RAY YAZZIE (NAVAJO)[1]

MYTHS AND LEGENDS have played, and continue to play, an extremely important role in the lives of the Native Americans of the Southwest.[2] People say the myths have been, and still are, a reflection of their culture, presenting an enduring system of values on which they continue to base their lives. Some regard the myths as a complete source of learning, and although the myths have their pragmatic or serious side many are also a source of entertainment. Told by elders on long winter nights,[3] they can produce awe or wonder, amusement or terror. Though the stories are often for the benefit of children, any adults present listen too.

Today the myths are a basis of learning and are integral to Southwestern ceremonial life.[4] The practice of sandpainting, which the Navajo are famed for, has no ceremonial meaning unless accompanied by a recitation of the appropriate myth. Myths affect normal, everyday life too: when Morris Opler recorded Jicarilla Apache myths in the 1930s, he noted that bad behavior was explained by saying, 'He doesn't know any better. The poor fellow never had a grandfather to give him the stories.'[5] Children were taught obedience by telling them a tale which showed them the consequence of their bad behavior, and adults continue to regard such stories as a source of moral guidance. Similarly, many Hopi stories praise the work ethic, which is a central component of their culture, or they demonstrate the terrible consequences which can occur because of dissension and loss of respect for the elders of the tribe.

The oral tradition of myth-telling has meant that although legends have preserved their form across long periods of time, several versions of the same tale can exist. Cottie Burland, writing about Navajo myths in the 1960s, suggested that the storytellers may have felt inspired to make alterations where they felt clarification was needed. The cultural dynamic is also seen in the alteration of traditional tales to include modern influences and objects.[6]

The survival of so many myths and legends today is a testament to cultural resilience in the face of over 400 years of active onslaught. Indeed, the myths have played a major role in keeping the culture alive. Between the suppression of native religion and the punishment of its leaders by Spanish colonials, and the eventual extension of religious freedom to Native Americans in 1934, the myths were a link which provided a fundamental expression of native spiritual belief. Today they form the basis of inspiration for the economically vital production of arts and crafts which are sold to tourists.

In the Southwest the ceremonies and rituals performed today are the same or similar to those performed for centuries, and are done by the same cults, clans, and societies. Although the Roman Catholic Church is an important spiritual force, native beliefs still provide the vital basis of peoples' spirituality.

This weather-beaten face of the Southwest (left) belongs to *Nasjaja Hatali*, or Wind Doctor, a Navajo medicine man. Most Navajo ceremonies seek to cure illness and relieve pain, and this thoughtful-looking shaman would have been at the center of religious life. He is wearing the typical turban and German silver necklaces. Sometimes these solid necklaces were enhanced by the addition of turquoise, the colorful mineral used in much Southwestern jewelry. Also typical of the region was the Navajo blanket work (right and far left), its vibrant color tones reflecting those of the environment.

The *Soyalkatsina* (above left) is, by tradition, the first to launch the kachina season cycle at the winter solstice when it opens up the *kivas*. The kachina's arrival in the village is the invitation to other masked dancers to appear and commence the rituals.

27

ORIGIN MYTHS

In a Navajo religious ceremony the sandpainting is the 'altar' and is central to the ritual. The 16 examples of Black God in this sandpainting (below) emphasize the essential act of concentrating on both spiritual and Earthly duties to ensure bountiful harvests. Black God carries a string of small blue cakes, a fire stick, and a medicine pouch of 'star rocks' which he arranged in the night sky. This role is symbolized by the Pleiades constellation visible on Black God's cheek (below, right).

'My uncle has been telling that story about where we came from ever since I was a kid. Most of that story I can't tell you. My uncle said, "Keep it to yourself." '

LOUIS NUMKENA SR. (HOPI)[7]

The emergence myths are the most sacred and the most secret to many of the Southwestern peoples. A general emergence myth might be told to children, while the real story may only be revealed when a person is initiated into the *kiva*[8]. As a result, traditional religious leaders are opposed to the origin myths being recorded. The Tiwa people at Isleta pueblo have been brought up in the knowledge that telling the sacred stories to strangers shortens their lives. Among the Cochiti it is taboo to tell whites the stories even if they are accepted and valued as friends. This secrecy surrounding the origin myths is for several reasons. The Navajo regard their origin myths as having great power: the telling can heal the sick, initiate an aspirant to religious experience, and unite people with nature. The Hopi insist details of individual clan origins, as

revealed in the origin cycle of stories, are secret and are the property of the clan concerned. This secrecy is respected and regarded as a source of strength. In the past, confidences have been exposed in books by scholars and this led to even greater reluctance to divulge them.

Multiple Worlds

The origin myths are the longest and most complicated of the legends. Both the Navajo and the Hopi tell of the existence of several worlds. To the Hopi the present world is the fourth, while to the Navajo it is the fifth.[9] Their worlds are stacked like plates, floating one above the other, and the emergence involves climbing from one to the next. Similarly, in the Zuni creation myth the people travel through four underground cave-wombs before emerging to the Upper World of Knowledge and Seeing. The idea that the preceding worlds were too small or became flooded or contaminated by witchcraft is a common thread. The move to the next world is usually essential and often in the form of an escape. The Navajo stack four mountains on top of each other[10] and then plant a reed which they climb up to get from the third world, which had flooded, to the fourth.

The Creators

The worlds themselves are usually made by a Creator who wishes them into existence, or makes them using substances from their own body. In a Papago myth the Earthmaker, or

Earthdoctor, creates the world from sweat and dust rubbed from his skin. He and other creators also use this recipe for making humans. Among the Navajo *Estanatlehi,* or Changing Woman, creates people using corn dust and water mixed with skin from her breasts. In Pima legend the Magician, or Man Maker, decides to make humans of clay and builds an oven; however, Coyote interferes, first telling Man Maker that the people are ready prematurely (whites) and then persuading him to leave them in the oven too long (blacks). White people and black people are made and put overseas before Man Maker gets it right and creates the Pima.

Explanations for the existence of whites occur in other myths. In Navajo myth they are sent along with war and pestilence by *Atse Hastiin* and *Atse Asdzan*, or First Man and First Woman, who are jealous of Navajo prosperity. In the Yaqui creation myth, the *Surems*, little people who hate noise and violence, are told of the coming of the whites. Given a choice between going away and staying to face the future, some of the *Surems* go, but the ones who stay grow tall and strong and eventually become the Yaqui and fight off the whites when they arrive.

People who have been created invariably need to be taught how to do things. The Apache deity *Usen*, after creating the people, teaches them how to find herbs to make medicine when they become ill. *Montezuma*, creator of the Papago, teaches the people to hunt and to grow maize. The original creator of the world or the people often disappears and this led to them being named Vanishing Creators by Ruth Underhill.[11]

The most common reason for the destruction of past worlds and peoples is that they have been bad. In Navajo myth, First Man and First Woman send monsters to destroy people who anger them by claiming that happiness is their own creation. In Papago legend the first people quarrel with *Montezuma* who creates a new human race which destroys the first. An Apache tale tells how misbehaving people are destroyed by a flood, as does Pima legend too.

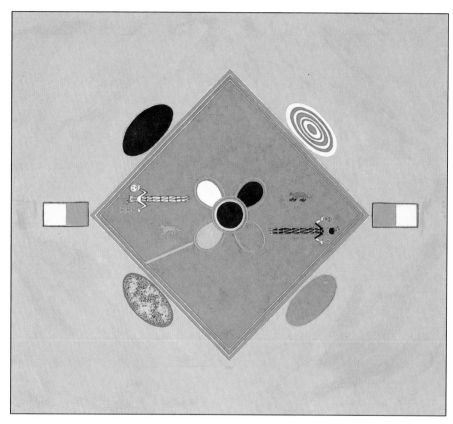

Blessingway is the most important Navajo ceremony. This sandpainting from it (above) shows a blue block representing water, a rainbow perimeter, and four sacred mountains. The black circle at the center is the place of emergence; the two women are the sisters White Shell Woman and Changing Woman. In the Wide Cornfield Painting (left) which is used to ensure a good crop, Changing Woman, who symbolizes nature and the mystery of birth, is again represented. She is surrounded by a rainbow.

'Masauwu *is very supreme in the universe, but he's an evil supreme. He's in the atmosphere. He's in the spirit. But he's not good.'*

HOMER COOYAMA (HOPI)[12]

The most powerful spirits are often shared by several cultural groups, and have similar names and characteristics. There are numerous spirits of nature, such as Rainbow Maiden and the spirits Thunder and Hail who control nature. In addition there are several notable spirits who are supremely powerful, but are more specifically related to one people.

Masauwu

Masauwu, the Hopi deity of fire and death, rules the whole Hopi world, both the surface of the Earth and the underworld. He is terrifying and mighty, wears a bald and bloody mask upon his head, and is clothed in raw animal skins. Every night he walks around the edge of the world carrying a flaming torch. People cannot bear to look at his face; if they do they are likely to die of fright, since he has the face of death. A more recent Hopi story tells of how Dr. Fewkes, a Smithsonian archaeologist and ethnographer, was visited by *Masauwu*. Dr. Fewkes was studying ceremonies in the village of Walpi in 1898 and during the sacred part of the *Wuwuchim* Ceremony, he was told to go and stay in his house as *Masauwu* was due to arrive. There he was terrified by the god, who had turned himself into a straw and entered through the keyhole. According to the Hopi this was the reason for the departure of Dr. Fewkes back to New York, not the dose of smallpox which he claimed!

Usen and Earth Mother

Some creators vanish, but others are a continuing source of power. The Apache deity *Usen* is an all-powerful god. Even so, other Apache gods are of considerable importance, such as the *Gahan*, or Mountain Spirits, who have power to help or harm people, and White Painted Woman, the mother of the Twin Brothers. Both she and the

Twin Brothers have parallels throughout the Southwestern cultural area. To the Navajo she is known as *Estanatlehi*, or Changing Woman, and to the Hopi she is Hard Substances Woman. She is most often seen in the role of Earth Mother. In all three cultural groups she is mother to the Twin Brothers and often re-populates the world after disasters.

Twin Brothers, Spider Woman, and Coyote

The Twin Brothers, whose father is usually the Sun, are known by various names including Twin War Gods and the Beloved Two. Most often they play the part of heroes, and their activities are usually crucial to the prosperity of humans. Similarly, in Papago myth there is a god called *Iitoi*, or Elder Brother, who is created by Earthmaker. He was the first born, when the sky came down and met the Earth. Elder Brother helped Earthmaker to shape the people and the world, and is a protector of the Papago. While the twins are powerful in their own right, the Sun is often there to help them. The Sun is regarded as a father, or Father Sky, to many groups in the Southwest and Hopi babies are still presented to the Sun God *Tawa*, who is told that a new life has begun.

Another powerful spirit is Spider Woman, variously referred to as Spider Old Woman, Grandmother Spider, Spider Lady, Grandmother or Grandma, and one people may know her by several of these names. The Hopi name for her is *Gogyeng Sowuhti* and she appears either as an old woman or as a small spider. The Hopi regard her as living medicine: she often gives medical advice, comes to the aid of people in danger, is kind and can always cope with any situation.

In contrast Coyote has power but is indiscriminate in its use. His actions bring both good and disaster. Coyote has similar characteristics in all of the Southwestern cultural groups, and is known as a trickster or buffoon. His exploits make him more of a mythical hero than anything else, but he is often integral to Creation and can use his power to perform good deeds. In Navajo

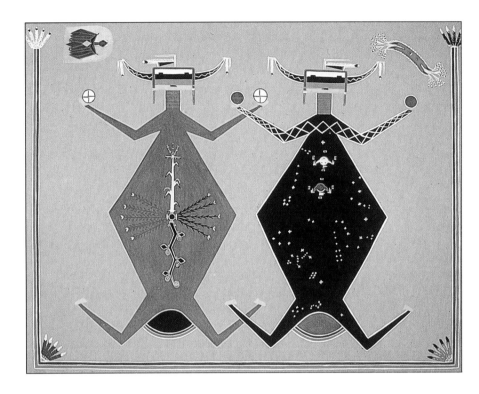

myth he is the catalyst forcing people to move from one world to another, and often he is responsible for the stars being scattered in the sky.

The Kachinas

Kachinas are at the center of Hopi religious life and are also particularly important to many other peoples of the Southwest. They are perhaps the most well-known supernatural spirit beings. The kachinas have varying origins and purposes but overall have the well-being of the people at heart. The Hopi believe that when good people die they become kachinas and are associated with clouds. Rainfall is extremely important for agriculture in the arid Southwest, and the kachinas are seen as the bringers of rain. The Zuni know them as *Koko*, or Raw People. They are associated with rain, and with the ability to give people the good things in life including longevity, fecundity, power, strength of will, and good fortune. However, rather than being powerful in their own right, the kachinas are often seen as beings who communicate people's wishes to the gods.

Mother Earth and Father Sky are two of the most important Navajo deities, and are shown here in a sandpainting made for the fourth day of the healing ceremony known as the Shootingway. Father Sky (in black) is depicted with the Sun, the Moon, the North Star, and various constellations, including the Milky Way. Mother Earth (in blue) has four plants (corn, squash, black bean, and blue tobacco) with four rainbows. Connecting their mouths is a yellow line of corn pollen, symbolizing positive energy. Corn is a central feature in Southwestern culture and *Avachoya*, or Spotted Corn (left), is one of many Hopi kachinas.

One of the most important Apache rituals is the ceremony for girls reaching puberty. This robe (below) would have been worn, and now carries a depiction of just such a ritual. The girls are with their guardians, wrapped in a blanket, and dancing around the purifying fire. Joining them are powerful Mountain Spirits known as the *Gahan*, four in number for the four directions, wearing exotic headdresses (below, right), who were once sent to Earth by *Usen* to teach people how to live reverent lives.

'In those times, and in that place, the people were unhappy and afraid. Tsakapi'yadya roamed the land, capturing and eating the people. Nearby lived Twin Boys who had great power. The people asked the boys to help them . . .'

JEMEZ STORY[13]

The inhabitants of Jemez pueblo feared a monster called *Tsakapi'yadya* who caught people and ate them, and kept all the game animals. Villagers asked the Twin Boys to help them, and after four days preparation they all set out to the monster's home, but half-way there the Twin Boys told the villagers to turn back. When the twins arrived the monster was very nice, it complemented them on their strength, bravery, and singing, and offered them food. It said they would have a competition to see who could shoot an arrow to a mountain in the south, and told them to bet their lives on it. The twins appeared doubtful and said that they could not shoot an arrow so far, but the monster insisted. The older twin agreed so long as the monster took the first shot. The monster shot his arrow to the base of the mountain. But the twins shot their arrows right over it, then killed the monster using a small piece of petrified wood. The monster's body fell into the canyon, breaking into many pieces. The twins rescued people the monster had imprisoned, freed the captured animals, and they all went back to their homes.

The origins of monsters vary. In some myths they are not explained, but are seen as having always been there; in others they are the gods' offspring, or have been created by the gods as a punishment when people have been bad. Where there are monsters there are usually heroes to kill them and put an end to their reigns of terror. However, the exploits of the culture hero Coyote are usually humorous, such as the recent Apache tales of how he outwits the whites.

Child of Water

Monsters occur most frequently in origin myths. In the Chiricahua Apache myth, recounted by Geronimo, the beginning of the world was full of

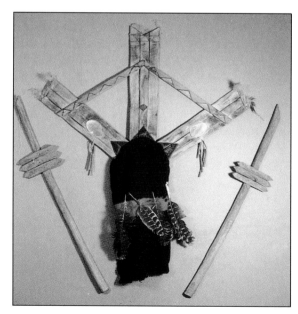

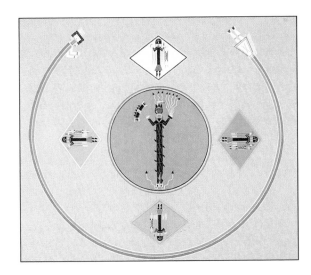

monsters which were continually killing humans. Many monsters were killed in the battle between the beasts and birds. Eagle killed one of the most hideous monsters, who was impervious to arrows, by flying high and dropping a boulder on its head. Afterward there were still some monsters left including a most horrific dragon who had four coats of scales and ate all the children. Only one child, whose mother hid him in a cave, survived. One day the boy, Child of Water, went out hunting with his uncle. The monster smelt their cooking and after he and Child of Water had wrestled over the meat, Child of Water challenged him to a contest which he won by penetrating the four scales above the monster's heart with four arrows. Thereafter people lived and prospered.

Terror in the Navajo Worlds

Monsters play a large role in the Navajo emergence myth. The water monster *Tieholtsodi* floods the third world after Coyote kidnaps his two children, but when people escape to the fourth world *Tieholtsodi* follows and floods that too. At last, when the people are emerging into the fifth world, they discover the children and throw them back to the monster who disappears and the floods retreat.

There are more monsters to contend with in the Navajo fifth world, sent by First Man and First Woman to punish the people. They include *Yietso* who, along with his children, eats human prey; *Delgeth*, a flesh-eating antelope; The People Who Kill by Lightning in Their Eyes; and The Kicker, a giant who kicks travelers off mountain trails.

Flesh-Eating Monsters

Many monsters have flesh-eating predilections in common. This is a characteristic of the Papago monsters, Killer Eagle and *Ho'ok*, both of whom are killed by Elder Brother. Most monsters are killed by being outwitted: *Ho'ok* is trapped in a cave and smoked to death; Killer Eagle has his head chopped off by Elder Brother who enters his cave disguised as a fly.

The people of Acoma pueblo tell the story of the hunter *Kasewats* who came home to discover that his wife had been taken by *Sko'yo*, a giantess. To find her he went to the spring his wife had been snatched from and made a lot of noise. The same giantess came, snatched him up and carried him to her home where he found his wife with many other frightened people whom the giantess was fattening up. *Kasewats* than tricked *Sko'yo* and killed her. He freed the people and returned home with his wife.This is a typical myth where intelligence overcomes force.

The mythical Navajo hero figure of Monster Slayer stands at the center of this painting of a ceremonial sandpainting from the Nightway, copied prior to the final act of ritual – its destruction. Monster Slayer is dressed in obsidian armor and guarded by four stars, each one containing a Black God.

These Hopi kachina dancers (below) were photographed during the *Powamu*, or Bean Planting Ceremony. The kachinas wear masks which represent both the incarnations of ancestors – who divided the year between the Hopis and the subterranean world – and ogres meant to frighten children into obedience to their parents.

'This land is a sacred home of the Hopi people . . . It was given to the Hopi people the task to guard this land not by force of arms . . . but by humble prayers, by obedience to our traditional and religious instructions and by being faithful to our Great Spirit . . .'

HOPI ELDERS, 1949[14]

The most widely held view among the Native Americans of the Southwest is that the land itself is a living being. The Zuni regard it as a spiritual relative; everything which makes up the landscape, the trees, the rocks, and clouds, are seen as being interconnected. The Navajo call this *hozho*,[15] which translates as balance or harmony, and they strive to maintain this harmony. Within the whole landscape particular features are regarded as especially sacred. The overriding importance of water is reflected in the reverence felt for springs. The Zuni see many aspects of the landscape, for example buttes, lakes, geological formations, and religious trails, as important and offerings are left at these sites, and prayers made for them. The land is dotted with shrines: places which may be significant to many people or only

to individuals, but this does not diminish their sacredness. Zunis consider the Middle Place to be the heartbeat of the world. After they came into the world they searched for it for many years, and eventually found it near the center of Zuni pueblo. It is equidistant from four oceans, and is believed to be the center of their six directions.

Places of Emergence

Many places are holy in mythology and continue to be sacred today. The Hopi place of emergence, known as *Sipapu*, is located at the bottom of the Grand Canyon. According to myth, the Hopi dead go to a house below this opening. At this place is a yellow pool located at the confluence of the Colorado and Little Colorado rivers in the Grand Canyon, 60 miles (96 km) east of Oraibi. The Hopi say their ancestors could talk freely with the Creator through *Sipapu*, but today the opening is almost always closed, due, they say, to mankind's departure from the correct path. In Navajo legend the dead also return to the place of emergence, while in Zuni myth the spirits of the dead go to the confluence of the Zuni and Little Colorado rivers. This is different to the Zuni place of emergence which is thought to be either in the Grand Canyon or the Mohave Desert.

Eight important shrines mark the extent of traditional Hopi territory: to the north is *Tokonave*, or Black Mountain, which the whites call Navajo Mountain; the second is on the Supai Trail west of Grand Canyon Village; there is one at *Kawestima* with some ruins which lie to the north of Kayenta; one near Williams, Arizona, called *Tesaktumo*, or Grass Hill; one on the San Francisco Peaks; one on Woodruff Mountain south of Holbrook; the seventh is at a place called *Namiteika*, near Lupton; and the last is on the Apache Trail on Mogollon Rim. The Hopi regard all land between the shrines as being theirs. They say the shrines mark some of the last staging points in their migrations to the three mesas. [16]

Places of Deeds

Mythology provides explanations for some of the

The pueblo of Zuni (below), photographed in 1879 by John K. Hilliers, looking east-southeast toward *Taaiyalone*, or Corn Mountain. Rising some 1,000ft (3,000m) above the plain the mountain is sacred to the Zuni people who maintain many shrines there and make pilgrimages to it at certain times of the year.

stranger elements in the landscape. A prominent mountain called Cabezon (the eroded plug of a volcano) is known to the Navajo as *Tse Najin*, or Black Rock. According to mythology, it is the head of the giant *Tieholtsodi* who was killed by the Twin War Gods (*Nagenatzani* and *Thobadestchin*) on Mount Taylor. They struck off the

giant's head, which rolled and bounced to its current resting place. Nearby lava beds are said to be the coagulated blood and gore from the giant's body. Canyon de Chelly is the site of Spider Rock, the home of Spider Woman, and today it forms part of the Navajo Reservation. Visitors to the canyon are requested to treat it with 'reverence and respect'. According to the Navajo, Spider Woman lives on the top of the tallest of two needles which make up Spider Rock. The top of the rock is white rather than red, and this whiteness is said to be bones of naughty children captured by Spider Woman and carried off to Spider Rock where they were devoured.

The directions of the compass are important and are usually associated with sacred colors. Before the Tewa people emerged from Sand Lake, the Two Little Boy War Gods were created. They were sent from the lake to report what they could see. They shot off their arrows, and the direction that the first arrow went was established as north and this was associated with the color blue. The other directions and colors followed: west was yellow, south red, east white, the zenith above was speckled, and the nadir below black.

Spider Rock (top left), an 800ft (244m) high spire of sandstone in Arizona's Canyon de Chelly, is named after Spider Woman who, among other things, was said to have taught Navajo women how to weave. Her home is on the white top of the tallest needle of rock, that of Talking God being on the lower one. It is he who keeps Spider Woman informed about the behavior of children.

Hopi Point in the Grand Canyon (bottom left), the magnificent series of valleys cut by the waters of the turbulent Colorado River which are sided by sheer cliffs rising thousands of feet above the canyon floor. Breathtakingly beautiful in itself, the magnificent sunsets of the Southwest only add to the spectacle on offer. The Hopi have a legend which relates that humans first emerged from a hole at the bottom of the canyon. The Papago believe that sunsets are a gift of the creator.

'Animals do not look like people, but they think like people do, and they really are people under their pelts.'

HOPI SAYING[17]

Animals in myth may act as messengers, guards, advisors, and servants. Mythological animals are essentially human. They think, speak, and act like humans but also have the abilities of their animal forms. Some are major deities such as Coyote and Spider Woman, but other common sacred spirit animals include bears, antelopes, deer, eagles, badgers, and wolves. Eagles are particularly important and their feathers were used in ceremonies, though now these have largely been replaced by turkey feathers. The Hopi believe that there is another land up in the sky where eagles go to breed before returning to Earth. They believe that children can be transformed into eagles and are cared for by eagle parents.

Animals not only act like humans but really are human under their skin. People entering *kivas* tell how animals remove their skins and hang them up like clothes. In Hopi myth the animals all have homes and when they need to rest they go and live there in their human form, though sometimes humans stumble upon them. A Yaqui man hit a snake which was lying across his path; later, he came to a village and was taken to the chief, beside whom was a young woman wearing a bandage around her waist who accused him of hitting her in the stomach.

Helpers

One of the most common animal roles is as helpers. Many emergence stories show animals are important in getting from one world to the next. In one version of the Navajo origin myth, Turkey is the last in the queue to climb up the reed from the third world to the fourth. When the flood waters reach his feet, he gives the signal to climb. Badger and Locust are important in getting from the fourth world to the fifth: Badger digs away at the earth to get from the fourth world and Locust outwits the challenge of four colored swans, so that all the people are let into the fifth world. Similarly, in Hopi myth four birds

The Mud Owl's Warning by Tom Lovell (right) shows a group of Apache warriors returning to camp at sunset after several days out on the trail. They are confronted by the mud effigy of an owl which has been placed on a branch of a tree as a warning that their camp has been struck by pestilence. The owl would have been one of several placed on the route. Spirits and ghosts permeated the world of the Apaches and the owl was considered by them to herald disaster and therefore to be a 'messenger of death.'

Line of Eight Dancers by Awa Tsireh of San Ildefonso pueblo, one of six Tewa-speaking pueblos in New Mexico. The animal dances in these pueblos are usually winter ceremonials and the number of participants varies. It usually includes a pair of Buffalo Dancers (as shown here), one of whom represents Buffalo Woman, Mother of All Game. The others impersonate deer, antelope, elk, and mountain sheep. The aim is to assure the hunter of success when he hunts real game in the spring.

are sent out to investigate the world above.

The living, as well as the dead, become animals but sometimes this is done by trickery. Once a Tewa man's wife and friend set out to get rid of him. The friend was a witch and invited the man to see a new dance, to which he asked all his witch companions. They all leapt through a hoop and turned into coyotes, then leapt back and returned to their human form. The man was encouraged to go through the hoop and he too turned into a coyote, but the witches took the hoop away before he could jump back through it. Similar metamorphoses take place in several stories but usually the humans are eventually recognized as such and helped to return to their human form while the perpetrators get punished. In the Tewa story the witch agrees to make a new hoop, and afterward dies of shame.

Destroyers

Animals are not always helpful or benevolent. One Navajo story tells how Frog and Turtle intend to catch some human women but people from their village catch up with them and attack them. Frog and Turtle, while acting like humans, use the advantages of their animal forms to escape. When hit, Frog hides in Turtle's shell which doesn't break, and when put in an oven, Frog puts the fire out with water from his mouth. In White Mountain Apache myth the actions of Big Owl are always destructive.

Clans

Many clans and societies in the Southwest region are named after animals, who may be thought of as direct ancestors. A Hopi male ancestor married the daughter of a snake chieftain and their descendants became the Snake Clan. To members of this clan, snakes are seen as relatives and are never killed. Snakes are widely revered, and both the Zuni and Hopi believe that they take messages to the gods. The Hopi, or course, also perform the famous Snake Dance in honor of Great Snake.

In Zuni mythology sacred animals guard the cardinal six directions. Mountain Lion guards the north, Badger the south, Bear the west, and Wolf the east, while the sky is looked after by Eagle, and the inner earth by Mole. Hoofed animals are associated with certain directions and also with kachinas, as Zuni kachinas may become hoofed animals when they die. Likewise people who die return as animals: girls and uninitiated boys are said to become turtles or water snakes.

The eagle is a highly sacred animal to Native Americans. Its plumage is used in some healing ceremonials and is also valued for its frequent use in ceremonial regalia. This Zuni man is leaning on an eagle cage made of stakes and adobe.

'And they played the drum, the heartbeat of our Mother Earth, in their ceremonies while the people dance in honor of the Creator and all living things. They danced in thanks for good crops and all the things the Creator provides through respect and love.'

EAGLE WALKING TURTLE[18]

Ceremonies are conducted to maintain or restore harmony. This is true of both the kachina and the sandpainting ceremonies and rituals which may benefit all people or just an individual. Ceremonial life is integral to native culture. Hopi ceremonies are described as being intertwined with daily life to the extent where one could not exist without the other. There are many different types of ceremonies: some are arranged calendrically and only performed at certain times of the year, while others occur whenever they are thought necessary. Many Southwestern ceremonies have their origins recounted in myth. White Mountain Apache legends about the

Water, Hawk, and Snake ceremonies are regarded as holy and are seen as being of much greater importance than the emergence myths.

Stories recount the origins of ceremonies and give direct inspiration on how to conduct them. One Jicarilla Apache legend describes the contest between Killer of Enemies and One Who Wins and is used as the basis for the purification ceremonies conducted for people who have come into contact with the dead. Anyone who has been so contaminated needs to be brought back to the 'life-side'. The ceremony involves a singer who takes the role of Killer of Enemies and fights the forces of evil personified by One Who Wins. Songs and prayers recount the bitter contest which was finally won by Killer of Enemies.

The Hopi Snake Dance

Several ceremonies are believed to have been brought to the people by heroes. The Hopi Snake Dance was discovered by *Tiyo*, or The Youth. Myth tells how *Tiyo* set out to find the source of

One of the Hopi tribe's most important rain-making ceremonies was the Snake Dance. The participants, pictured here at Oraibi in 1900 (right), are costumed to represent the heroes of the Hopi myth. Wooden prayer sticks, carved and painted to represent snakes (above), are used by the leading priest and the participants carry live rattlesnakes in the mouth, making for a dramatic spectacle. Afterward the snakes are set free in sacred places situated at the four cardinal directions of the Hopi, and the dancers take an emetic.

living things and are held from late winter until the end of the July rituals. The dances are offered to the Creator for people's health and welfare, and in thanks for good crops. In myth the kachinas were actual beings sent by the gods until they had taught the ceremonies to the Hopi priests. Today, dancers are members of the Kachina Cult. There are many different types of kachina, including clown kachinas who are naughty and provide entertainment between the ceremonies.

Sandpainting

The Navajo perform many rituals to maintain harmony between humans and the spirit world, such as songs, chants, and the creation of sandpaintings. Like the Hopi Snake Dance, sandpainting was taught to the Navajo by a mythical figure. A young woman called *Gilspa* found the Snake People's village where she was tutored by Snake Man, and when she returned to her people she taught them the ceremonies she had learnt. There are said to be hundreds of different Navajo sandpaintings, each of which is accompanied by its own song. The Apache are reputed to have around 50 different types. Traditionally, the sandpaintings are made on the floor of the *hogan* (dwelling) by the *hataali*,[19] or singer, out of cornmeal, sand, charcoal, and pollen, and can take several hours to complete. Their beauty and their depiction of the spirits' power attracts the spirits themselves. The actual power of the spirits is then used in ceremonies which may last over a week. At the end of the ceremony, done either for the benefit of an individual or for the greater good, the paintings are destroyed. Commercial sandpaintings contain errors so as not to offend the spirits.

the Colorado River. Eventually, with the help of Spider Woman, he was shown the source of the river by Great Snake, and after he had proved himself *Tiyo* was initiated into the Snake Clan. Finally, he returned home with his wife Snake Maiden and taught the Hopi how to perform the Snake Dance. The Snake Dance is still performed today and public performances attract huge crowds. It is said that the Snake Priest at Walpi still uses the original *tiponi* (medicine bundle) that was made by *Tiyo*. The Snake Dance is performed by initiates of the Snake and Antelope clans and requires two weeks of ritual preparations. Snakes are caught from the four directions and are made 'brothers' in the Snake Society, before they are taken back to the desert carrying the Hopi prayers for rain. The ceremony is most famous for the Snake Dancers' ability to hold snakes in their mouths without being bitten.

The Kachinas

The kachinas are of prime importance in many rituals including those of the Zuni and Hopi, and at Acoma pueblo. The Hopi feel they are spirit essences who show their presence by rainclouds or mists and they stay with the Hopi for seven months every year until July. Then after 16 days of rituals they return to their homes in the San Francisco Peaks, near Flagstaff. Kachina dances restore and maintain harmony in the spirits of all

The Winter Mixed Dance by Waldo Mootzka (left) depicts a dance performed at the opening of the kachina ceremonials beginning in January or February, depending on the village. The masks are incarnations of ancestors. The leader (extreme left) wears a snake dancer's kilt and carries a carved prayer stick. The design of such kilts (below) is said to represent both a lightning strike and a snake. The motif within the design is a frog's tracks and the striped band is a rainbow – both these things being symbolic of rainfall.

THE PLAINS

> *'The first experience of the Plains, like the first sail with a cap full of wind, is apt to be sickening. This once overcome, the nerves stiffen, the senses expand and man begins to realize the magnificence of being.'*
>
> COL. RICHARD DODGE, 1877[1]

THE GREAT PLAINS are the very heartland of North America. A land of grass, sun, and wind almost 1,000,000 sq miles (2,590,000 sq km) in extent and stretching from the North Saskatchewan River in present-day Alberta and Saskatchewan, south almost to the Rio Grande in New Mexico and Texas. An area of sudden and stark contrasts, both in terrain and climate, its one major characteristic is a level surface of great extent, largely devoid of forest and having only limited rainfall. There are, however, within this vast region, outcrops of timber, high hills and deep valleys, lush green lands, and many rivers and streams. In historic times, the area teemed with wildlife, including herds of buffalo and antelope.

The historic Plains tribes – the buffalo-hunting, tipi-dwelling, equestrian nomads – arrived comparatively recently on the Plains, moving into the region with the introduction of the horse in the mid-18th century. While the Plains culture lasted for no more than a century (1780-1880), it was forceful, dynamic, innovative, and resilient. And during this period, there were many changes, some of surprising rapidity.[2]

There seems to be something within the unique environment of the Great Plains which causes a people to live with such vivid intensity and an awareness and wonder of the things around them. The Plains Indian was so much in daily association with his environment and so dependent upon it, that not only animals but plant life and even some inanimate objects were believed to have a spiritual existence. There was an awareness of a great power – the energy or moving force of the universe – which, in the sacred language of the Lakota shamans, was called *Skan* or *To* and the blue of the sky symbolized its presence. This was distinct from physical power and it could act in different ways for good or evil. It was against this background that ritual and ceremonial of the Plains tribes was set – the harnessing of this power to best effect, both at the individual and tribal level.

The importance of mythology was paramount in Plains Indian ceremonialism and the description of any ceremonial was invariably in terms of myth; such myths explained the topography of the Plains, with its lakes, mountains, Badlands, and majestic prairies, with repeated reference to the warpath, buffalo, and quest for supernatural powers. Perhaps the most widespread are the versions of Old Man Coyote myths which relate to the origin of the Earth and Man: human heroes, too, are popular, animal figures often being transformed into humans (and perhaps back again) at various stages of a myth.

Myths expressed a fundamental pattern of conduct which regulated, and to a certain degree regimented, the population, the ceremonies being dramatizations of the sacred myths, and so, at least in theory, the complex details of a ceremonial continued unchanged through successive generations.

As with the eagle whose feathers he prized so highly, this Cheyenne, Crooked Nose (left), evokes the atmosphere and spirit of the Great Plains of North America; as, too, do the beaded designs on a Lakota pipe bag (right and far left) representing lofty mountain outcrops with cuts of colored earth and symbols of arrows for war and the hunt. Protection by supernatural powers was very much a part of the ethos of the Plains. The umbilical cord of an infant was placed within a beaded amulet case to ensure the baby's growth and health. A case in the shape of a turtle (top left) identifies it as being for a girl, the Lakota believing that the turtle has power over illnesses peculiar to women.

Powerful influences from the highly developed Mississippian cultures have been identified in the northern Plains tribes. Stone buffalo effigies of ancient origin (below) have been found as far north as Alberta and Saskatchewan. The incised design on the body is similar to a Thunderbird, underlining that Mississippian cosmology had integrated with that of the northern buffalo hunters. Such figures were probably used on an earthen altar in ceremonials intended to call the buffalo.

'We love our country because it is beautiful, because we were born here. Strangers will covet it and some day try to possess it, as surely as the sun will come to-morrow.'

PLENTY COUPS (CROW)[3]

The creation of the world from a sample of mud, brought to the surface by a diving animal, frequently occurs in the mythology of the Plains tribes.

Napi or Old Man

The Blackfeet sages referred to the time when there was nothing but water, together with *Napi* or Old Man, the original culture hero, who sat on a log with four animals[4] pondering the possibility of something beneath the water. He persuaded them to dive down and explore; only the muskrat returned, bearing a sample of mud, which *Napi* took, rolling it in his hands while it grew rapidly

before falling back into the water, assuming such dimensions that he was able to stand on it. He then released a wolf which ran across the partially dried mud, and whenever it stopped a deep indentation appeared, producing a valley. His further movements gave rise to the mountains and plains, while water flowed into some of the indentations to produce the lakes and rivers. The role of animals in the origin of the world was commemorated in the elaborate ceremonial of the Beaver Bundle which contained, at least in theory, representations of all the animals associated with Blackfeet cultural history – all except the frog which was excluded since it could neither sing nor dance!

First Creator of the Mandans

While the Mandan origin myths also make reference to diving animals and the formation of the Earth, the origin of the tribe itself was explained in terms of emergence from underground. Emerging, for example, from the butte of the Black Tailed Deer[5], they brought corn up with them. Their chief at that time, Good Furred Robe, taught one group, the *Awigaxa*, special songs for success in growing corn. He also had a special robe that, if sprinkled with water, would cause the rains. The Mandans moved progressively north, and in one particularly dry year two men, First Creator and Lone Man, appeared.

These two culture heroes are credited with the origin of the Buffalo Dance, telling the tribe that whenever there was a shortage of food they should perform this dance to call the buffalo to the vicinity of the village. Mandan legend relates that there was a progressive development of the ancient and simple Buffalo Dance which led to one of the most complicated of Plains ceremonials, the *O-kee-pa* Ceremony.

Pawnee Sky Powers

While most of the Plains tribes explain their origins in terms of emergence from the earth, the

Pawnee credit *Tirawahat*, the One Above, supreme and changeless, with making all things. He gave the stars great power, in particular the Morning Star whose younger brother was the Sun. In the east were those stars representing men and ruled over by the Morning Star and Sun; in the west were those stars like women, with the Evening Star and Moon as their rulers. The lengthy myth results in marriages between the Morning Star and the Evening Star and, after reconciling their differences, between the Sun and the Moon. Children were born to each couple and placed on Earth, who in turn married, populating the Earth.

 The obstacles in the myths symbolically represented the sicknesses and troubles that humans experienced throughout life, and the teachings were that only by elaborate ceremonials, invoking the helping powers of the Morning Star and Sun, could these evils be overcome. Such myths led to the development of a complex sacred bundle system which was believed to have been given in ancient times by various of the heavenly powers, hence linking the powers to Earth-bound Man.[6]

Underwater and Sky Powers of the Crow

The Crow Indians' version of the origin of Earth and Man combines underwater and sky powers. Thus, Medicine Crow, the informant for this myth, related that many years ago there was no earth, only water, and the only creatures were ducks, and *Isā'katā'te*, or Old Man. One day, Old Man came to meet the ducks, saying, 'My brothers, there is earth below us. It is not good for us to be alone,' and instructed a red-headed mallard to dive down and bring up some earth, but he was not successful. Then a pinto duck, blue-feathered duck, and hell-diver were ordered to do the same thing but only the latter was successful, emerging with a little mud in his webbed feet. So, in company with the successful duck and with mud in hand, Old Man, travelling from the east, spread the mud around, thus making the Earth. Travelling across the Plains, they found a medicine stone, *bacō'ritsi'tsè*, which Old Man said was the 'oldest part of the Earth,' able to reproduce itself, thus explaining why there are stones to be found all over the Earth. Finally, they saw a human who Old Man said had been a star but now was Earth-bound, but on approaching him he transformed himself into a tobacco plant – regarded by the crow as the first plant on Earth. Medicine Crow then explained that it was believed that the stars had assumed this form and if the tobacco was taken, raised in the spring, and appropriate ceremonials performed – the Tobacco Society rituals – all the needs of the people would be met.

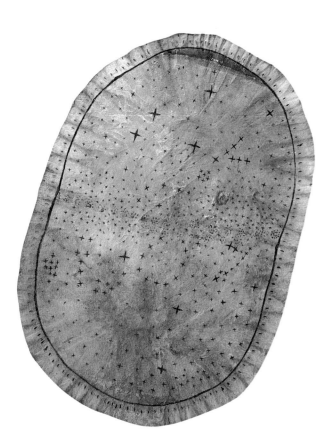

The importance of sky powers to the Plains tribes is no better illustrated than on the *Skidi* Pawnee star chart (left). A great deal of Pawnee mythology relates to star powers, and this buckskin chart identifies constellations such as Corona Borealis, Ursa Major, and the Milky Way. It was believed to incorporate the powers of the stars and bring these powers to the people when it was used and displayed in complex ceremonials. Sky powers were also invoked by the Crow in their Tobacco Society ceremonials (above). Tobacco was considered to be the most distinctive of Crow medicines, Crow oral tradition stating that tobacco seeds were a special gift from the Creator and should be planted each year. Those seeds on which appeared the figure of a star – taken to be the Morning Star – were regarded as especially potent.

43

One of the most complex of Plains ceremonials was the Sun Dance (right) which was highly developed by the Cheyenne, its central theme being world renewal and called by them *Oxheheom*, or New Life Lodge. Its origin myth attributes its introduction among the Cheyenne to their culture hero *Tomsivsi*, or Erect Horns, who was instructed by the all-powerful spirits, *Maiyun* and Thunder. This scene, by Cheyenne artist Richard West, depicts the third day of the ceremonial. At the center is the pledger; the Thunder Spirit nest, containing a broken arrow, buffalo meat, rope, and a rawhide effigy, is attached to the center pole.

'In the beginning was Inyan, *who had no beginning, for he was there when there was no other, only* Hanhepi, *the Darkness.* Inyan *was soft and shapeless, but he was everywhere and he had all the powers. These powers were in his blood, and his blood was blue. His spirit was* Wakan-Tanka'

LAKOTA ORIGIN MYTH[7]

The mythology of the Plains Indians provides valuable data on their culture, insights into their religion, and into the way they viewed the powers associated with the spirit world. It also enables interpretation of much ceremonial of their, often elaborate, regalia.

The Adventures of Scar Face

The Blackfeet Scar Face myth, which makes reference to the powers of the Morning Star, the Sun and the Moon, concerns the adventures of a poor young man referred to as Scar Face because of a long ugly scar on his cheek. He was in love with the daughter of a chief but she was unwilling to marry him unless he could find a way of removing the scar. Desperately seeking supernatural aid to this end, he leaves for the Land of the Sun, a journey encountering many adventures and culminating in the killing of seven large white geese and seven aggressive cranes, the heads of which Scar Face took to the Sun. Thus, the Blackfeet explain the origin of scalping – proof that an enemy had been overcome – by reference to this mythological episode.

So impressed was the Sun with these feats of courage that he presented Scar Face with a fine costume embellished with weasel skins. The shirt had a quilled disc on the chest and back, symbolic of the Sun, and seven black stripes painted on the sleeves to represent seven of the birds, while the leggings were embellished with seven bands, symbolic of the defeat of the other birds.[8] Scar Face subsequently married the chief's daughter and became one of the most successful of Blackfeet ceremonialists.

The Spirit World of the Crows

The Crow Indians' concepts of supernatural powers are explained in the myth relating to *Eehtreshbohedish*, Starter of All Things or First Worker, who was said to be composed of the many vapory elements that existed before the world was formed by him. They said that First Worker gave to *all* things both a purpose and a power, which was referred to as *Maxpé* or medicine. It could be bestowed upon individuals by a supernatural helper to assist them throughout their Earthly life, but they did make a distinction. For example, in their most important ceremonies, such as the Sun Dance and Tobacco Society rituals, the Crows offered prayers directly to First Worker.

The Lakota Concept of Power

The stand these people took toward the rest of mankind was to regard themselves as superior, but before the awesome forces of nature they presented themselves as humble and weak suppliants, yearning to gain – through a vision or dream – some of the powers which daily they observed around them. The Lakota perceived an all-pervading force, *Wakan*, the power of the universe, which was manifested in the blue of the sky or in the brilliant colours of the rainbow. Then there was the terrifying crash and reverberation of the thunder and associated destructive power of the lightning. All these, together with the wind and hail to name but two, were viewed as potential sources of power which, if symbolically harnessed, could be used to personal best effect. Thus, most of these powers were appealed to in the Sun Dance and Spirit Keeping ceremonials. The totality of the creative force of the Lakota universe was *Wakan-Tanka*, the Great Mysterious. Although it was recognized that *Wakan-Tanka* could at the same time be both one and many, it was only the shamans who attempted a systematic classification with the *Tobtob Kin*,[9] a system not fully comprehended by the common man. The shamans also said that *Wakan-Tanka* could communicate with humans

through the *Akicita Wakan*, or Sacred Messengers. Those who had had visions sometimes drew what they had experienced, and both realistic and conventionalized representations of such messengers and spirits are found on Lakota accoutrements, such as shields and warshirts;[10] the key to their interpretation lies in an understanding of the *Tobtob Kin*.

The Pawnee Universe

In Pawnee mythology it was *Tirawahat* who reigned supreme. The blue of the sky was associated with *Tirawahat* and he was ever-present in all things, particularly the storm. Pawnee mythology relates that in winter the gods withdrew from the Earth, the first thunder in the spring being a signal that they had once more turned their attention to it; thus commenced the Thunder and other ceremonies in succession. This first thunder was believed to be the voice of *Paruksti*, the deity who was a messenger of *Tirawahat*; and so as *Paruksti* traveled above the land with thunder as his speech, the Earth was reawakened and life rekindled. His return was celebrated by the commencement of the Thunder Ceremony, which traditionally ushered in the ceremonial year, and thanks were given by the people to the all-powerful spirits for renewal, the growth of crops, the birth of animals and birds, and the return of the buffalo – the cycle of all life on Earth.[11]

Pledgers often received visions during the course of the last four days – devoted to the public dance in the Sun Dance Lodge. Such an experience is vividly illustrated by the Kiowa artist *Wohaw* (left). Here, the pledger stands in front of the lodge, raising his arms and face to the sky, and sees in his vision two gigantic Thunderbirds, the Sun, Moon, and Morning Star – all creatures and objects which figure prominently in Plains mythology.

HERO CREATURES AND MONSTERS

'The buffalo horns are on my head and I speak for the Buffalo God. I am now the buffalo bull and you are a young buffalo cow. I will show you what the bad influence would have you do. I will show you what the good influence would have you do.'

LAKOTA BUFFALO POWERS[12]

A Sioux rawhide shield (above) with eagle and hawk feathers did not protect against rifle fire; rather, it was the objects attached to the shield – referred to by the Lakota as the *wo'tawe* – which they said imparted an all-embracing protective power. Thus, eagle feathers evoke thunder power and suggest the owner had some rapport with that awesome power of nature; hawk feathers evoke the acute sight and swiftness of that bird.

In common with other regions, heroes in Plains culture came in many guises but more often than not drew directly from the animals in the world around them. Coyote was considered particularly powerful, for instance, in Crow mythology, being credited with attaining life by his own efforts. He transforms from animal to man and back depending on the circumstances.

Old Man Coyote and Summer

In this tale, the summer and winter are kept in different colored bags which are owned by Woman with the Strong Heart, but all she would release to Crow country was the winter, while the south always had summer. Despairing of the climate, Old Man Coyote tells a youth that he is

going after the summer and obtains four male animals to help him – a deer, coyote, jack rabbit, and wolf – and he assesses how far they can run. In order to arouse sexual passions, Old Man Coyote changes himself into an elk and arriving at Woman's tipi, exposes himself; on hearing shouts, Woman leaves her abode and Coyote takes the opportunity to slip in. When Woman returns, she is confronted at the door by Coyote who subdues her by rubbing medicine paint on her face. Coyote then carries off the bag containing summer, running with it until he is tired when the jack rabbit, deer, and finally wolf carry it in turn. On reaching Crow country, wolf opens the bag and agreement is reached that each country should now have a summer and winter.

The Little People

Dwarf-like creatures are a common ingredient in Plains mythology, in particular the Crow named Pryor Creek as *Aratace*, or Arrow Stream, at the request of a mythical dwarf who wanted arrows shot into the clefts of so-called Arrow Rock as an offering to him. Offerings are still made today to a spirit who guided the last great Crow chief Plenty Coups, on his first mountain-top vision.

Not all Little People were exclusively benevolent, however. The Dakota and Lakota Tree Dweller, *Canotina* or *Canotili*, was a powerful spirit who generally appeared as a little man and dwelt in the forest ready to confront solitary hunters. He was generally malevolent and to be avoided for he caused people to be lost in the woods. His appearance struck terror in humans, since if they actually saw *Canotina* one of their close relatives was said to be doomed to die.[13]

Blackfeet Star Myths

The chief characters in the Blackfeet star myths either appear as heavenly bodies or become such at the end of their Earthly careers. A number of these myths explain the acquisition of tipi designs, the origin of buffalo-calling, and ceremonial episodes such as those associated with the Sun Dance. Generally, animals take an

Spirit of the Buffalo (left), painted by Joseph H. Sharp, suggests an episode from the Lakota *Alo'wanpi* ('to sing for someone'). This ceremony was closely associated with the mythological White Buffalo Maiden and her visit to the tribe. The central idea was the affection of a father for his child and the desire that only good should come of it. Buffalo power is invoked here: as one Lakota informant related, White Buffalo Maiden was sent by the Buffalo tribe. She was pure white and without blemish – this being the principal desire of the father for the character of his child.

Thunderbird myths were widespread on the Plains. The Blackfeet said they received one of their most sacred pipes from the thunder; while the Lakota referred to the Thunderbird as *Wakinyan*, whose flapping wings and flashing eyes were said to give rise to thunder and lightning. This petroglyph (opposite, below) at Legend Rock, near Worland, Wyoming, may be 1,000 years old and suggests that these ideas prevailed on the Plains at a very early period – possibly due to influences from the highly developed Mississippian cultures to the south and east.

important part in these rituals, being persons in disguise and identified in descriptions as Otter Woman, Crane Woman, Beaver Man, and Elk Woman. The latter refers to the medicine woman who was principal leader in the Sun Dance and, in Blackfeet mythology, dug a forbidden turnip out of the sky.[14]

Power of the Morning Star

In Pawnee mythology, Morning Star is a leader of men, helping with the creation of the universe. Morning Star travels with his brother, the Sun, to the land of the western stars in an attempt to overcome the power of the Moon who has killed all previous approaching man-stars. This hero figure uses the power of a sacred bundle and an associated war club to overcome the obstacles

Moon puts in his way and thus enter the women star village.

Water Monsters

Water Monsters figure prominently in Sioux mythology, the Lakota referring to them as *Unktehi*, their greatest powers being in water where no other forces could trouble them. They were thought to make the floods which they spewed out of their mouths, and they were said to catch people or animals and to eat them. Their power was in their horns and tails which they could push out or draw in as they wished. They were in a continual state of war with *Wakinyan*, the mythological Thunderbird. The subordinates of the *Unktehi* were said to be serpents, lizards, frogs, ghosts, owls, and eagles.

HOLY PLACES, SACRED SITES

'The Ground on which we stand is sacred ground. It is the dust and blood of our ancestors . . . A few more passing suns will see us here no more, and our dust and bones will mingle with these same prairies.'

PLENTY COUPS (CROW)[15]

The Great Plains, as stated earlier, was a place of topographic diversity with areas of outstanding beauty, desolation and privation, and – given the right season – abundance. In common to all was the fact that they were nature's gift, few man-made sites existed.

The Home of the Sun

One of the most fascinating structures in the Plains region associated with the early occupants of the area is the Medicine Wheel, located in the Bighorn Mountains of modern-day Wyoming.[16] It is a circular outline of piled stones, approximately 69ft (21m) in diameter but flattened on one side. It was discovered by Euro-Americans in the 1880s and is documented as a vision quest site by the Crow Indians. This was *not* the original use of the Medicine Wheel, which dates from not later than 1700, and it is speculated that some of the earlier ceremonies of the Mountain Crow, close relatives of the Hidatsa, were practiced there when they were a sedentary people. Crow informants referred to it as the 'home of the Sun,' rather firmly tying it in with the Sun Dance and the Mandan *O-kee-pa*. The Medicine Wheel is now more than a remnant from the past for many Native Americans; as one Crow spiritual leader explained, 'this Medicine Wheel is our church . . . it is a United Nations for Indian people.'[17]

Pryor Mountains : Crow Vision Quests

Vision quest sites were located on eminences in terrain such as that Guthrie described for the Crow in Montana and northern Wyoming:

'An enormous world, a world of heights and depths and distances that numb the imagination . . . the mountains are loftier . . . the streams are swifter . . . the wind fiercer . . . the air sharper . . .'[18]

Among the best known of these, exclusive to the Crow for their favorite fasting place, are the Castle Rocks, just south of Billings, Montana, on the northeast edge of the Pryor Mountains. Here, fasters would sit in a small U-shaped stone structure, facing the Morning Star which was considered to have great supernatural power. According to the Crow chief, Two Leggings, the Castle Rocks had additional sacred associations, being the home of the Little People, mythical beings who had great physical strength and supernatural powers. Similar sacred sites for the Lakota are Bear Butte and Harney Peak in the Dakotas, still favorite sites for vision quests.[19]

The Dakota Badlands

East of the Black Hills are the South Dakota Badlands, it is known as an area rich with the fossil remains of extinct animals. The Lakota said the Badlands was the home of *Wakinyan*, the mythological lightning or thunder spirit. Petroglyphs and pictographs depict him as a great bird but sometimes he assumes a partly human shape. On war whistles or warshirts, he is represented by a zig-zag line to evoke communication with that awesome power. The lightning was said to be the flashing of his eyes and the thunder his voice, his awesome power apparent in the large treeless zones of the Lakota domain,

One episode (top right) in the Arikara Buffalo Society's Medicine Bundle Ceremony. This clan or society of the Arikara combined buffalo-calling and thanksgiving rites with curing functions embodying much of Arikara mythology and ceremonialism. Here the members of the society are massed in prayer before the earthen medicine lodge; to one side stands the sacred cedar, a symbol of tribal unity. In the days when the traditional tribal religion of the Arikara was still vital, all of the society bundles were housed in this medicine lodge, which for this reason has been called the 'tribal temple'.

where animals and humans were struck not infrequently, while his voice reverberated through the sacred *Pa Sapa*, Black Hills, and the canyons of the Badlands.

Dog Den Butte

The third day of the Mandan *O-kee-pa* Ceremony, The Everything Comes Back Day, comprised most of the bundle owners of the village. Animal rites were performed, Mandan mythology relating that these originally belonged to the Buffalo People who were created in the vicinity of Heart River by Lone Man and who were, together with all other animals on Earth, imprisoned by *Hoita*, or Speckled Eagle, in Dog Den Butte. *Hoita* then put on, for the first time, the Buffalo Dance in Dog Den Butte and called all the buffalo away from the villages. Every living thing was brought in and the people faced starvation. Eventually the cooperation of *Hoita* was obtained and he set the animals free.

Chief Mountain

The highest mountain on the Blackfeet Reservation in Montana has origins in *Napi*, or Old Man, whose powers were being tested continually. Challenged by the Great Spirit to demonstrate his strength, Old Man made the Sweet Grass Hills and then brought Chief Mountain to its present location and named it.

Sacred Enclosure of the Mandans

It should also be emphasized that there are less spectacular sacred places of which today only the initiated are really aware, and of all these the sacred cedar is paramount. First Man, the mythological Creator of mankind, founded the *O-kee-pa* ceremonial and established the custom of leaving an open area within each village for dancing, thus every Mandan village traditionally had an open plaza reserved for ceremonials. At the center stood a cedar post which was painted red and symbolically represented not only the body of First Man but also tribal ancestors. This sacred enclosure was a central pivotal point for the *O-kee-pa*, symbolizing the integrity of the Mandan as a people. Today, this ancient and holy shrine, sometimes referred to as The Ark of the First Man, is still located within the traditional territory of the Mandan tribe.[20]

Devil's Tower, Wyoming (below). This striking demonstration of the way nature molded and reshaped the Earth's surface, as if by some master sculptor, is in the Wyoming portion of the Black Hills country. Not surprisingly, such marvels of nature often had sacred significance to the Indian tribes of the region and, as with other nations, bloody wars were fought because of these religious sites. High mountain-tops or buttes were often vision quest sites but the steep sides to this particular formation precluded its use for ritual. However, the Lakota referred to it as *Mato-tepee*, or 'the home of the bear,' a prominent figure in Plains Indian mythology.

An Arikara warrior, Black Fox (right), wearing a grizzly bear claw necklace attached to an otter skin collar embellished with strips of white ermine skin. The otter turban with eagle feathers completes a costume replete in animal symbolism: the powerful bear, the brave weasel, the amphibious otter, and the mighty eagle.

This stuffed bald eagle holding a weasel skin in its talons was used as a tipi flag by a Blood Indian around 1880. It was tied near the top of one of the tipi poles and believed to bless the owner with special spiritual power.

'He made men and women. They asked him, "What are we to eat?" He made many images of clay, in the form of buffalo. Then he blew breath on these, and they stood up; and when he made signs to them, they started to run. Then he said to the people, "Those are your food." '

OLD MAN IN BLACKFEET MYTH[21]

In common with many Plains tribes, the Lakota recognized that all living creatures and plants derived their life from the Sun. A deeper knowledge of particular animals was greatly desired because not only was it believed to have been taught its ways by *Wakan-Tanka*, the Great Mysterious, but also that all animals were of benefit to one another. The acquisition of some of their powers was possible by a dream or vision of one of them, whereupon the creature was adopted as a helper and part of it worn on the person.[22]

The Powers of the Elk

A dream of an elk and acquisition of elk power was of particular significance among young men. In much of Plains mythology reference is made to the many desirable attributes of the elk – beauty, gallantry, lightness of foot, and great physical strength. The elk was also considered to live in harmony with its surroundings and was blessed with a long life. Above all, however, the male elk was known to have great influence over the opposite sex. It was observed that the elk would stand on a hill and call or whistle, bringing the females to its side. This intangible power was greatly desired and the flageolet (a type of flute) was used to imitate the elk call. Sioux, Blackfeet, and Plains Ojibwa mythology all have myths for working the charm with a flageolet, and additionally the Sioux made use of a special courting blanket which usually displayed the painted figures of an elk, a spider, and whirlwind.[23]

Crow Love Medicine

Among the Crow, the elk was considered to be primarily the giver of love medicines, generally associated with personally owned bundles, which

In most of the complex ceremonials, the buffalo was recognized as the life-giving gift of the higher powers. The mythology associated with the rare white buffalo epitomizes the revered animal mythology. White buffalo were particularly swift and wary and for this reason, together with their rarity, they were difficult to secure. When a white buffalo was killed, the fatal arrow was purified in smoke from burning sweetgrass, and before the animal was skinned the knife was similarly purified; no blood was to be shed on the hide. Only men who had dreamed of animals were allowed to eat its flesh and only a woman who was noted to have lived a pure life could tan it. In an annual ceremonial of the Omaha, the albino was represented by the skin of a small white buffalo with the horns and hoofs intact. It was considered one of the tribe's most revered objects and symbolic of the tribe's continued survival.[25]

The Blackfeet Beaver Bundle

The place of revered animals is perhaps no better illustrated than in the mythology associated with the Blackfeet Beaver Bundle which invokes the power of the legendary figure Weasel Woman – the name based on observations of the weasel's bravery and therefore a patron of warriors. Weasel Woman's husband was the owner of a Beaver Bundle, the most complex and ancient of all Blackfeet medicine bundles. Owners of Beaver Bundles were often referred to as *ijoxkiniks*, 'those having the power of the waters,' and they were obliged to show no fear of water in any form. A very important duty of the Beaver Bundle owners was to take on the role of buffalo-callers,[26] during which the power of Raven was invoked, calling the buffalo down to the vicinity of the village. Raven was considered the wisest of all birds, its superior abilities being recorded in the myth referring to the contest between it and the Thunderbird, when Raven made it so cold that the only way the Thunderbird could keep from freezing was by constantly flashing his lightning. He finally conceded defeat!

The weasel was considered alert, skillful in evading pursuit, and aggressive for its size. A carved weasel crouches on the Oto club (below) as a symbol of war; its ermine has also been used on the buffalo horn headdress (left) of the Crow shaman Sees-the-living-bull.

had been taken as a result of the grief caused by unrequited love. Such medicine power was not confined to one sex and both men and women possessed these various medicines, seeking to attract the person of their choice.

Buffalo Power

While the elk emerges as a symbol for love and gallantry, it is the buffalo which, above all, is woven into ceremonials and figures most prominently in Plains legends. Its origins are explained in terms of emergence, such as in this Omaha legend:

'The buffalo were underground. A young bull browsing about found his way to the surface . . . the herd followed . . . As they went they came to a river. The water looked shallow, but it was deep. As the buffalo jumped in, the water splashed and looked gray in the air. The herd swam on and over the stream, where . . . they found good pasture and remained on the earth.'[24]

RITUALS AND CEREMONIES

A torture scene in the Mandan Medicine Lodge on the fourth day of the *O-kee-pa* Ceremony which acted out the legends and mythological history of the tribe. Those participating, particularly in the torture episode, were subsequently looked to as leaders and keepers of tribal ceremonial. The *O-kee-pa* was performed annually and few white people ever observed it; one notable exception was the artist and traveler George Catlin who visited the Mandans in July 1832 and recorded what he saw for posterity (below). While there was some controversy relating to Catlin's descriptions and illustrations of the *O-kee-pa*, his work has now largely been vindicated.

'Wakan' yan	In a sacred manner
mica'kelo	he made for me
nagi Ksa pa wan	a wise spirit
maka'hewaye	I met

CHARGING THUNDER (LAKOTA)[27]

Among the most important of Plains Indian religious practices was the quest for personal supernatural power, which was usually acquired by the visitation of a guardian spirit in a dream induced by fasting, praying, and perhaps self-mutilation. The guardian spirit could be almost anything, animate or inanimate,[28] but was often the Moon, Morning Star, or a bird or animal invested with supernatural power. The vision quest generally took place in complete solitude on a high eminence and could last up to four days,[29] usually being preceded by a ceremonial sweat bath; this purifying of the body in sage or sweetgrass smoke removed the human odor which might be offensive to the spirits.

The Circle of Life

A recurring theme in Plains Indian ceremonialism is that of regeneration and harmony expressed by the symbolism which the Sioux associated with the circle or hoop. To them it emphasized the relationship between mankind, the buffalo, and all the rest of the universe, which was perceived as existing in cyclic harmonious balance. The Sun Dance of the Lakota, as well as their other major ceremonies such as the Spirit Keeping and *Hunka*, emphasized this theme, and the mythological figure of the White Buffalo Maiden who represented the Buffalo tribe and gave the Lakota the ceremonial pipe was intricately woven into these ceremonials. By correctly observing annual ceremonials, the unity of the people was maintained, and the great hoop of life remained intact; if this hoop was broken, the people would be destroyed.

The *O-kee-pa* Ceremony

The Mandan believed, in common with most Plains tribes, that many animals and birds and even some inanimate objects, possessed some spirit power which they called *xo'pini*. Such power, they said, could be transferred to individuals by involvement in certain rituals, the most important of which was the *O-kee-pa* which, prior to the virtual extermination by smallpox of the Mandans as a tribe in the summer of 1837, was without question the most complicated and colorful of those performed on the northern plains, probably strongly influencing the nomadic tribes such as the Lakota, Blackfeet, Kiowa, and Cheyenne in their developments of the Sun Dance. The *O-kee-pa*, a four-day ceremonial performed at least once every summer, acted out the mythological history of the tribe. It was a dramatization of the creation of the Earth, its people, plants and animals, together with the struggles the Mandan endured to attain their present position, and in addition it enabled key participants to renew the coveted *xo'pini*. One of the most striking episodes was when young suppliants were suspended from the ground by splints through the muscles of the chest or back, the sight of which, one observer reported in 1832, 'would almost stagger the belief of the world.'[30] Naturally, this act took courage and caused the

tribe to speak of them as brave men and to look to them for leadership.

Sacrifice to the Morning Star

While the torture episode in the Mandan *O-kee-pa* is a dramatic example of penance, that of the *Skidi* band of Pawnee was perhaps the most extreme,embracing as it did the sacrifice of a young girl. Analysis of Pawnee mythology leaves one in little doubt of the great powers associated with the Morning Star which was viewed as a personification of manliness and conceived of as a great warrior who drove before him in the sky the other stars, identified as people in Pawnee mythology. The sacrifice, however, was actually considered as the symbolic overcoming of the Evening Star by the Morning Star and their subsequent union from which sprang all the life on Earth, the young girl being perceived as a personification of the Evening Star. When she was ritually killed – by an arrow through her heart – the life of the Earth was symbolically renewed. Human sacrifice was an unusual custom among Plains Indians and there was increasing opposition among the Pawnees to its performance. In 1818 the custom was finally abandoned.

Black Elk's Lament

Annual ceremonialism and ritual, so vital in the ethos of the Plains tribes, was progressively suppressed during the early reservation period. The effect was devastating and it led to the Ghost Dance ceremonial and tragedy at Wounded Knee in December 1890. The despair was captured in Black Elk's now famous lament:

'You see me now a pitiful old man who has done nothing, for the nation's hoop is broken and scattered. There is no center any longer, and the sacred tree is dead.'[31]

As a 'rite of passage' into manhood, a young Plains Indian teenage boy was urged to undertake a vision quest, as captured here (left) by Tom Lovell in The Vision Seeker. Several days of purification, perhaps in a ceremonial lodge, was the prelude to the vision quest and then the vision-seeker would retire to some remote butte or mountain-top, often a place designated as a sacred site, and fast for several days. Such vision quests might be repeated on several occasions in a person's life, whenever it was considered necessary to seek help from the higher powers. Sees-the-living-bull, for example (see headdress on page 51), sought visions on four occasions and the spiritual help which he acquired gave him the reputation as a great medicine man with powerful war medicine. Not all fasters were so successful, however; the cold, hunger, and lack of sleep was not always rewarded and it would be necessary to repeat the ritual at another time. While it was usually males who were encouraged to seek power through such a visitation, women too might seek the advantages of a supernatural helper at any of life's critical moments.

PLATEAU AND BASIN

'I hear what the ground says . . . The water says the same thing . . . "Feed the Indians well." The grass says the same thing . . . The ground says, "The Great Spirit has placed me here to produce all that grows on me, trees and fruit." The same way the ground says, "It was from me man was made . . . take good care of it and do each other no harm . . ."'

YOUNG CHIEF (CAYUSE)[1]

THIS REGION, constituted by two culture areas rather than one, is most difficult to summarize. Indeed, anthropologists long believed that neither the Plateau, which extends outwards from the Columbia and Fraser rivers, nor the Great Basin, formed between the Rocky mountains to the east and the Sierras to the west, had any distinctive cultural features of their own but were amalgamations of the customs of those around them. (And it is true that Plains influence can be detected in both areas,[2] and in the Basin some peoples shared features with adjacent California cultures.)

Also, since traditionally the people of the region, especially those of the Basin, were hunter-gatherers, and anthropology as a social science discipline arose during a period much infected with hierarchical notions of race (with 'civilized' Caucasian city-dwellers at the top, downward through agricultural and pastoral peoples), these tribes were considered 'primitive' and uncomplicated. The Shoshonean-speaking peoples, who showed notable ingenuity in surviving for countless generations in the extremely hostile aridity of Nevada and Utah, were designated by incoming whites as 'Digger Indians', a derogatory term that referred to their practice of digging for roots and wild vegetables. In fact, of course, the cultures of these peoples were highly complex and, due to the marked geographical variation across the region and the sheer number of different tribes, extraordinarily diverse. The contrast between the canoe-owning Kutenai in the far north, into present-day British Columbia, and the Chemehuevi, a Southern Paiute group who used to roam the Mohave Desert and now reside mostly on the Colorado River Reservation, could hardly be greater.

Despite such differences, all Plateau and Basin peoples believed, above everything, in the sacredness of all life. They held these views in common with most other Indians, but perhaps with greater passion or, at least, intensity of expression, and in treaty negotiations with whites they frequently voiced reverence for the Earth in statements like that from Young Chief quoted above. It is therefore not surprising that important inter-tribal religious movements, such as the Ghost Dance,[3] originated in the region, or that they had a richness of origin myths for their staple foods. In the Plateau these told of the genesis of the need for hunting and fishing, and included stories of the theft of salmon. In the Wishram version Coyote freed the fish from two old women who kept them in a lake, appearing to them as a baby boy and secretly digging a channel between their lake and the Columbia River. The old women were then turned into swallows. In the Basin the equivalent myth was that of the theft of piñon nuts.

It is important to remember that all cultures are dynamic. Here it is possible to give only a sample of the variety of beliefs and practices of this range of peoples, and no inkling of the changes that have occurred over time.

This unidentified Shoshoni man (far left) is recognizable as being from the Plateau due to several things: the upswept hairstyle, free on one side braided on the other, with a massive feathered hackle plume at the back; a multi-strand necklace of bone or ceramic beads; and ermine strip fringes on the shoulders of his jacket. The Plateau and Basin region was not renowned for its material culture, many things being acquired from neighboring regions. Possibly the most distinctive manufactured items were Nez Perce cornhusk bags in pleasant colors and patterns (right and far left). The deer figure made of rushes (top left) was collected from the Thompson Indians. It was a highly symbolic item in mourning ceremonials, being shot at with a special bow for four nights after a person's death.

ORIGIN MYTHS

A Kutenai headdress (right) embellished with human hair, ermine skins, and eagle feathers, and surmounted with antelope horns, is of a typical elaborate style used by Plateau men in dances and other rituals. It is replete with animal powers – the fleetness of the antelope, the bravery and majesty of the eagle, and the tenacity and fighting abilities of the weasel.

A petroglyph on the Columbia River shows the huge eyes of the woman chief *Tsagigla'lal* (below right). Wishram mythology relates that Coyote told her that the world would change and there would be no women chiefs. She was then turned into stone to become a guardian of the tribes in the area.

God created the Indian country and it was like he spread out a big blanket. He put the Indians on it . . . and that was the time the river started to run. Then God created fish in this river and put deer in the mountains . . . Then the Creator gave us Indians life; we walked, and as soon as we saw the game and fish we knew they were made for us . . . we grew and multiplied as a people.'

CHIEF WENINOCK (YAKIMA)[4]

The peoples of the Plateau and Basin, in common with those of other cultural areas, explained the origin of the world out of primeval waters. In most stories the Creator, while floating on the water, called on the animals to fetch mud from the bottom and the Muskrat, Chickadee, Toad, Turtle, Beaver, Duck, and Mink were among those who were successful in various versions. The Creator then flattened and stretched the

mud to create a new earth. In one Shoshoni and Bannock version the sky and people were also formed from this mud. As with much Indian mythology, the occasional existence of many versions of a myth among one tribe shows that each was not believed as a single truth, but as one reasonable explanation among several.

In a Northern Paiute version, the flood was decreed by the Creator to follow a great fire. After the world dried, the people began to make war and the Creator went away southwards with his wife. In one Northern Shoshoni version, the flood resulted from Coyote's desire to wash the world, and in another, Wolf and Coyote in the Upper World created land by throwing soil down into the world ocean below. For the Kutenai and the Flathead, Chief Eagle of the Mountains fired an arrow to stop the flood rising, thereby leaving behind what is now called Flathead Lake.

The Scattering of Tribes

The predominant Plateau myth concerning the dispersal of people depicted Coyote defeating a giant monster who had swallowed all the animals. In Kalispel mythology the creature was actually a huge whippoorwill. In the Nez Perce story, Coyote deliberately allowed the monster to swallow him; while in the Flathead and Kalispel versions he was carrying a tamarack tree with which to block the monster's mouth, but was swallowed involuntarily. The tree took root where the monster threw it away, near what is today Arlee, Montana.

After being sucked in, Coyote severed the monster's heart and instructed the animals to run out through the creature's openings as it died. The last animal to escape varied in different versions, but included Woodtick, Ant, and Muskrat. Coyote then created the Indian tribes by scattering sections of the monster's body. In the Nez Perce story, Fox reminded Coyote that he had not made any people in the valley in which they stood. Coyote created the Nez Perce from the blood on his hands sprinkled with water, explaining that they would be few in number, but very strong.

In other myths humans originated from the offspring of Coyote and two women whose supposed vaginal teeth he broke. When Coyote was sent away with the children in a container, he opened it out of curiosity and the ancestors of all Indian tribes jumped out.

Fire

Usually fire was obtained by theft from a guarded mountain-top or from the sky, very often masterminded by Coyote; occasionally Rabbit was the hero (Southern Paiute), or more frequently Beaver (Nez Perce, Cayuse, Sinkiuse). In all these versions, the central character tricked the guardians of fire (for example, Coyote let his headdress trail in it and then ran away when it caught light) and all the animals were vital in relaying it to safety, many of them being killed by their pursuers along the way. In alternative Nez Perce versions, fire was kept in the sky by the Creator, but a small boy managed to shoot it down with an arrow on to an abalone shell; or Coyote's son was kicking a tree stump around in such a way that it split and made fire.

In Paiute myth Walker Lake (above) was said to be home to two of the Creator's four children. (The other two were sent farther north where they became the ancestors of the Bannock.) It was also the place where, in 1869, a Northern Paiute shaman initiated the Ghost Dance movement. The dance cult quietly faded after a few years but was revived some 20 years later with devastating results.

'The time was when Our Father, who lives above the clouds, loved our fathers, who lived long ago, and his face was bright, and he talked with our fathers.'

CHIEF WASHAKIE (SHOSHONI)[5]

In the Basin area, and to a lesser extent in the Plateau, most powerful spirits were elements of nature and not separate deities. The most important deity, as such, of both sets of people was the Creator, who was usually known as Our Father. In the Basin this was often the sole supreme being, whereas in the Plateau other powerful spirits were sometimes mentioned. Among the Cayuse, *Hon-ea-woat* was the Great Spirit; among the Lillooet, he was Great Chief; among the Washoe, he was This Man Up Here.

Our Father was important not only to indigenous religions, but also to such inter-tribal movements as Peyotism, a religion centered upon the ritual consumption of the mind-altering peyote cactus.[6] Peyotism, which spread to Basin peoples in the last two decades of the 19th century and reached its peak in the 1940s, included among its paraphernalia a Father Peyote fetish. The Eastern Shoshoni and others had a Father Dance in which they gave thanks to *Tamapö* and prayed for his continued blessings; it was also a plea to keep children healthy against the smallpox.

Some debate whether the Our Father concept was influenced by contact with Christianity, but it seems likely that it was of aboriginal origin. In any case, the fact that *all* of these myths have been translated, and altered from oral to written forms, means that precise meanings can never be ascribed.

Wolf

Wolf was sometimes an interchangeable substitute for the highest god. The Eastern Shoshoni called him *Pia Apö*, or Big Father, and called Coyote *Tei Apö*, or Little Father. Among the Northern Paiute the Creator was *Nümüna*, or Gray Wolf. Wolf was regarded as the creator of people and the solar system, and was also known as Father by some Northern Shoshoni and Bannock, the Ute, some Southern Paiute, and some Western Shoshoni, who believed the power of a wolf gave cunning and strength.

Sun

'All the products of the Earth are children of the Sun, born of the Earth.'[7] This is how Kate McBeth, a missionary, explained the Nez Perce view of the world. They would ask for the blessings of Father Sun and Mother Earth, and before every meal the food vessel was silently turned, in imitation of the Sun's rotation.

Among the Kalispel, Flathead, and Coeur d'Alêne, *Amotken* was the Big Spirit Above, or Highest Mystery; other names for him were Sky Chief, Power of the Upper World, and He Who Sits on Top of the Mountain. The creator of the Sun, Earth, and other worlds, *Amotken's* symbol was the Sun, and myths told of *Amotken's* son,

Rock art figures, often painted in red pigment, abound in the eastern Wyoming region. It is believed that many were produced by the Shoshoni prior to their retreat to the Plateau region. This figure (right) may be a female water spirit who figures prominently in Plateau myths. This solitary spirit dwelt in springs, lakes, and streams. She stole unguarded babies or pulled people into the river. Old and young alike are still said to believe in her existence today.

Spokani, being the Sun and the Moon. In the spring, when the first bitterroot and camas were dug, the chief would offer prayers to the Creator, to the Sun, and to the Earth before the harvest was eaten. The daily morning prayers of the Kutenai were addressed first to the dawn, for the young of the family, and then to the Sun, for children outside the family.

Master of the Animals

Most of the peoples of the Plateau and Basin had a spirit which they identified as having power over the animals, especially those which they sought for food. The Ute and Southern Paiute believed that bears, mountain sheep, elk, and deer were controlled by a snow-white being who lived high in the mountains.

Thunder

Thunder was a spiritual entity for many tribes, and frequently less powerful only than the Creator. Among the Wishram and Wasco, Thunder was a large bird which caused lightning when it spat. The Northern Paiute told of Thunder Badger, who lived in the sky, and when he felt that the land was too dry, put his head down to the ground and dug, sending clouds up in a flurry and thundering curses at the earth.

The weasel (below right) was highly esteemed by Plateau and Plains tribes. This was due to its ability to change the color of its pelt from brown to white in winter, and to the effectiveness with which it killed its prey – including many larger than itself. Joseph Rotunda, a Nez Perce boy pictured in 1900 (below left), is wearing an otterskin necklace and a shirt embellished with two fine long-tailed weasel skins.

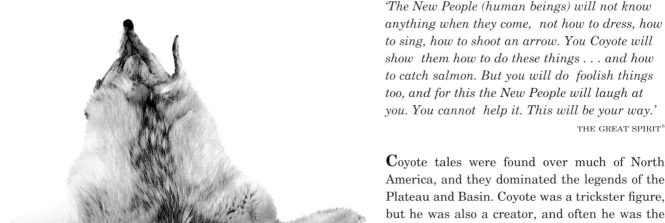

'The New People (human beings) will not know anything when they come, not how to dress, how to sing, how to shoot an arrow. You Coyote will show them how to do these things . . . and how to catch salmon. But you will do foolish things too, and for this the New People will laugh at you. You cannot help it. This will be your way.'

THE GREAT SPIRIT[8]

Coyote tales were found over much of North America, and they dominated the legends of the Plateau and Basin. Coyote was a trickster figure, but he was also a creator, and often he was the younger brother of the more responsible Wolf. The stories in which Coyote figured tell of his exploits during the course of his journey eastward along the Columbia River from its mouth. The task he was given by the Creator was to prepare the Earth for the imminent event of the coming of people. Although he heroically rid the land of evil monsters, he also inadvertently made many errors which were both amusing and tragic, and he ordered the world in ways that were not always the most logical or just. Coyote tales are simultaneously comic and solemn. He died many times, but was always brought to life by Fox in order to continue his duties. Although Coyote's adventures could be traced to particular locations along the river, their chronology was irrelevant.

Thus, several stories exist concerning Coyote and women, some of them his wife – but in one Flathead and Nez Perce version his wife was Mole, in a Northern Paiute one she was Weasel, and in another she was the wife of Thunder and was stolen by Coyote. In the mythology of the Kalispel, Flathead, and Coeur d'Alêne tribes, Coyote labored to overcome the malevolent actions of *Anteep*, the wicked chief of the Lower World.

Coyote was at once a hero and a comic figure. He created the world as people knew it and was

A preserved pelt (right) of one of the central Plateau mythology figures – Coyote. A Nez Perce creation myth tells of a great monster which devoured most of the animal people by inhaling them. Coyote – described as The Great One – tricked the monster into swallowing him, then stabbed the monster in the heart and released the animal people inside. He then cut the monster into pieces and flung them to the Wind gods and they became different tribes of men. He then shook the blood from his hands to create the *Nee-me-poo*, the Nez Perce, the noblest men of all. Acts such as these embody the heroic and trickster aspects of Coyote.

therefore revered as a creator and transformer, but he was also depicted as both a cunning trickster and a greedy fool. At times it was his avarice, stupidity, curiosity, or lack of foresight which were blamed for the hardships of humans, such as hunting, childbirth, winter, and death.

The Water Monsters

Water Babies featured in the legends of most of the peoples of the Plateau and Basin. Neither sex was specified in the original languages, but they were usually depicted by those who had seen them as female, and they were typically solitary. They were generally described as small people with long hair, and they were responsible for the creation of hot springs. For most tribes, they were evil creatures who stole unguarded babies at night and pulled people into rivers and lakes. In the Plateau, the Nez Perce saw them as benevolent, and a child was expected to offer discarded teeth to them; the Northern Paiute had the same custom, but the offering was made instead to Old Sage Woman. Among the Northern Paiute, the water babies were sometimes regarded as messengers to the Lower World.

Other water monsters were told of, such as the Washoe great bird of Lake Tahoe (present-day California), the giant water serpent in Pyramid Lake, and the white water buffaloes in Bull Lake (both present-day Nevada). Some tales ascribe the primeval flood to the vengeance of a water baby (Washoe) or water ogre (Shoshoni).

Giants, Cannibals, and Dwarf Spirits

Giants and cannibals occurred in many stories. Sometimes they had only one leg or eye, or their eyes glowed with supernatural brightness. The Washoe feared a one-eyed giant who lived in the Pine Nut Mountains near the Carson Valley, Nevada. Other tribes often had legends in which mountains were inhabited by giants: the Kalispel, Flathead, and Coeur d'Alêne told of the *Natliskeliguten*, or Killers of Men; the Northern Paiute told of *Nümüzo'ho*, or Crusher of People. Stone manos, metates, and mortars were all said to have been created by *Nümüzo'ho* and displaced to the edges of lakes which he jumped into when the world was burning. The Wishram told of a cannibal woman called *Atata'tiya* who was outwitted by a girl and boy.

In much of the Plateau and some of the Basin, a dwarf spirit was the master of the animals. He was described as a little green man who fired invisible arrows which caused sickness in both humans and animals. Although many tribes had a taboo against saying his name, in the Plateau he was not always seen as an evil spirit, but one who actually helped hunters and good shamans.

The origin of the Bear Dance (below left) is explained in the Ute legend where a hunter was instructed by a bear that he would gain hunting and sexual prowess if he appeased the bears by performing the dance. During the dance sessions, women selected male partners who danced opposite them, forming male and female lines as seen here at Uintah Reservation.

The Snake River area, with the majestic Grand Tetons in the background, has been Eastern Shoshoni territory for at least 500 years. The mythological beings and animations of all nature and its powers were of central importance to the Shoshoni who, through the Sun Dance or visits to sacred and remote places like these, gained the blessing and help of the higher powers.

'I buried him in that beautiful valley of winding waters. I love that land more than all the rest of the world. A man who would not love his father's grave is worse than a wild animal.'

CHIEF JOSEPH (NEZ PERCE)[9]

The Wallowa River runs through the Wallowa Valley in northeastern Oregon. It is not only where Old Joseph was buried, it is also the spiritual heartland of the Nez Perce, and its loss to the United States in 1863 was one of the contributory causes of the Nez Perce War of 1877. Chief Joseph spent the last years of his life campaigning for its return to his people.

Lake Waha (meaning 'beautiful'), situated in the mountains above Lewiston, modern-day Idaho, was one of the places to which Nez Perce children were sent for their spirit quests.

Many of the flood stories mention a local high point which either remained above the water or was the first dry land to emerge, and for the Nez Perce tribe this point was Steptoe Butte in the southeastern part of present-day Washington State.

Ancient Wishram Shrines

For the Wishram, *Nixlu'idix*, today called Wishram, was where Coyote found the woman chief *Tsagigla'lal* and told her that the world would soon be changing and women would no longer be chiefs. She was changed into a rock to watch over the people at this place. A petroglyph face, with huge eyes, marks this spot on the Columbia River, upstream from The Dalles.

Not far away from Wishram, or *Nixlu'idix*, is a cave on the river bank called *Tca'mogi* whose entrance is under water at high tide. There is also a big rock in the water at *Waca'k'ukc*, nearly a mile below the village of *Cqô'anana*. Both of these sites were sacred to the Wishram and children were sent there on vision quests.

Plateau Sites

Near Elko, British Columbia, the images of three spirits are found on the cliff. To the Kutenai they represented *Kukluknam* (Weariness), *Kukisak* (One Leg), and *Kaklokalmiyit* (There Is No Night to Him); the latter being the highest and most difficult spirit to obtain. The Kutenai also believed that in the future the dead would return to the shores of Lake Pend Oreille, Idaho, where rocks above it are marked with sacred paintings.

Medicine Tree in Bitterroot Valley is now in Montana State Park south of Darby. Here, according to the Flathead, Coyote killed an evil mountain ram, leaving its horns imbedded in the tree. People left gifts at the site for the Creator.

Volcanic Mount Hood, Oregon, is where the Cayuse claim that fire was guarded by demons before Beaver and Woodpecker masterminded its theft. Woodpecker still continually taps trees with his beak to show people where fire may be found.The John Day River is said to have been created by the path of melted snow which Beaver left behind him as he ran.

To the Kalispel, *Kaniskee*, or Spirit Lake, Idaho, was a feared place at which the loveliest bride of each moon was believed to be in danger of being stolen by witches. The accompanying tale involved the tragic death of two sweethearts from enemy tribes drowned when forced to meet in secrecy. The Coeur d'Alêne had the same story about Hayden Lake, Idaho.

Sacred Places in the Basin

In Malheur Cave in southeastern Oregon, which was also called Water Cave by the Paiute, water babies, Indian-crushers, and cannibals were said to have lived and been responsible for the piles of rocks found there. These evil creatures were banished by the Creator to the earth-hole near Sucker Lake (Pyramid Lake, Nevada). Malheur Cave is now a meeting place for various Indian fraternal orders.

For the Paiute, Mount Grant, near the southwest end of Walker Lake, Nevada, was the first

mountain to emerge from the primeval deluge. This mountain was also the place to which Sage Hen retreated with fire to save it from the surrounding water by fanning her wings.

Dinwoody Canyon and Bull Lake, Wyoming, are holy places marked with pictographs. Like other sacred sites, especially caves, these places were believed by the Eastern Shoshoni to be former entrances to the subterranean pathway which led to the Lower World.

The encampment at Nespelem (above) of the Nez Perce band led by Chief Joseph in 1902, just two years before his death. The Nez Perce had tried valiantly but in vain to hold on to the Wallowa Valley land that was sacred to them. Joseph's father had told him, 'This country holds your father's body. Never sell the bones of your father and mother.'

Mount Hood (left) was the place where, according to the Cayuse, fire was found. Mountains were said to be the home of spirits and sources of power. There, a shaman might converse with Wind, Cloud, and Rain, or learn a song for treating people.

' "I will take one of the powerful names," said Coyote. "The Mountain Person, Grizzly Bear, who rules all the four-leggeds, or Eagle, who rules the birds, or Good Swimmer, the Salmon, the chief of the fish people. These are the best names. I will take one of these names." Fox said, "Maybe you'll have to keep the name you have . . . People don't like that name. No-one wants it." '

PLATEAU MYTH[10]

The Nez Perce were expert horsemen and prized white horses with spots on the rump. They developed the fine breed known as the Appaloosa (below) to a very high quality within a comparatively short time after developing a horse culture. A Nez Perce or Umatilla warrior recorded his battle coups in paint on his horse's body.

The practice of sponsoring was widespread in the Plateau; the sponsor could be an individual, a family, or a band of families, who took charge of inviting other families, building any necessary structures, preparing the food, and hiring any

necessary singers for a dance dedicated to an animal by the first man to dream of it during the year. Often the need for the dance, or the appropriate time for it, was revealed to the sponsor in his dreams.

The Bear Ceremony

The bear had an important role for the Kutenai and their springtime dance was held to secure immunity from attack by grizzly bears which were soon to emerge from hibernation.

The Ute also held a Bear Dance, in late winter, which was a line dance and thus unusual for the Basin, although the Bear Dance itself was fairly common in the eastern area of the Basin. Bear was believed to give sexual and hunting prowess.

Bluejay and the Winter Spirit Dance

Bluejay, an important figure for the Northwest Coast, was central to the religious life of the tribes of the southern part of the Plateau, such as the Sanpoil, Spokane, Kalispel, Coeur d'Alêne, and Colville. He had a uniquely important and complex role for the Flathead, including healing, and had a vital part in the Winter Spirit Dance, the major ceremony of all these tribes, which was held at the winter solstice.

The dance lasted several nights, for the purpose of spirit singing, power contests, and shamanistic performance. It was sponsored by an individual shaman, or a non-shaman who possessed a guardian spirit, but participation was open to all who possessed a spirit, and attendance was open to the whole community. One of its features was the initiation of novices, and this involved the difficult task of extracting the youth's spirit song. The young man did not know the identity of the spirit who had given his song until it was interpreted for him by a shaman. Sweat lodge purification took place for three days before the ceremony, and it was accompanied by a feast or gift-giving, or both.

Gift-giving was one of the more variable features; for instance, it was not obligatory for the Sanpoil but was for the Wishram, although the

Sanpoil tended to give bigger things while the Wishram only gave little tokens. The Flathead and Southern Okanagan did not give to people at all but to the spirits, the gifts being hidden in the forest. Generally, gifts were hung on a special center pole. Typically, sponsors gave more than others and shamans more than laity. Among the Sanpoil, strangers were the first to be given gifts and the best gifts went to those who danced the hardest. In all cases the act of giving bestowed power on the giver.

During the dance, anyone whose guardian spirit was the bluejay – and there might be several – was transformed utterly: his face was painted black, he discarded clothes, spoke unintelligibly or not at all, and perched in the rafters of the ceremonial lodge, all to the accompaniment of fiercely shaken deer hoof rattles.

Horse

The horse was very important to the peoples of the Plateau and to those in the north and east of the Basin. Although it soon became more integrated into Plateau cultures, the horse was probably introduced through trade with the Basin's Shoshoni, the peoples in the Basin having had earlier access to horses through their proximity to the missions in California and the Southwest. The Basin habitat, however, was not conducive to supporting the animal because it needed the foods on which the peoples themselves depended, hence there was resistance to the horse found among the Western Shoshoni, Washoe, and others. In some cases, however, dominant tribes deprived weaker ones of the horse, in the manner in which the Shoshoni prevented the Gosiute from obtaining any.

In the Basin, the horse was most integrated into the cultures of the Northern and Eastern Shoshoni, and the Bannock. It was not highly incorporated into their religious life, however, as it was for many peoples of the Plateau. There, the horse was of prime religious significance to the Nez Perce and Cayuse.

The horse came to mean a great deal to many Plateau tribes, even being incorporated into religious life. When a Wishram man died, for instance, his best horses were often killed. In everyday terms, horses were a means and symbol of wealth. They were decorated in fine fashion to reflect this – as shown with the horses of this Flathead mother and daughter (above) – often with fine saddles and bridles obtained from the Crow in trade.

'As the Sun goes down, sit on the rocks facing him, watch him while he goes from sight, and look into that direction all night. When the dawn comes, go to the east and watch the Sun return to his people. When he comes to noon, go to the south and sit there, and when he has traveled low again, go to the west where you sat first and watch until he has gone. Then you start for home.'

FATHER TO HIS SON (NEZ PERCE)[11]

The central element of the religions of the region was the acquisition of spirit power through visions. The Plateau followed the Plains pattern, in that it was vital for a man to have at least one spirit helping him through life. In the Basin it was not as crucial, and it is generally true to say that visions were not sought there with such fervor as in the Plateau, and sometimes not at all.

In the south and southwest of the Basin, spirit power came from spontaneous dreams – more like the pattern of California and the Southwest. The Ute believed shamanistic power to come with life, and did not usually seek it, although some Ute shamans, unlike others in the Basin, did undertake vision quests. The Bannock and the Eastern and Northern Shoshoni were more like the tribes of the Plains.

In the Plateau, all boys and some girls were sent into the wilds to seek visions. Their return was celebrated with a feast, but they would not be asked about their experience, and did not tell of the vigil's outcome, until adulthood, maybe 10 years later. Vision quests continued among some peoples for years, the distance and difficulty of the child's quest increasing with age, sometimes into adulthood, until the desired spirit appeared. Each man's spirit would inform him of individual

Hope Springs Eternal – the Ghost Dance by Howard Terpning, a painting (right) which captures the desperate efforts of the Plains Indians to invoke spiritual help via the Plateau-derived dance which was originated by the Paiute prophet *Wovoka*. Instead of bringing Indian people back to life to replace the whites it resulted in the tragic massacre of 300 Sioux women, children, and old people at Wounded Knee in 1890.

food taboos. The Flathead revealed their spirit only at such a time as it was needed. A man's spirit song was learnt from him at his death, when others would sing it for him.

Shamans

Throughout the region, there was a strong belief in the efficacy of dreams and the power of prophesy. The Spokane did not start fishing at the beginning of the season until a man whose special role it was dreamt a predictive dream that was then verified.[12] Individuals who had certain spirit power became shamans, responsible for using their powers for the rest of the tribe and capable of healing, harming, or controlling the weather. In the Basin, there was a certain ambivalence toward the power of the shaman, and resistance to becoming one. This was partly because it was not known at first whether the person's power would take a beneficent or malevolent form. People rarely sought to achieve the power of a shaman unless they already were one; if power was offered and refused, a person became ill.

In return for his duties, the shaman was often made a rich and very powerful member of the tribe, although shamans of the Kalispel and Flathead sometimes refused payment for their services. A shaman would not begin practicing his power until he was around 50 years of age. The Basin was fairly unusual in that there were an equal number of men and women shamans; in the Plateau, women were capable of receiving power, but only practiced on their own sex.

Round Dance

Round dances were the most important, and sometimes the only, ceremony of the Basin peoples. They were held at times of thanksgiving, such as the piñon harvest, the first rabbit drive in the autumn, or the first antelope hunt of the spring. The Northern Shoshoni and Bannock held one in the early spring to ensure the return of the salmon, and another at the arrival of the salmon. They also held dances in the autumn or any other time of adversity.

The dances took place in a clockwise direction around a pole or tree, each person joining hands with those on either side, stepping to the left and bending the right knee; most lasted about four nights. The dances were primarily for pleasure and an opportunity for courtship, but in some places they also had a rainmaking function. It was a variation which became the Ghost Dance.

Mourning Cry

Some of the Basin tribes held an annual mourning ceremony known as the Cry. It ended formal mourning by the relatives of those who had died during the year and it included the ritual washing of the mourners, who had abstained from cleansing themselves since the death as a sign of their grief.

For the Southern Paiute it was the most important ceremony of the year. It took place in the fall among the Owens Valley Paiute, and was generally practiced by those on the border with California cultures; the Washoe may also have performed it. Generated in the south of the Basin, it was sometimes mixed with the Bear Dance of the eastern groups referred to before.

A ceremonial lodge packed with members of the Dreamer Cult led by *Smohalla*, a Wahapan. The cult advocated that the Indians cling to their traditions and found many followers among a people suffering great cultural dislocation.

CALIFORNIA

'Desolate it was
Desolate the earth
First they appeared
First they came out
First Mokat
First Tamayowit
These the chiefs
These the ancients . . .'

CREATION SONG (CUPEÑO)[1]

PRIOR TO THE COMING of Europeans in the late-18th century, California was one of the most densely inhabited areas of North America with an estimated population of 310,000. Archeological evidence indicates human presence in the California area for perhaps as long as 26,000 years, and native traditions affirm long residence there. Once one of the most linguistically diverse areas in the world, more than 60 'tribes' lived in the region. Some of the languages spoken by people of a single tribe living as close to each other as neighboring river drainages were as different from each other as Spanish is from French.

The California culture area can be divided into three main regions: northwest, central, and southern. Tribes in the northwest, such as the Yurok, Karok, and Hupa, developed a rich culture which relied on plentiful salmon, plant foods (such as acorn), and animals, including deer. They were skilled woodworkers, producing dugout canoes, split-plank houses, sinew-backed bows, and other objects. The women were fine basket weavers. Accumulated property (such as dentalium-shell beads) indicated wealth and was a means of acquiring status.

In central California people relied on the acorn as their principal food source, along with hundreds of other plant foods. Animals, including deer and elk, were also important to their diet. Homes consisted of the large earth-covered, semi-subterranean structures of the Nisenan, Valley Maidu, and Patwin in the Sacramento Valley; the brush-covered dwellings of foothill Maidu people; and the dome-shaped, tule-covered homes of some Pomo and Yokuts peoples. Women of all these groups developed coiled, and in some cases twined, basketry to a high art. Baskets were produced for every conceivable function: cooking and food preparation, storage, carrying loads, cradling children, and catching fish. Baskets became an obvious symbol of wealth, and village leaders insured their prestige at feasts by serving many large baskets filled with acorn mush. To honor the deceased, some baskets were made to be burned during mourning ceremonies.

In southern California, people adapted to a more arid environment. They lived in dome-shaped homes covered with brush, tule or grass, and women wove fine, coiled baskets. The Chumash, on the coast, had an elaborate ceremonial system and developed fine artistry in creating small steatite sculptures, beads and pendants, multi-colored rock art, and ocean-going redwood plank canoes.

Native people still live in California today, some practicing native beliefs. World Renewal ceremonies held in northwestern California use new regalia, created by talented contemporary artists, along with the old. In central California, the Pomo, Patwin, and Miwok people hold dances in newly created ceremonial roundhouses built at ancient village sites. And in southern California, too, groups such as the Chumash have worked diligently to revive ceremonies and insure that their ways will not disappear.

The lifestyle of the Californian Indian – generally peaceful and gently flowing – is reflected in the contented face of this Hupa Jumping Dancer (far left). This man displays his substantial means with his elaborate shell necklace and woodpecker scalp headdress, also considered by the Hupa to demonstrate a concern for the well-being of the community.
California's natural abundance provided ample time to evolve the finest type of basketry in the whole of North America, as evidenced by the decorative strip of a Wintu basket (right and far left); while among tribes such as the Pomo, the ornamentation of the body extended to elaborate feathered ear lobe decorations (above left) which were carved from bone or wood.

'My Grandma Sokaneh, *she used to tell me the story of creation at nights when I was little. She had a cane, and she'd thump it on the floor in time to the cadence of the words and songs as she told the story.'*

HENRY AZBILL (VALLEY MAIDU)[2]

Henry Azbill, an elder of the Valley Maidu people from Chico, recalled this story as it was told to him by his grandmother around 1900. Older tribal members commonly recounted the origin myths of their people, as in this way tribal history was passed on. Azbill retold *Sokaneh*'s creation story in the 1960s:

'In the beginning *Helin Maideh* created the water and the misty air. He was alone with Turtle on a raft, and since he was lonely, he brought *Kodoyampeh* (World Maker) into being to keep him company. *Kodoyampeh*

descended from the sky on a white feather rope and he had a face so bright that one could not look at it. After days of drifting on the water, *Helin Maideh* told *Kodoyampeh* that there should be earth and people, and he charged him with the task of creating them.

Kodoyampeh told Turtle to dive into the water and see what he could find. Three times Turtle dove, and found nothing. On the fourth day he made his dive and pushed deeper through changing colors of water until he felt something. He was gone a long time, and when he returned to the raft he seemed more dead than alive. When he was pulled on to the raft, small bits of mud were found under the nails of his hands and feet.

Kodoyampeh gathered the mud, rolled it into a ball, flattened it, and placed it upon the water. The power of *Kodoyampeh*'s

The beauty, elegance and symbolism of Californian basketry is evidenced in this oval-shaped tray with flaring sides (right), made in 1918 by Mission Indian Ramona Lubo using the interlocked coiling technique. Decoration is in the form of a splayed lizard on the base with a rattlesnake motif in dark brown running around the side – creatures which, according to a Maidu creation myth, predated mankind on Earth.

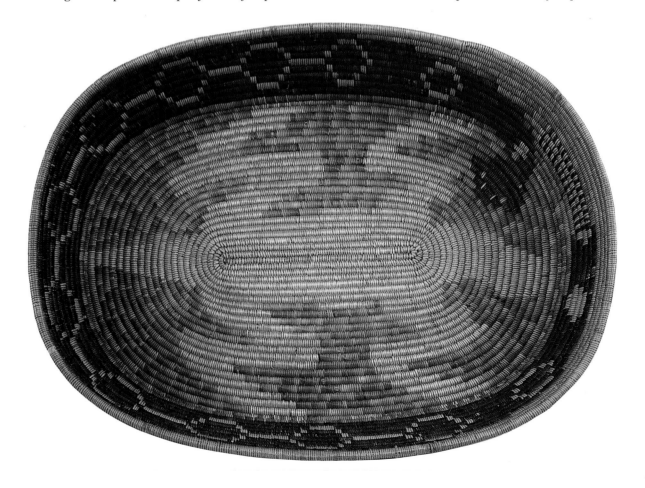

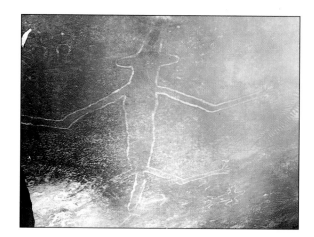

A pictograph found on the Tule River Reservation of a long-snouted animal (far left) is probably a Coyote, which figures in many creation stories of the Californian people. Generally, such myths intertwine the creation of land and people, there being almost none which refer to any movement to their present home from elsewhere; such stories thus substantiate a long residence for the Indians of California. Earth paints, shells, willow bark, rabbitskin, and eagle and condor feathers worn by Imperial Valley Tipai (left) underline the close association which these people had with their environment.

thought caused the little mud patty to swell and grow until it was the size of the world, with all the rivers, lakes, and mountains. In order to keep the world from floating away, *Kodoyampeh* anchored it at the north, south, east, and west with four ropes.

Helin Maideh had already created the animals, fishes, birds, and trees, and he said that there should be people. He told *Kodoyampeh* to cut two straight willow sticks, strip them of their bark, and hold one in each of his armpits when he slept. If he felt anything unusual in the night, he was to act as if nothing was happening and under no circumstances was he to move. In the early morning he felt movements and fingers tickling him all over his body. He looked up and saw a man and a woman. He rose from his bed and sent them to bathe and then to come and eat. He gave them fire, instructed them how to live, and gave them songs to sing as prayers. There was no sickness and no death. Life was good.'[3]

Most origin myths of the California people begin with a world covered in water. In a Sierra Miwok version, Coyote helps to create the world. Usually known as a trickster, Coyote behaves himself in completing that task; later he became a comic, ribald character prone to making mistakes. According to the Maidu, it was Coyote who sug-

gested that death would be good. When the first person to die was Coyote's son, Coyote regretted his idea, but it had become a fact of life which he could not change.

Diegueño Creation

The Diegueño people of the south tell another version of creation. The world was covered with salt water like a big sea, and two brothers lived under it. They had to keep their eyes closed or the salt would blind them. The older brother went up to look around, but he could see nothing but water. As the younger brother followed him up, he opened his eyes and was blinded by the salt. Since he saw nothing, he went back down. The older brother decided to make little red ants, and from them he created land. Then he made birds, but they couldn't see their way to roost. He tried to make a light from yellow, red, and black clays, but it was pale when he placed it in the sky. It became the Moon. He took more clay and made another object for the sky. It became the Sun. He then made a man and a woman from the clay.

'Don't you swim at that place, because if you do, the hohape will get you!'

Such admonitions would be told to Southern Miwok children who wanted to swim in certain pools of the Merced River. The *hohape*, river mermaids who caused people to drown, are but one example of the many spirits who controlled the world of California Indian people. The spirits included all-powerful spiritual entities that controlled much of everyday life, and lesser spirits who inhabited and gave life to every valley and creek. California Indian people constantly gave thanks to these spirits through prayer, dances, and offerings of food and beads.

The *Chingichngish* Religion

In southern California, the Luiseño-Juaneño, Gabrielino, and Tipai-Ipai practiced the *Chingichngish* religion, derived from the teachings of the shaman-like hero, *Chingichngish*. He dictated a moral code to live by and enforced it with spirits called 'the avengers.' These spirits, which included Rattlesnake, Spider, Tarantula, Bear, and Raven, watched to see that people obeyed the laws and they punished wrongdoers.

Nature Spirits

Among the Central Sierra Miwok, a class of nature spirits were called *suchuma*. They had the power to cause rain, violent windstorms or whirlwinds, and to roll rocks down on people. Miwok children were warned to stay away from spirits such as the *Nenakatu*, a two-foot tall, human-like creature with hair that hung to her heels.

The Miwok used the wormwood plant for protection from these spirits, to keep away ghosts, and to purify and protect those who had come into contact with evil forces. Some Southern Miwok people wore pieces of root from a rare plant strung around their necks to protect themselves from supernatural sickness, in much the same way as Central Miwok people tied folded wormwood leaves onto string necklaces.

As the Californian tribes moved into crises in the 1870s, due to disorientation by white impact, there was a modification of native religious systems. In the Ghost Dance, a prophet announced the destruction of all white people and the return of the land to the Indians. Although this failed to materialize, the foundations of the *Bole-Maru* Cult were laid. Popularly referred to as the Big Head Dance, due to the headdress depicting a male spirit, participants (right) could have a vision which would bring information from the Creator about a new cosmological scheme.

Some spirits lived in specific geographic locations that were often shunned by native people. In Yosemite Valley, Miwok and Paiute people avoided the areas around waterfalls because of the *nunu*, the spirits who lived there and destroyed people who ventured too close. In Central and Northern Miwok country, limestone

A bone whistle with a figure of the Big Head deity engraved on it (above), was used by a Pomo shaman and *Bole-Maru* dreamer in both healing and diagnostic functions which were inherited from the older religions. The Big Head deity was thought to live in a large house at the south end of the world. When the whistle was sounded, it supposedly represented the speech of Big Head which helped effect a cure of the sick patient.

These Pomo and Patwin dancers (left) are members of the *Hesi* Society (who were paid for enacting ceremonial roles) and are dressed in elaborate costumes of willow rods and feathers. The figure at the far right is *Moki* and this is a rare example of a *Moki* feather cape being seen in use. The *Hesi* Society members celebrated not only all the seasonal events but they also conducted a cycle of dances to the animal spirits – dances which continue today.

caverns were thought to be the home of *Chihalenchi*, an evil, hair-covered man who ate people who ventured into the caverns, and of *Ettati*, a man-eating, snake-like creature.

Other spirits in certain locations were sought out by shamans, and it was from them that some shamans obtained their power. Maidu men, for instance, obtained shamanic power by swimming in certain places. After diving into a deep pool and losing consciousness, they were often able to communicate with animal spirits. When they came-to, they would have been deposited on the shore by the spirits. Later, they would be able to speak with the spirits, dream of them, and after a long quest, obtain power and help in curing from them. These spirits were sometimes those of animals, but others could be those of deceased people. One Maidu shaman had as a helper spirit a gold miner who had died 50 years before.

The Power of *Moki*

One of the most powerful spirits in central California was known as *Moki* by the Valley Maidu and neighboring Patwin, and *Kuksuyu* by the Nisenan and the Sierra and Plains Miwok. The Sierra Miwok believed that the *Kuksuyu* was a wild spirit who lived in the forest and could sometimes be seen on a moonlight night. A brave dancer who saw the spirit on such a night sang for him instead of running away. Subsequently, the dancer copied the spirit's costume and began impersonating it in dance ceremonies.

The Valley Maidu likewise believed the *Moki* was extremely powerful and potentially danger-ous; some believed the spirit was actually the Creator itself. In dance ceremonies, the *Moki* was impersonated by a man dressed in an all-envelop-ing feather cloak. The dancer had to observe numerous taboos and strict rituals, for a mistake could be very dangerous for the dancer and other people present at the ceremony. So great was this spirit's power that just the act of touching the feather cloak would cause common people to be-come violently ill.

'Those caves, stay out of them or the Ettati *will get you.'*

CHIEF RICHARD FULLER (CENTRAL SIERRA MIWOK)[5]

Chief Fuller's warning to family and friends concerns the monstrous snake which lived in limestone caverns in the Sierra Nevada mountains. Elsewhere, too, wonderful heroes and terrible monsters fill the mythological world of the California people. Characteristic of many such creatures is the Southern Miwok story of *Uwulin*:

'Long ago, the bird and animal people lived in Yosemite Valley, and they lived well. But then came *Uwulin*, a great giant from the north who began to eat people

He was as big as a pine tree and his hands were so huge that he could hold 10 men at a time in each hand. He traveled with a great sack on his back into which he placed the people he had captured. His sack was so big that it could hold the entire population of a village. He caught so many people that he cut them into small pieces and made jerky of their meat. He hung the jerky to dry on a huge granite rock near the Merced River, and to this day that rock is stained with the blood from his making jerky.

The bird and animal people tried to kill the giant in every way, but they failed. Arrows and spears could not penetrate *Uwulin*. Finally, the bird and animal people asked Fly to help them. They told him to bite the giant all over his body to discover where he could be hurt. Fly searched for the giant and finally found him asleep. He bit *Uwulin* everywhere. The giant did not flinch until Fly bit him on his heel, which caused the giant to kick his massive leg.

Fly returned and told the bird and animal people of his discovery. The bird and animal

people decided to make a number of long, sharp, deer-bone awls, like those used in making baskets. They arranged the awls with the points up along the giant's trail, so that he could not avoid them.

When *Uwulin* came down the trail, he stepped on many of the awls. Finally, one pierced his heel where his heart was. He died immediately. The bird and animal people decided that they must destroy his body with fire, and they all carried wood and covered *Uwulin* with it. They watched his burning closely to insure that no part of his body escaped the flames, for they feared that such a part could grow and let *Uwulin* come back to life.'[6]

The Story of *Oankoitupeh*

There are other stories of heroes and monsters, as in the Valley Maidu and Konkow stories of *Oankoitupeh* who was miraculously born to the

A fine coiled-weave basket (right) from the Luiseño Indians of southern California. The eagle motif on the base and the flower and insect motifs on the sides are suggestive of Luiseño cosmology which centers around a dying-god motif and a creator-culture hero called *Wiyot* whose death changed the nature of the universe and led to the creation of the existing world of plants and animals, with each species in a productive, hierarchically-arranged and mutually-supportive relationship.

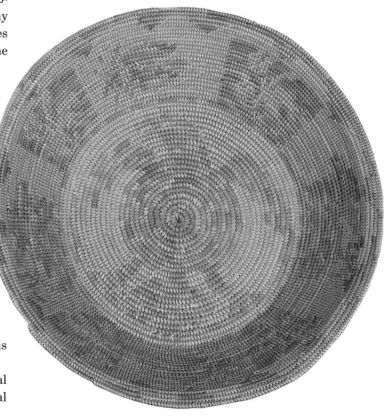

daughter of the chief in dire times. He grew to manhood in four days and set about making the world right. He drained the Sacramento Valley by breaking away mountains where the Carquinez Straits are today, and he destroyed both a fierce, human-sized black eagle and a She-Devil that had been killing people. Finally, he traveled to the north and challenged the doctor *Haikutwotupeh* to gamble with him for the return of the people *Haikutwotupeh* had won from *Oankoitupeh's* grandfather. *Oankoitupeh* won his grandfather's people back and restored every tribe to its original place.

The Cannibal Head

Throughout central and northern California stories are told of a cannibal head that rolls about the countryside eating people. Most of these stories start when a man who has accidentally injured himself first wipes away the blood, and then starts to lick his wound. The blood tastes so good that he devours his entire body, leaving only his head and shoulders. From then on, he bounces and rolls around, searching for and eating people. In one Maidu version, the monster dies when he bounces into a river and drowns.

The *Antap* Religion

Among the Chumash, the Sun was the basis for the *Antap* religion. *Antap* consisted of a society whose members were primarily tribal leaders of wealth and power. By means of a lunar calendar, members of the *Antap* Society set the schedule for important ceremonies to renew the world, especially at harvest time and the winter solstice. Society members presided at ceremonies where the Sun was worshipped as a threatening male deity, and Wind, Rain, and Fire as female deities. The powerful deities were somehow connected to the power and wealth of the *Antap*'s members.

The stories of monsters are not limited to legendary times. Even today, some Miwok parents warn their children against going into the limestone caverns of the Sierra Nevada, for the huge, snake-like *Ettati* is said to be living there still.

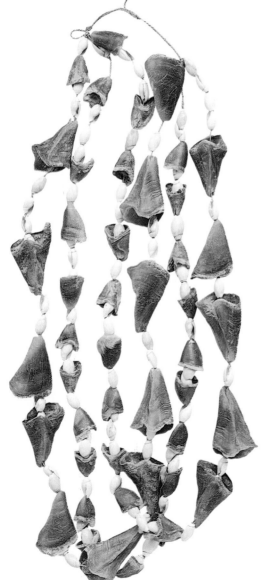

A human-like figure with extended arms and legs appears in this ancient pictograph at Mutau Flat (top left). Such figures – referred to as rock art – were probably painted by shamans and seem to be abstractions connected with the supernatural and maintaining a bond between Man and the mythological hero figures of the past.

A Hupa shaman's necklace (bottom left), made of deer hooves with olivella shells strung between, probably makes reference to one of the myriad of supernatural beings referred to in Hupa mythology and legend. Not least of these were the spirits who tended the deer, and to whom appeals were made at the time of embarking on hunts in order to keep them content.

This pictograph on rock (below), probably painted by ancestors of the Chumash Indians, is one of the many to be found on the Corrizo Plain, an enclosed basin directly north of Santa Barbara. Unusual rock formations were often considered to be sacred places of great power. The majority of paintings found in this region consist of circles which are quartered, rayed, or toothed. It is suggested that they were to maintain the essential balance between what were regarded as the dynamic supernatural forces in nature, such as restoring the seasonal round or turning the Sun's course at solstice.

'The first people lived on the Kaweah River a long time before our people, the Wukchumni, came. They had a bird and animal village at Tiupinish, *the little pointed hill near the station at Lemon Cove. This village was called* Shono'yoo. *When the Wukchumni came, the old-time people went away to the mountains and plains and left* Shono'yoo *for us.'*

TAWP'NAW (WUKCHUMNI)[7]

The Wukchumni elder *Tawp'naw* told this story in the 1930s as part of his people's creation story, and it illustrates how, to the Indian people of California, all of the land has a history making it sacred or holy. Many places were sacred because of their association with legendary events, while other sites were known to be home to spirits.

Rock Art

Chumash shamans produced elaborate rock art using native pigments at hundreds of locations. Many of these sites are in nearly inaccessible locations, while others are more easily accessible on large rock formations. One such site, where a mass of sandstone rocks rise 30-40ft (9-12m), was a solstice shrine called the House of the Sun.

Among motifs found painted in the rock shelters there is a large red disc with lines radiating from it, perhaps denoting the Sun. There is also a black circular design with a red outline which may represent an eclipse. Other images at this site, as well as at other Chumash sites, suggest mythological figures such as Bear, Condor, and animals of every sort. Another rock art site near the Chumash village of *Tashlipunau* consists of work spread through four caves. The images include large circular motifs with concentric rings, zoomorphic and anthropomorphic figures, dots, bifurcates, and zig-zag forms. They are painted in black, white, yellow, cream, red, orange, green, and blue-green. The orange and green paints have only been found at this site and it is possible that they were obtained by the Chumash when they sacked mission supplies in 1824. The use of the paint in the pictographs may have been an effort to gain supernatural control over the Chumash's Mexican enemies.

Sacred Mountains

Prominent mountains were often considered to be sacred places. Mount Diablo, just east of San Francisco Bay, was held sacred by many tribes in central California. To the east of Mount Diablo, the Central Sierra Miwok claimed that the *Lileusi* Dance came from the mountain, while other Sierra and Plains Miwok people place legendary events such as the creation and acquisition of fire as taking place on the mountain. The Patwin people to the north declared that some medicine people went to Mount Diablo to pray for prosperity and health. The Nisenan (Southern Maidu) believed that the dead crossed the mountains on their way to the land of the dead and that spirits watched from Mount Diablo's peak for wrongdoing. Among some of the Ohlone (Costanoan) people, a site just below the summit was an area where people gathered for a major autumn ceremony.

Mount Shasta figured prominently in the lives of Wintu people, who believed that the mountain possessed benevolent spiritual power and was

the 'main one' in the Wintu inventory of sacred mountains. When burying the dead, bodies were generally oriented toward the north and funeral orations directed souls on their journeys to Mount Shasta and the heavens. It was believed that the soul of a dead person went first to Mount Shasta before rising to the Milky Way, from where it would travel south and then east to the hereafter.

Wintu people today still consider Mount Shasta to be the sacred place it has always been to their people. Some Sierra Miwok and Ohlone people remember the importance of Mount Diablo in their spiritual background, and many Chumash people revere the sacred rock paintings of their ancestors. With the rapid growth and development that has taken place in California in the last century, many sacred sites have been lost to native people. Most of the Gabrielino village of *Puvungna*, birthplace of the *Chingichngish*, founder of the Gabrielino religion, is covered by the campus of the California State University at Long Beach. The small portion of the site which had not yet been built upon was recently slated for development, but the site was saved after a vigil by Gabrielino people. Today, Indian people are fighting to protect their sacred sites.

Rising alone from the surrounding rocks, the Great Dome in Yosemite (left) is the type of unusual rock formation considered by the prehistoric population to be a sacred place of great power, as was Mount Shasta (below) in the territory of the Wintu of northern California. The Wintu believed that the spirit of the deceased – which was 'like a whirlwind and one can feel a chill' – traveled northward to Mount Shasta and from there ascended to journey along the spirit trail in the Milky Way.

'The eagle, he's a messenger spirit who takes your wishes to Helin Maideh, *the big man.'*

HENRY AZBILL (VALLEY MAIDU)[6]

Participants of the White Deerskin Dance, such as these Hupa of northwest California (below), held albino, or other oddly colored, deerskins aloft on poles, carried beautifully chipped obsidian blades or wore long pieced-together feathers of the condor bird (right). The dance was not only a sign of wealth, but also invoked the powers for world renewal, as epitomized by the sacred Condor. Pictographic images of this are still to be found, and sometimes they are rendered in a human-like form (below right) as symbolic of the ascending hopes of mankind.

Like most California Indian people, the Maidu considered certain animals to be sacred. They believed that the eagle was a messenger to the Creator, and that by using eagle feathers in ceremonial dance regalia, or on a special flag to be hung in front of the ceremonial roundhouse on sacred occasions, one's prayers would be conveyed to the Creator. Among the Diegueño, the Eagle Ceremony was held to honor deceased leaders. A captured eagle was ceremonially killed by apparent supernatural means (which usually involved strangulation). Its wing and tail feathers were plucked for ceremonial regalia and its body carefully buried in a ceremony similar to that which would be held for a person. Skeletons of eagles, vultures, and condors have been found in archeological sites buried like humans; some of these burials date back 2,000 years.

The Supernatural Condor

The condor was the largest bird in California, with a wingspan of nearly 10ft (3m), so it is not surprising that California Indian people considered it to be a special animal, capable of providing communication with the supernatural world. The condor appeared frequently in the legendary history of many California Indian people. Legends among widely scattered peoples (including Central Sierra Miwok, Wiyot, Valley Nisenan, many Yokuts groups, Western Mono, and Chumash) related many supernatural and powerful acts performed by Condor during the early days of the world. The condor was considered a 'bird chief' among the Central and Northern Miwok, and some Central Miwok shamans acquired their power from the condor,

allowing them to suck supernatural 'poisons' from their patients' bodies.

Dances honoring the condor, in which dancers represented the bird, were widespread in central California. Most of these dances among the Sierra Miwok, Patwin, and Pomo involved a dancer wearing a condor skin with its feathers still attached. Southern Californians sometimes used condors in ceremonies similar to the Diegueño Eagle Ceremony, and used condor feathers to create ceremonial skirts and feather-quill bands. Far to the north, Yurok, Karok, and Hupa people sometimes pieced together several condor feathers to make what appeared to be one enormous feather, 20in (51cm) or longer, which was worn by participants in the White Deerskin Dance.

The Bear

In the 1970s, Northern Sierra Miwok elder Alice Pruitt admonished her grandchildren, 'A bear is just like a person. You don't want to eat him because you might be eating your grandfather.' Such views about bears, grizzly bears in particular, were held by many Miwok, Maidu, and other California people. Some Sierra Miwok people believed that the spirits of deceased, malevolent shamans might inhabit a grizzly bear, and thus they avoided them. Some regarded the bear as almost human, and others thought it was a messenger spirit. Out of respect, they would not eat bear meat, but would use the hide as a robe, for bedding, or for ceremonial regalia.

The Pomo greatly feared 'bear doctors' who, dressed in a bear disguise, waylaid and killed hunters and travelers for their goods. These bear doctors reportedly dug caves in a secluded, mountainous region. There, the doctor and his or her assistants would construct the special regalia which would imbue the doctor with the power of the grizzly bear. A similar belief in bear doctors was found among the Konkow and Maidu people, but they believed that bear doctors were sometimes so powerful that they were able to turn themselves into bears, and did not need to resort to dressing in bearskins.

Although grizzly bears are now extinct in California, and the California condor is on the verge of extinction, many native people still revere the supernatural power of these animals' spirits. In the Sierra Nevada, the Maidu still perform the Bear Dance every spring in honor of the grizzly, and the Condor Dance has recently been revived among the Chumash. In many contemporary California Indian homes, elders and parents instruct their children in the importance of respecting the power of these animal spirits.

The regalia (below) of a Pomo bear doctor consisted of a complete bearskin which covered the head and body of the wearer. When dressed in it the bear doctor could assume the powers of a bear and was greatly feared. Ceremonial daggers of elk antler were worn with the skin.

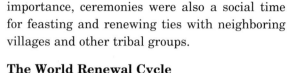

This Karok dance hat (below) of deerskin embellished with woodpecker and flicker feathers, some of them tipped with 'spirit-evoking-breath' plumes, was part of the regalia of the Brush Dance. Traditionally, this dance was performed to cure a sick child, being an appeal to the supernatural powers for healing.

'The dance is a celebration of life. It . . . represents a vehicle that preserves the life force – its joys, its uncertainties, and, above all, . . . it increases the awareness of one's own being.'

HARRY FONSECA (NISENAN-MAIDU)[9]

Rituals and ceremonies were an integral part of the lives of California Indian people. Special ceremonial observances were held to mark the changing of the seasons, give thanks to the spirits, and mourn the dead – although these ceremonies differed greatly from group to group throughout the region. Many of the rituals and ceremonies were given to humans in legendary times by the Creator or various spirits. Besides their ritual

importance, ceremonies were also a social time for feasting and renewing ties with neighboring villages and other tribal groups.

The World Renewal Cycle

In northwest California, the Tolowa, Karok, Yurok, Hupa, and Wiyot had an elaborate ceremonial life. Rites conducted by priests and their assistants were often secret, and part of the World Renewal cycle of ceremonies. Those held in public included two major dances: the White Deerskin Dance and the Jump Dance. In the White Deerskin Dance, a line of dancers held elaborately decorated hides from rare albino deer up on poles. The dance, which sometimes lasted as long as 16 days, celebrated the world's renewal. Through a display of regalia that got markedly more elaborate each day of the dance, it climaxed in a stunning display of wealth. In the Jump Dance, male dancers wore headbands made of woodpecker scalps and carried sacred dance baskets. These dances were each hosted by different ritual centers at distinct times of the year, and an extensive network of wealthy sponsors was required in order to organize and sustain the events, each of which might draw over 1,000 people.

Secret Societies

The term *Kuksu* describes a secret male dance society that flourished in most of central California, sometimes assisted by a similar women's dance society. The society performed dances, particularly during the winter months, to insure prosperity and health. Boys were initiated into the society as adolescents and were taught the dances, regalia, songs, and rituals that accompanied each of the ceremonial performances. The ceremonies were markedly different from one tribal group to the next, and sometimes even from village to village. Individual religious leaders had some leeway to practice their own ideas and beliefs while respecting long-established tribal beliefs about 'correct' ritual procedure. Among almost all of these central California

groups, the donning of regalia and the act of dancing brought forth a manifestation of supernatural power. This power, while not evil in nature, was believed to be so potent that bad luck could strike those who did not demonstrate proper respect in handling dance regalia or in performing rituals. The impressive array of regalia used in the dances included headbands made from the scraped quills of flicker feathers, woven belts which incorporated scarlet woodpecker and iridescent green mallard scalp feathers, and cloaks made of feathers from larger birds (i.e., eagles, hawks, and herons).

The Whirling Dance

The Tipai-Ipai, Luiseño, Gabrielino, Cahuilla, Cupeño and others had an elaborate ceremony to commemorate the anniversary of the death of a

chief or dance leader. Young condors or eagles were taken from their nests, raised, and then used in a ceremony which culminated in the bird's death by strangulation or from pressing on the heart. The bird's wing and tail feathers were used to create a fringe at the ends of a net-skirt, worn in the Whirling Dance. Among the Tipai-Ipai, the Whirling Dance was part of an elaborate ceremony performed after the death of a member of the *Toloache* Society, and involved a single male dancer who carried two sticks and wore only the skirt, a head ring, and plumes of owl feathers. The dancer's skipping and turning caused his feather skirt to whirl away from his body, giving the dance its name.

Today, some California Indian people still gather to practice old rituals. Among the Yurok, Tolowa, Karok, and Hupa there has been a strong revival in the production of ceremonial regalia and the resurrection or continuation of ceremonial dances. In the central part of the state, an unbroken chain of seasonal dances continues in a few places, while in other communities certain dances and ceremonies which have been preserved in the memories of elders have recently been reconstructed and reintroduced after a hiatus of 40 to 50 years. Since the 1970s there has been a revival of Chumash ceremonial life, many of them not seen for a century or so.

Hupa participants in the Jumping Dance (left) photographed at the Yurok town of *Pekwon* on the Klamath River in 1893. As with the White Deerskin Dance, the performers wear deerskin aprons and a profusion of dentalium shells, but here they also carry tubular baskets filled with straw which they shake as they perform the leaping and then crouching movements characteristic of the ritual. The headdresses worn were embellished with dozens of woodpecker scalps (above) attached to a band of deerskin taken from the animal's belly.

THE NORTHWEST COAST

> 'And when the last Red Man shall have perished, and the memory of my tribe shall have become a myth among the white man, these shores will swarm with the invisible dead of my tribe, and when your children's children think themselves alone . . . they will not be alone. In all the earth there is no place dedicated to solitude.'
>
> CHIEF SEATTLE (SUQUAMISH/DUWAMISH)[1]

THE STORIES OF THE Northwest Coast peoples are the transporters of hereditary rights, ethical behaviors, and appropriate interactions in the powerful interchanges between social, natural, and supernatural worlds. The people had a distinctive and ingenious response to explaining the universe to themselves, to ongoing generations, and to us, the outsiders. They did this with a wealth of stories, rituals, and visual images that ignited imaginations and drove the dullest mind into action. Their myths are histories of human and ancestral events. Their rituals are the means to make visible these stories, to bring to life and to memory the complex constellation of relationships between humans, nature, and the supernatural. Brilliant yet subtle, the stories are still being told. Dominated for a while by other societies and thoughts, the stories still speak to the people, and transcending, time and space, to us.

For centuries the Northwest Coast people lived in a uniquely mild environment on the North American continent. The people had many diverse languages, but shared a similar maritime culture that is considered one of the world's most distinctive. They included the Tlingit, the Haida and Kaigani Haida, the Tsimshian (comprising the Gitskan, Nishga, and Coast Tsimshian), the Salishan-speaking Bella Coola, the Northern Wakashan (formerly called the Northern Kwakiutl or Bella Coola), the Kwakiutl, the Nuu-chah-nulth (also called Nootka) and the closely related Makah, and the Coast Salish.

If we are to characterize the stories of the Northwest Coast, not in an effort to 'de-mystify' or to catalog them, but to provide a framework for them, then there are some aspects of their culture relevant to understanding the tremendous forces that inform and guide these people. Abundant with the stuff of life – ample food from the sea and land, cedar rain forests to furnish everything from cradle to coffin, and a temperate climate – the Pacific Northwest ecology provided the appropriate setting for permanent villages of planked houses. These abundances also provided the leisure time to develop an amazing array of material culture. The visual and oral arts especially flourished and reflected the peoples' deep spiritual response to this generous environment. If the physical setting provided leisure and abundance, their spiritual life provided an environment of deep contemplation and explanation. One seems necessary for the other, a concept that may elude contemporary western minds. For without contemplation of the laws of nature, human conduct is without moral laws or rules and thus is alienated from the supernatural.[2] This fundamental assumption in Northwest Coast spiritual life was probably never intended to be stated so simplistically, and this chapter's simplification of complex mythological and ritual structures is only intended to be a broad framework with which to view some of the ingenious and diverse responses to the synthesis of the social world with nature and the supernatural.

Faces of the Northwest Coast (far left), Tlingit men and boys in dance costume in 1895. Some of their clothing displays crests which indicate lineage or clan. The crests were a representation of their totem, often consisting of mythical animals, birds, fish, and so on.

Tales of how an ancestor obtained the crest often furnished the theme for a clan song, a number of which were sung during the spectacular masked dances the region was renowned for. The raven mask (top left) is Kwakiutl and would have been worn by a *Hamatsa* dancer in a winter ceremonial.

The region was also famed for its material crafts, both for carving as demonstrated in the masks, but also for many other things. The distinctive patterns of the Chilkat blanket (right and far left), for example, were immediately identifiable.

Raven on top of a clamshell which contains the creatures who will become the first Haidas. The myth behind this beautiful yellow cedar carving by Bill Reid is that when the creatures mature they will challenge the power of the ocean and wrest from it a rich livelihood.

'In the world today, there is a commonly held belief that, thousands of years ago, . . . Mongolian nomads crossed a land bridge . . . and became the people now known as the American Indians. The truth of course, is that the Raven found our forefathers in a clamshell on the beach at Naikun[3]*. . . Another part of it is that . . . the Great Halibut . . . shed his tail and fins and skin, and became the first man. Thunderbird then took off his wings and beak and feathers to become the second man . . .'*

BILL REID (HAIDA)[4]

Among the thousands of myths on the Northwest Coast many origin stories begin with accounts of supreme beings living in an upper world. This world has many layers, fits like an inverted bowl over the curved Earth, and is the residence of the supreme beings who have human forms and live in human-style dwellings. The Bella Coola call this *Nusmata*, or the 'place of myths; legends; stories.'[5] The stories are often told in the past tense, because the events took place so long ago.

A Supreme Being

Most of these cultures believe that the supreme being was not himself created, but always existed and is responsible for creating primordial life forms and the geographical features of the world, either singularly or by delegating the task to other lesser deities. Supernatural transformative creatures then created the world as we know it today. The Haida people, for example, speak of *Nanki'lsLas-lina'-i*, or He-Is-Going-to-Become-He-Whose-Voice-is-to-be-Obeyed, a nebulous creature who eventually became Raven and who formed the world by a complex recipe that is typically elusive and vague. The Yakutat Tlingit describe *Nas-caki-yectl*, or Creator, as the supreme but nebulous power of the universe that made all living things, including humans.[6] The Bella Coola people describe a 'supreme deity', *Atl'kwntam*, having no particular form, but who is addressed as 'highly respected one'.[7]

Primordial Darkness

The beginning of time was a period enveloped in darkness and was inhabited by humans, animals, and ghosts. In the primordial darkness all three had similar cultures, forms, and souls. Humans were decidedly less knowledgeable and less capable than animals or ghosts, though they did possess some power and had a potential to obtain it. Animals of the land and sea had more power because they had the ability to transform their human bodies into animal forms at will. In their natural realm, they lived within a ceremonial and social structure that paralleled that of

humans. Ghosts triumphed over animals and humans because under cover of darkness ghosts were invisible and dangerous in their constant quest to devour souls as well as food.

Daylight and Fire

The first time of darkness ended when a transformative being, Raven, brought the first and most important gifts to the world: daylight and fire. Ghosts, who hated light of any kind, fled to distant darker regions and, though still dangerous, became less of a threat. Animals became more covert about transforming themselves into human forms. People generally acquired more power and wisdom and entered a relationship of reciprocity with plants and animals.

Birth of the People

Sometimes Raven found people, as he did on the beach at Naikun where, hearing muted sounds coming from inside a large clamshell, he discovered infant humans: the ancestors of the Haida of the Queen Charlotte Islands. In another story, this Haida Raven was said to have summoned four different tribes out of the ground: the Tsimshian, Haida, Kwakiutl, and Tlingit.[8]

Other cultures of course, have their own origin stories. Many of the Kwakiutl clans and families trace their origins to supernatural beings who in animal forms descended from the sky, out of the sea, or from the underground to specific localities, removed an animal mask and became a human ancestor.[9] The Bella Coola's *Atl'kwntam* created four supernatural carpenters to create land features, plants and animals, and humans. The Salish trace their origins to the all-powerful *Swai-swei* rising out of the Fraser River and creating the first woman and mother of all men.

These creation or origin stories attempted to answer universal human questions about where we came from and why. Origin stories acknowledge the beginnings of human consciousness while recognizing the quality of the eternal, of time without beginnings, of creators who themselves knew no creation. They are a handle for speculating on the trajectory of human endeavors, while forming explanations about the elusive and sometimes paradoxical worlds around us.

This Clayoquot dance robe (above) displays a Thunderbird image with lightning serpents at the lower edge. In much coastal mythology these serpents are often described as Thunderbird's harpoon and belt. The Clayoquot are Nootkans from the Kennedy Lake region and some features of this role indicate the influence of more northerly Kwakiutl art styles.

'We-gyet was craft without wisdom, power without regard for consequences. He was as unheeding and petulant as a spoiled and pampered child and yet often as appealing as an unloved one . . . We-gyet was caught between spirit and flesh. He was no man, yet all men.'

TSIMSHIAN STORY [10]

Raven has many names on the Northwest Coast. He is *We-gyet* or *Txamsem* among the Tsimshian, *Yehl* among the Tlingit, *He'mask.as* (Real Chief) among the Bella Bella, *Kwekwaxa'we* (Great Inventor) among the northern Kwakiutl, and *Nankil'slas* (He Whose Voice is Obeyed) among the Haida. Raven was an instrument of the Creator.[11] In the beginning of time, he traveled around the world and throughout the cosmos, a hero finishing the job of creation. Although wisdom and integrity were not the wily Raven's strongest features, he often unwittingly became the benefactor to many human communities, bringing the first salmon, the first berries, and other gifts such as the Sun, Moon, stars, the tides, rivers, and streams.

The Sun and the Box of Daylight

Most Raven stories begin with an account of how he stole the Sun. First he impregnated the Sky Chief's daughter by turning himself into a conifer needle she swallowed in a drink of water. She gave birth to a boy who was really Raven in disguise. (In some stories, Raven simply appeared after the birth, scooped the child out of its skin and assumed the boy's identity.) The grandson of the Sky Chief grew rapidly and, as young children will do, the toddler became irritable and cried when he could not have his own way. The doting grandfather, like all grandfathers anxious to please, and perhaps just as anxious to placate the screaming child, gave him the box containing the Moon. The box was broken open and the Moon escaped into the sky. The crying resumed and the next toy proffered was a larger box containing the Sun: the Box of Daylight. Seizing the prize he came for, the child transformed back

Yehl, or Raven, crouches over the Box of Daylight with the Sun disc between his ears (far left). This Taku Tlingit headdress is probably the finest illustration of this famous myth. Raven has been rendered in semi-human form and grasps the lid of the chest which contains the daylight – represented by the inlaid mirror.

into Raven and escaped through the smoke-hole of the chief's great house. (Some story-tellers claim that this is why the Raven's feathers are the color of soot, for in the time before the liberation of light Raven was a white bird.) Raven traveled around the world, opening the Box of Daylight, not only bringing light to the spirits of the world, but giving many of them the physical forms that they have today.

Thunderbird

All the First Nations of North America tell stories of Thunderbird, of its monumental size and power. A swift death-bringer, Thunderbird's awesome supernatural power is represented by two 'horns' on top of its head. This being is so enormous that extinct volcanoes cradle its nest. Called *Hagwelawremrhskyoek*, or Sea-monster Eagle, by the Tsimshian, this giant bird swoops from the sky and devours whales. When the bird blinked, lightning flashed, and thunder crashed from the flapping of his great wings. In the Coast Salish (Comox) Thunderbird Dance, a small amount of gunpowder was ignited near the ceremonial house entrance to represent the flash of his eyes.[12] For the Tlingit, seeing or even hearing a Thunderbird made a person wealthy.[13]

The Whale

Of all the groups on the Northwest Coast, only the Nuu-chah-nulth hunted whales, the 'salmon of the Thunderbird'. In their stories, Thunderbird had Lightning Snakes under his wings that he hurled down to kill a surfacing whale. The whalers painted the image of Lightning Snake on the prow of their canoe, then concealed it with black paint: the power of Thunderbird's lethal weapons was thus transferred to the hunters.[14]

Thunderbird, Lightning Snake and Moon by Tim Paul (above) examines common Northwest Coast themes. The Quileute attributed thunder, lightning, and certain rains to the *Tistilal*, or Thunderbird, whose lair was the Blue Glacier on Mount Olympus in the southeastern part of traditional Quileute territory. Eclipses were caused by monsters such as Lightning Snake who had bitten away chunks of the Moon. These designs were rendered on the front of planked houses

HERO CREATURES AND MONSTERS

Gonaquadet (below left) is a supernatural underwater being and source of wealth. The carving shows a Haida hero dressed in *Gonaquadet*'s skin and holding a whale. The *Yagim* (below right) appeared in the *Tseyka*. This powerful monster could start storms and destroy entire tribes.

'My ancestor at the beginning of mythical-times was Stone-Body. His skin was made hard as stone when his father, Head-Winter-Dancer, washed him with the blood of the double-headed serpent. His son was Odzestalis, *and the child of* Odzestalis *was Property-Body. Oh, why should I continue to enumerate the great names of the chiefs, my ancestors?'*

POTLATCH SPEECH (KWAKIUTL)[15]

Monumentality is a feature of Northwest Coast material culture exemplified by the towering crest poles in front of huge planked houses. These gabled dwellings not only housed many families, they were metaphorically large enough to contain the cosmos during the winter ceremonials.[16] Monumentality is also a feature in the description of all-powerful spirits of the coast including those amalgamations of natural forms that we call 'monsters'. Many of these monsters can assume any shape. Often, monsters provide people with monumental wealth, but sometimes they are also the source of almost unthinkable fear and danger.

The Trickster

Raven's importance to the world as the transformer-hero is paralleled by his role as the supreme trickster. In his voracious search for food and sex, Raven is a transforming monster, a randy jester, and frequently a shamed fool. In

some stories Raven loses or injures parts of his anatomy while attempting to steal food or sex; in others, he assumes various human and animal disguises to obtain illicit sexual favors.

In one series of the Raven stories, an old fisherman tricks Raven into stealing bait from a hook, and he loses his beak in the escapade. He sulks shamefaced around the man's village, a blanket covering his face, until he recovers the beak. In some of the more risqué tales, Raven's penis is so long that he has to coil it over his shoulder like a lasso. In a few of these adventures Raven succeeds in seducing various beautiful women (and men); in others, his amorous ruses are sometimes humiliatingly and sometimes painfully exposed. Tales of humiliation and triumph, of noble and foolish behavior, of reverence and irreverence, Raven stories illuminate the fundamental paradoxes of human life.

Water Creatures

The waters of the Northwest Coast provide the wealth of food, as well as awesome and often invisible dangers of the unpredictable and ever-changing watery environments. What better place to discover monumental monsters?

Among the northern tribes there is a powerful sea being called *Gonaquadet* among the Tlingit, *Ginaxcame'tk* among the Tsimshian, and *Wasgo* or *Su'san* among the Haida. A wealth-bringing monster who lives in the sea or in a lake, *Gonaquadet* and his ilk can assume any shape.[17] These monsters often had toenails, claws, teeth, hair, canoes and other belongings made of copper, the regional symbol of wealth throughout the Northwest Coast area.

Many of the stories reveal that the *Gonaquadet* has given his skin to a human cultural hero, usually a misfit of some sort, who performs amazing supernatural feats, such as rescuing the village from certain starvation by providing his people with inexhaustible food supplies. The hero's reward is immortality. Clothed in the monster's skin, the hero is the mythological analogy for the spiritually enlightened and wealthy chief

in Northwest Coast society. So, the distinctive emblems of chiefly power – the raven rattle, the Chilkat dancing robe, the frontlet headdress, and the chief's box to contain this potlatch paraphernalia – are all said to have originated with *Gonaquadet*.[18]

Kwakiutl stories describe the power of *Sisiutl*, a giant double-headed serpent with darting tongues and a human face in the center of its body. Each of the three foreheads of the *Sisiutl* are adorned with horns of power, like those found on the great Thunderbird, its major predator. Noted for swiftness and a voracious appetite, the *Sisiutl* is a daunting carnivore that looks like a serpent, swims like a fish, yet can travel on and under land. Seeing it, touching it or even its slimy trail, can turn people into stone or foam, or cause them to vanish altogether. The *Sisiutl* can transform itself into a variety of forms including a self-propelling canoe that must be fed seals. Yet when killed properly, the creature's skin can be worn as a belt. The owner of such a belt, usually a warrior, is protected from death. This awesome protective power of the *Sisiutl* is represented visually on many housefronts, masks, and dancing paraphernalia.[19]

A double-headed serpent with curving, darting tongues is referred to by the Kwakiutl as *Sisiutl*. This monster is generally depicted with a human face at the center of its body which is surmounted by horns. *Sisiutl* was in constant conflict with Thunderbird. The painting style is typical of Northwest Coast formline art. When the design is rendered in mask form for dancing, the sections representing the serpent are hinged so that they can move back and forth and add to the drama.

HOLY PLACES, SACRED SITES

'Every part of this soil is sacred in the estimation of my people. Every hillside, every valley, every plain and grove, has been hallowed by some sad or happy event in days long vanished . . . and the very dust upon which you now stand . . . is rich with the dust of our ancestors and our bare feet are conscious of the sympathetic touch.'

CHIEF SEATTLE (SUQUAMISH/DUWAMISH)[20]

The sea and the forest are two places in Northwest Coast belief which teem with mythical power. The Kwakiutl's chief of the undersea world is *Goomokwey* (above), a source of prestige and wealth for those who gain his good will. The forbidding nature of the Northwest's forests provided fertile ground for the imagination, and they are thought to be home to the terrifying, child-eating *Tsonoqua*.

In western cultures, places for worship and sacred sites are distant from everyday lives. In traditional Northwest Coast cultures, sacred events are held in the places where people work and live, reflecting the comprehensive, holistic world view that connects the spiritual and the profane. Their clan houses, for example, are living spaces for most of the year, but for parts of the winter they become sacred sites as ceremonial settings and metaphorical containers of the cosmos.

Holy and sacred are not necessarily concepts tied to place, but may express a condition – as in the sacred time of the winter ceremonies. Or 'sacred' may describe a kind of event – as in the offering of tobacco dipped in the water on the end of an oar to placate Swell Woman who has made seas dangerously high. 'Sacred' may also designate places such as grave sites. Unlike those in the western culture, these are not the sites of pilgrimages or places of homage. From a native view, these are places where ghosts may reside, and most are not places that people revisit after fulfilling their duty to the deceased.

Understanding the three important realms of Northwest Coast consciousness – earth, sea, and sky – will illuminate the Northwest Coast concepts of sacred places. These realms intersect and provide an axis of human interaction with the supernatural forces of the universe.

Earth

The Earth is a complex plane, basically divided into three sectors. The beach is the first, where powerful and dangerous creatures pose enticing threats to human sanity. The Land Otter Man of the Tlingit and *Pook-ubs* of the Nuu-chah-nulth were spirits of drowned men who appeared as humans on lonely beaches, and were dreaded because of their great supernatural powers to entice humans, rob them of their senses, and turn them into Land Otter spirits.[21]

The second Earth plane is the forest, dark and equally dangerous as the beach, full of perils and rewards known and unknown to the hunter. The Kwakiutl *Bukwus*, or Wild Man of the Woods, and the *Pu'gwis* of the Tsimshian are remarkably similar spirits of deep woods. Each has a human-like countenance, but with the skin and facial features of a corpse: stretched facial skin, lips curled back from the teeth, and the fleshy parts of the nose decayed to reveal large nasal passages. The danger of this creature is that it has the ability to imitate humans, and to seduce or

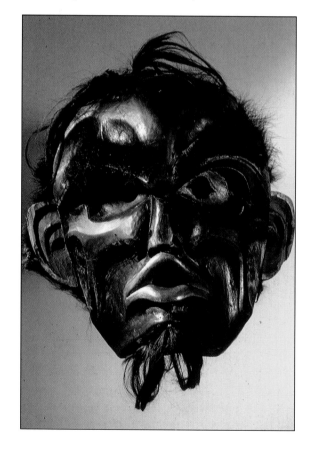

capture them by rendering them senseless or foolish.

The woods are also the home of the mysterious *Tsonoqua* or *Dzonokwa*, the Wild Woman of the Woods. She is a cannibal woman known to the Kwakiutl and Bella Coola. Her lonely cry is heard in the woods as a low, long whistling sound: 'u, hu, u, u.' The image of *Tsonoqua* is a black-faced, sleepy-eyed woman with pursed lips. She sometimes appears in the winter ceremonial, an ogress threatening to snatch away children. For all her fearsomeness, she is also known to bestow power and great wealth: the abundance of food at feasts and great shield-like coppers.[22]

Humans occupy the third Earth plane: that thin strip of habitable land between beach and forest, between sea and sky. In that humble position of liminality, they contemplate their own power in relation to the sacred spaces of the universe around them. It is there that they give voice, image, and memory to the contemplation of that tenuous and fragile existence in the tension between the natural and the supernatural.

Sea

Before them, the sea provides the wealth of food and the dangers of an alienated ecology. People need the sea for survival, yet every day they risk their lives interacting with it. The wealth of the sea lures the people, and it is personified in numerous supernatural creatures. For example, the Kwakiutl tell of the great chief under the waters, *Qlo'mogua*, or Wealthy, the controller of all sea life and consequently of great wealth. He is sometimes referred to as Copper Maker and his masks are adorned with parts of sea animals: spines, fins, tentacles, and suckers as well as with copper or images of coppers. He is generally a benevolent spirit, bestowing great gifts on those who encounter him.

Sky

Sky beings occupy the layers that make up the solid vault above the Earth and sea. Home of the all-powerful ones who figure in the creation

stories, the sky is also home to the spirits of Wind, Rainbow, Cloud, Sun, and Moon. This heavenly realm, where the Milky Way is known as the Seam of Heaven in Kwakiutl thought, is similar to the Earthly plane. There one finds the good life, freedom from pain and sorrow, and timelessness. Humans have been known to travel to and from this realm, and to receive messages from it via supernatural birds. Many Northwest cultures view this upper world as the place of origins, the dwelling place of creators; as well, it is the place of endings, the dwelling place of ghosts, of the dearly departed.

Rialto Beach in Washington State (above) is typical of the Northwest shoreline. It is a region with a relatively mild climate and temperate rainforest, and a sea rich enough in marine life to allow the creation of an economy and a culture for the indigenous peoples.

Marine animals, naturally enough, played the most prominent role in Northwest culture. This war helmet (bottom) is a killer-whale holding a seal in its mouth. It was worn in battle by a Tlingit nobleman who fought the Russians at Fort Archangel Michael in 1802. He belonged to the Wolf clan with the Killer-Whale crest. Non-marine animals though were important too. The great horned owl mask (center) was used by the Bella Coola in the *Luwulaxa* Ceremony, but probably the most important crest animal was the grizzly bear. It is represented here (top) by this Tlingit mask of bearskin, teeth, wood, iron, copper, and abalone. It belonged to a noble family of the *Nanyaayi* clan, acknowledged as 'the chief ones owning the grizzly bear.'

'Whale, I have given you what you wish to get – my good harpoon . . . Please hold it with your strong hands. Do not let go . . . Whale do not turn outward, but hug the shore, and tow me to the beach . . . for when you come ashore there, young men will cover your great body with blue-bill duck feathers, and with the down of the great eagle, the chief of all birds; for this is what you are wishing, and this is what you are trying to find from one end of the world to the other, every day you are travelling and spouting.'

A PRAYER (NUU-CHAH-NULTH)[23]

Earth, sea, and sky are inhabited by powerful and revered animals in Northwest Coast story and ritual. Animal spirits appear in natural and personified forms to enter into states of super-natural reciprocity with humans. Some of the most important animals of the coast – salmon, whale, killer-whale, bear, wolf, eagle, and raven – demonstrate this concept in stories that illuminate the cosmic balances and spiraling cycles of life. Many of the revered animals figure as ancestors, and are thus celebrated in the songs, dances, stories, and visual images that are the personal property of individuals and clans.

Killer-Whale

Interestingly, humans are not considered to be superior to animals. Neither is independent of the other, for supernatural ancestors of the people were often transformative animal spirits. The Tlingit and Haida, for example, regard the Killer-Whale People as a superior race of beings, even though the Tlingit maintain the first killer-whale was made by a man out of a piece of yellow cedar. Haida women would take children down to the surf generated by a passing *Orca* pod, and dip the children's feet into the water while uttering a prayer that the powerful Killer-Whale, or *Sga'na* – which also means 'shaman' and 'power', would give them strength, good health, and wealth.[24] The Kwakiutl prayed to it to give them food and placed mountain goat tallow, cedar bark, or, in later times, tobacco in the water. Tsimshian sea

monsters use killer-whales for their canoes. Many of these seafaring peoples believe the souls of drowned relatives became killer-whales and live with the powerful beings in their village under the sea. This may explain why killer-whales are never hunted for food.

Wolf and Bear

On land, revered animals included the wolf and the bear. The Nuu-chah-nulth describe the connection between the wolf and killer-whale as originating from the time when the sea mammal beached on the shore and its spirit transformed into Wolf, which explains why the wolf has the same black and white markings. Wolves are both admired and feared as canny relentless hunters, swift and skilled. Supernatural wolves are a prominent feature of the Nuu-chah-nulth winter ceremonial known as the *Klookwana*, where they are responsible for taking initiates to the forest to begin the ritual process of joining a secret society. In a similar Kwakiutl ritual, wolves bite and then greedily devour the initiate; later, the guilty supernatural wolves revive the dancer.[25]

Although wolves are not hunted for food, bears are. The grizzly bear, the Salmon-Eater, shares an important role with eagles and with humans as omnivorous hunters. All North American First Nations have a profound respect for the bear, and Northwest Coast people share with them many ceremonial aspects of bear-hunting. Hunters fast and abstain from sexual intercourse before the hunt, and prayers are said to the bear thanking him for giving his body for food. After the kill, the head and skin are positioned in the same manner as a human chief lying in state. The head is sometimes painted and anointed with red ochre and eagle down; the bones are handled carefully, not only that the bear might be reincarnated in perfect form but so that the dead bear's friends will not kill the hunter.

Most important food sources, plant or animal, are thanked in simple prayers, such as this Kwakiutl one to a slain grizzly bear which illustrates their special relationship:

'Thank you friend, that you did not make me walk about in vain. Now you have come to take pity on me so that I may obtain game, that I may inherit your power of getting easily with your hands the salmon that you catch . . . O Friend! Now we press together our working hands that you may give over to me your power of getting everything easily with your hands, friend!'[26]

Prayers often conclude with a request for the slain animal to tell all its relatives that it has been well-treated and they should continue to come to the people with their ultimate offering.

The salmon is associated with a cosmos situated below the ocean where marine mammals and fish exist in human form. The salmon can transform at will into any other being or object and come each season as fish to give their flesh to humans. This headdress (above) was used to act out this myth.

Body tattoos were also used to mark clan crests. Johnnie Kit Elswa (left), a Haida, has a bear on his chest and a dogfish on each wrist. A potlatch would have been given in his honor when he was a child, entitling him to wear marks of his status in the form of tattoos.

'You will be known all over the world, as far as the edge of the world, you great one who safely returned from the spirits.'

HAMATSA SONG (KWAKIUTL)[27]

Synthesizing the social, natural, and supernatural worlds, the ritual and ceremonial practices of the Northwest Coast people make visible and memorable the social and supernatural worlds. In events that define, separate, and then unite the sacred and the profane, the movement of human spirits between social and spiritual realms is marked by ritual births, deaths, transformations, and regenerations.

First Salmon Ceremony

Most Northwest Coast people hold First Salmon ceremonies in the spring, thus beginning the harvest of their primary food source. Swimming from their underwater villages to their natal streams every four or five years, the Salmon People assume fish form. Complex and solemn rituals accompany the first salmon to be taken from the river. The salmon is their gift of life and accordingly the animal is honored with prayer, song, and ceremony. The Kwakiutl have a prayer to these great supernatural beings who are addressed as 'Swimmers' or *me'mE∑ yo'xwEn*:

'Oh Swimmers. This was the dream given by you, to be the way of my late grandfathers when they first caught you at your play. I do not club you twice, for I do not wish to club to death your souls so that you may go home to the place where you came from, Supernatural One, you givers of heavy weight [meaning wealth/supernatural power] . . . Now you will go.'[28]

The fish is then cut up by the chief's wife, who offers a special prayer of thanks. The parts of the salmon are distributed to members of the group, consumed, and then all the bones are carefully collected and returned to the water for the Salmon spirit to reflesh and regenerate. Enacting this 'ritual of rightness' the people enable the reincarnated salmon to swim back to their villages. The continuity of life, for the people and for the salmon, is thus ensured.

Cannibal Ceremony

The First Salmon Ceremony marks the opening of the profane season of food gathering and ritually sanctions the devouring of supernatural animals by humans. The Kwakiutl *Hamatsa*, or Cannibal, Ceremony marks the devouring of humans by the supernatural. The *Hamatsa*, a secret society of the Kwakiutl and Bella Bella, is performed in the *Tseyka*, or sacred season of the winter ceremonials. Neighboring tribes have similar cannibal societies: the *U'lala* or *Wa'lala* of the Haida, and the *xg.edt* or *U'lala* of the Tsimshian.

In these societies, an initiate begins a spirit quest, separating himself from the villagers by going into the forest and fasting for several days. While in isolation, the initiate 'travels' spiritually to the house of *Bakbakwalanooksiwey*, Great Cannibal at the North End of the World, and is

The power of this *Skhwaikhwey* mask lies in its essential use in cleansing and purifying ceremonies. These are associated with important times of change in human lives, such as puberty, marriage, and even death. It is wood decorated with feathers, beads, and cloth. This mask is identified with the trickster Raven, but other masks detail different creatures.

The *Hamatsa* or Cannibal Ceremony stood highest in rank in the *Tseyka*, or winter ceremonials, of the Kwakiutl. This incredible wooden mask (left) is embellished with cedar bark and painted with standard black, red, and white colors.

devoured. In the belly of this monster that has an insatiable hunger for human flesh, the initiate's cultural identity is metaphorically digested and the raw, natural human spirit is either vomited or excreted. The initiate, stripped of his cultural attributes, is naked, has no language or song, walks on all fours, and has an appetite for human flesh; he is the protégé of the Man Eater. Eventually the *Hamatsa* is 'captured' by members of the society and returned to the winter ceremonial house where he performs dances.

First appearing with darkened face and wearing only hemlock boughs, the *Hamatsa* dances with the assistance of helpers. With trembling outstretched hands he moves around the fire. Sometimes he lunges at people, biting them; sometimes, he appears to devour the flesh of a corpse. Later, with shredded cedar bark covering most of his body, he wears one of the supernatural bird-like masks that represents the creatures in the household of *Bakbakwalanooksiewey*. The masks are striking in the raking firelight: first the Man-eating Raven, then *Galokwudzuwis*, or the Crooked Beak of Heaven, and finally the long-beaked *Hokhokw*, or Cannibal-bird, that crushes men's skulls. The dancers appear one by one, until up to four of the great supernatural birds are around the fire. When they depart, the initiate dances alone: upright, proud, the inspired frenzy vanquished. As the wildness leaves his body, he once again resumes a tame and cultured life. However, the dancer is always a *Hamatsa*, a

human transformed in the belly of the great supernatural one. Forever changed, with a new name and a new identity, he is reintegrated into society with an elevated spiritual status.

Wealth and great spirituality are the coinage of power on the Northwest Coast. Myth and ritual help ensure that power is made visible and memorable. The synthesis of power between natural and supernatural realms is thus enacted and made viable for human spirits questing and dreaming through the universe.

The setting of the *Hamatsa* (below) and its dancing epitomized the dramatic nature of Kwakiutl ritual. The initiate danced into the firelit room wearing the powerful, long-beaked mask (center) that was said to be used to crack open human skulls and eat the brains.

THE SUBARCTIC

'In falltime you'll hear the lakes make loud cracking noises after they freeze. It means that they're asking for snow to cover them up, to protect them from the cold. When my father told me this, he said, "everything has life in it." He always used to tell us that.'

KOYUKON HUNTER[1]

THE SUBARCTIC CULTURE area spans the North American continent from the coast of Labrador to the lower Yukon River in Alaska. Its northern boundary approximates to the tree line, while the southern boundary runs from the lower St Lawrence River, just north of the Great Lakes and along the northern edge of the prairies to the foothills of the Rocky Mountains in northern British Columbia. For the most part the land is level and low-lying with lakes, streams, and bogs, but toward the west it rises, becoming rugged and mountainous. The landscape is dominated by coniferous forests of spruce, pine, cedar, and larch which thin out to open woodland and tundra toward the north. The winters are long and bitterly cold. The summers are warm, but short.

Population density has always been low. It is estimated that at the arrival of the first Europeans there were no more than 60,000 inhabitants scattered over this vast area of some 2,000,000 sq miles (3,219,000 sq km). The native people spoke one of two major languages, Athapaskan or Algonquian, each one made up of numerous dialects. The Athapaskans included the Ingalik, Tanaina, Koyukon, Kutchin, Tanana, Ahtna, Han, Tutchone, Inland Tlingit, Tahltan, Hare, Yellowknife, Dogrib, Slavey, Beaver, Carrier, and Chipewyan. Among the Algonquians were the Western Woods Cree, West Main Cree, Northern Ojibwa, Lake Winnipeg Saulteaux, East Cree, Naskapi, Montagnais, and Attikamek. How far these groups can be identified as 'tribes' is perhaps debatable, since any form of political unity or integration was generally lacking. The pattern throughout much of the area was of small, autonomous extended family units, isolated from one another and often highly mobile. Not unnaturally, such a pattern bred independence and individuality.

The quest for food was all-important. People lived primarily by hunting and fishing, with trapping gaining in importance following the advent of the fur trade. Caribou and moose were the principal large game animals. Smaller game included hare, beaver, muskrat, squirrel, and porcupine. Bears, although never a major food resource, were sought after for the fat they provided. Waterfowl and fish were also important, the latter especially so along the streams of the Pacific drainage system.

Subarctic mythology reflects the precariousness of human existence in a harsh, often hostile environment. Myths and legends provided reference and reassurance for the inexplicable or unpredictable aspects of daily life. They also provided a source and explanation for the multitude of rules which governed people's behavior. Such rules ranged from specific prohibitions, like that against women scraping skins at night, to complex instructions for the ritual treatment of a killed wolverine. Taken together, myths equipped their listeners with the means of understanding the natural world and their own place in it and established a code of proper behavior toward the environment and its resources.

The earliest descriptions of the Ahtna referred to them as tall, fine-looking people with smooth olive complexions and well-kept hair, who wore ear and nose ornaments of metal or shell and dentalium shell necklaces. The picture (far left) of these Ahtna girls from the Copper River Valley is testament to the accuracy of such writings.

The Kutchin are a neighboring group; the patterns of their decorative beadwork seen here (right and far left) had their origins in earlier distinctive quillwork. Also artistic, but far more numerous, are the Cree who are dispersed widely across the continent. The stuffed goose head (top left) was collected from the Cree at James Bay, Quebec, early this century, and would have been kept as a charm or a hunting trophy.

'Nobody made it up, these things we're supposed to do. It came from the stories . . . My grandfather said he told the stories because they would bring the people good luck, keep them healthy, and make a good life.'

KOYUKON HUNTER[2]

All Subarctic communities have a vast repertoire of myths and legends relating to the origin of the world and everything in it. They are set in a remote primordial world and describe, often at great length and in great detail, how the present order of things was established.

The Distant Time

The Koyukon name for this series of myths is *Kkadontsidnee*, meaning Distant Time. In the Distant Time, all living things – people, animals and birds, trees and plants – were related. They all had human form, spoke the same language, and lived in the same way. The stories explain how these human beings were transformed into the animal and plant species we know today. Certain trees, for example, were once women who were told of the death of their husbands. One cried and pinched her skin and was changed into the spruce tree with its rough and pinched bark. Another cried and slit her skin with a knife, and became the poplar with its deeply cut bark. Such stories, attractive in themselves, have a deeper purpose, for they remind people that even trees have spirits and need to be shown respect before they are 'killed' by being cut down.

The scope of Distant Time stories ranges from the cosmological to the minute. They explain the origins of the Sun, Moon and stars, winds and thunderstorms, mountains and lakes, as well as those of mosquitoes. The Northern Lights, for example, was once a hunter who broke his bow shooting at caribou and was burned up in a fire.

The Raven Trickster

The central figure in this ancient world is the trickster, known as Raven or Crow to tribes like the Tanaina, Kutchin, Inland Tlingit, and Kaska, as *Wisakedjak* to the Cree, as *Nanabush* to the Ojibwa, and as *Djokabish* to the Naskapi. Whatever his name, he is the same wonderfully contradictory figure – at one moment he is a creator, transformer, and manipulator of the forces of nature, at the next a mischief-maker, buffoon, coward, thief, and glutton. It was Raven, for example, who first created human beings out of stone, but then finding that they never died, recreated them from dust so that they became mortal as they are today.

Predictably perhaps, most Distant Time stories relate to animals. In their simplest form, the stories explain, often in a comical way, how an animal's present physical appearance came about. For example, a Tanaina myth describes how the beaver and muskrat originally had each other's tails, but decided to exchange them. The Koyukon said a lynx's black-tipped tail resulted from its having been burned, while the wolf received his dark markings when Raven tricked him by throwing caribou innards in his face.

Other stories refer to the ceremonial treatment accorded to certain animals after they have been killed. One of these tells how two powerful chiefs went on a long and unsuccessful hunting expedition. As they wandered on and on, they became thin and their clothes ragged. Their skins tanned and their hair grew long. Finally they began to live like animals and they were transformed, one into a wolf and the other into a wolverine. This is

The aurora borealis was associated with the stories of *Kkadontsidnee* or Distant Time. When it appeared in the winter sky (right) it was said by the Koyukon of northwestern Alaska to be the Northern Lights Man shooting arrows foretelling the appearance of caribou. The stories explained mankind's interconnections with nearly everything in the universe, teaching listeners to recognize the relationship between themselves and the natural world and to respect other animate and inanimate things.

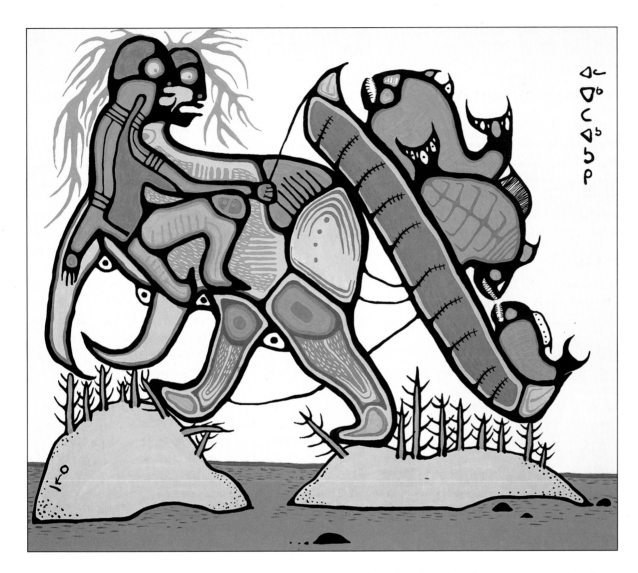

The Great and Mischievious *Nanabush* by Blake Debassige illustrates the Subarctic's creator-trickster figure under the name he is known to the Ojibwa. The Ojibwa saw him as half-man and half-spirit, his mother being the granddaughter of the Moon and his father the spirit of the west. His origins enabled him to transform into anything he wanted. In the painting he has become a giant so that he can travel further in search of food. He is actually crossing the Great Lakes, using the islands as stepping stones, and returning home with some 'fish' to eat which are in fact whales. *Nanabush* is depicted with another person inside him to symbolize the duality of both his personality and that of all other people too.

why, traditionally, whenever these animals were killed, they were hailed as great chiefs and given the place of honor at a funeral feast, 'remembering their hardships long ago.'

Each tribe or group of tribes also had myths relating to their own origins. For example, several tribes, including the Chipewyan, Dogrib, Hare, Slavey, and Yellowknife, shared a mythical ancestry from a woman who married a dog which turned into a man at night. It is this story which probably gave rise to the Chipewyans and other Athapaskans being designated by early European travelers as 'dog-sided' or 'dog-ribbed.' It may also be related to the taboos against eating dogs.

Codes of Conduct

Origin myths were not told simply as entertainment, they also established the rules governing the interaction between human beings and the natural world. These rules were based upon a vast range of taboos against behaving in a particular way toward animate and inanimate elements in nature. Although they seldom contain explicit moralizing, myths were often told for moral effect. Thus myths served as a code of conduct and a medium of instruction.

ALL-POWERFUL SPIRITS

Raven (top) and Crow (bottom) were central figures in the myths of many Subarctic groups; in fact they are among the nearest things in the region to an all-powerful spirit. These masks representing them are from the Ingalik Mask Dance, held to honor Game Mother.

*'*Manitou *was looked upon as the boss of the whole world. The Earth and everything was made by* Manitou.*'*

JEANNETTE SAGABA'KISKAM (CREE)[3]

This statement, made by an elderly Cree in the James Bay area in the 1930s, appears to be at odds with the many origin myths in which the work of creation is credited to the trickster figure, as represented by Raven, *Wisakedjak, Nanabush*, and so on. In contrast to the trickster, *Manitou* or *Kitche Manitou* – the Algonquian Great Spirit – is presented as a remote, mysterious, and omniscient being, playing no role in traditional myths, and not represented or personified in ceremonies.

Christian Influence

In seeking to rationalize such contradictions, it must be remembered that, as with other cultural areas, most Subarctic groups have been in contact with Christian missionaries since at least the middle of the 19th century, and, in the case of some groups, even earlier. This has not necessarily meant the loss of traditional beliefs, since Subarctic culture is characterized by a relativism which allows for the coexistence of different belief systems. Nevertheless, the intermingling of ideas which has undoubtedly taken place does tend to blur any reconstruction of the belief system which existed prior to the coming of Christianity. For example, the question of whether or not the concept of a supreme being (such as *Kitche Manitou*) is an indigenous one has been much debated.

It is true that, in the role of creator and transformer, beings such as Raven, *Wisakedjak*, and *Nanabush* do display attributes of an all-powerful spirit and supreme being. However, there were no cults or ceremonies associated with them nor is there any suggestion that they were regarded as deities. Indeed, it is clear from the myths themselves that the trickster figure could in no way be equated with the supreme being of Judaic-Christian tradition. Among the present-day Kaska, for example, creation is attributed to God who is called *Tenatiia*, a term designating a rich and powerful person. In their traditional creation myths, a major active role was taken by Crow, but no one regards Crow and God as identical.

The Power of Many

Indeed, as far as the Athapaskans are concerned there is no indication in their mythology of the existence of a supreme being. Rather, there was a concept of an impersonal immanent power in the universe which could be tapped by people in order to gain food, health, long life, or whatever was required. The same concept also existed among the Algonquians, *Manitou* being the term used to describe the power or spirit inhabiting all living things, objects, or natural phenomena; there were thus a great many *Manitous*, good and bad. *Kitche Manitou*, on the other hand, has been identified as a supreme beneficent force, dispenser of life and death, rewarder of goodness, and punisher of evil.

Those who argue that this concept was aboriginal point to 18th century references for support. For example, David Thompson, the late-18th century trader and explorer, records a narrative in which *Wisakedjak* was instructed by *Kitche Manitou* to show men and animals how to live peaceably together. *Wisakedjak* disobeyed and spread dissent and confusion instead. In anger, *Kitche Manitou* destroyed all creation in a flood, only *Wisakedjak*, a beaver, a muskrat, and an otter surviving. When the waters eventually subsided, man and all other life-forms were re-made, but *Wisakedjak* was stripped of his former authority and reduced to being only a trickster and deceiver. Whether or not the supreme being concept was traditional, it has to be said that this narrative and the characteristics ascribed to *Kitche Manitou* suggest more than a hint of Christian influence.

What seems more likely to be indigenous is the host of minor *Manitous* termed 'owners', 'masters', 'keepers' or, latterly, (in a borrowing from modern lumber camps) 'bosses' of game. This concept was based on the view, already described, that everything in the universe was animate.

Every fish, animal and plant species functioned in a society which was parallel in all respects to that of mankind. Every species had a spiritual 'owner' or 'boss' who controlled the individuals of that species. Thus, bears had an 'owner', as did beavers, caribou, otters, and so on. For a hunter to be successful, he had to win the help and favor of the owner of the game. Without this, individual animals could not be caught. If the owner of a species was insulted or alienated, the hunter would not be allowed to kill or even find a member of that species. For this reason, hunters treated the animals they killed with care and respect. The Athapaskan legend of the Game Mother reflected similar concerns. Failure by hunters to show proper respect would result in the animals being recalled to her home.

Subarctic religion was thus highly functional. While concepts of little immediate relevance remained poorly defined, those intimately bound up with the subsistence quest and physical survival tended to be much more elaborate.

This grouse mask (above) was collected, with the other two, at the turn of this century. It would have been used in the dance to honor the grouse and increase its numbers for the benefit of the tribe. For peoples for whom the hunt was so vital, beings who controlled the supply of game were very powerful indeed.

'Eredk'ali *was a man who lived for 300 years . . . He did so much it took a long time to tell how he began and his life story. It would take two days to tell . . . One time the Cree were after him, you know, and he ran right across a valley between two hills. He didn't even touch the ground . . . That's how he got his name . . .* Eredk'ali *means "to go across flying".'*

CHIPEWYAN HUNTER[4]

The archetypal culture hero is presented as a poor boy, perhaps an orphan or one abandoned by his friends and relatives, who, aided by his spirit helper, has a series of adventures in which he overcomes many obstacles and gains wealth and power. The myth cycle relating to the Beaver culture hero *Saya* or *Usakindji* is typical. It begins

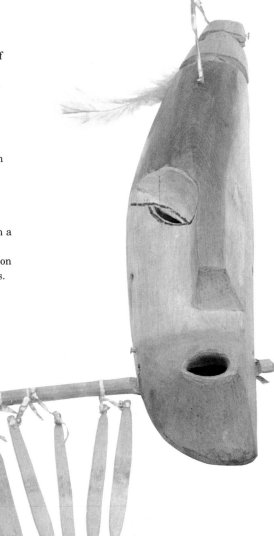

The Ingalik had seven major ceremonials, of which the *Geyema* or Mask Dance was one of the most important. It emphasized a symbolic bond between humans and the myriad of animals on which the people depended for survival. This half-man mask with its wooden rattlers suggests shamanic associations for the wearer who would have indulged in a powerfully dramatic display of communication with the higher powers.

with a young boy being abandoned on an uninhabited island by his father. He receives spirit help in a dream and with ingenuity and determination is able to survive the winter. Eventually he escapes from the island and travels round the world destroying the giant animals, which at that time preyed on people, and transforming them into the smaller animals which exist today.

Saya's adventures are replicated in the stories recounted by other tribes about their culture heroes – the Kutchin *Ataachookai*, for example, the Kaska *Kliatata*, the Chipewyan *Segalaze* and *Eredk'ali*. All are represented as benefactors who passed on to others the knowledge which they acquired during their travels. *Saya* taught people how to make arrows. *Kliatata* gave them bows and snowshoes and taught them to make fishing nets from willow bark.

Superhuman *Segalaze*

In carrying out their exploits, heroes often display strength and speed of superhuman proportions as in this story about *Segalaze*, recorded in the 1970s:

> 'Another time the people were walking up a big hill. When they got to the top there were two grizzly bears there. The people were scared but *Segalaze* was in back again. He loosened up his cape and he ran ahead to those grizzly bears and ran around them real fast. Pretty soon all you could see was just dust. He must have had some kind of medicine for that because there was no dirt there. And when the dust cleared away those bears were dead.'[5]

It is interesting to note that in modern renditions these traditional heroes are compared with comic book characters such as Superman, or with real-life contemporary heroes like boxers or athletes. This is entirely logical for, as well as being told for entertainment, culture hero stories were also a medium for instruction with the hero as role model. The story of *Saya* on the island, for example, is the story of a vision quest, something which all boys were expected to undertake. His adventures as a whole promote a philosophy of life in which self-reliance is combined with dependence on spiritual support.

The Malevolent

It is this instructional role which distinguishes the culture hero from the trickster. While Raven or *Nanabush* frequently perform feats appropriate to a hero, their heroic aspects are diminished by their corresponding failings. The culture hero helps and protects people in need; the trickster is more likely to take advantage of their weakness.

Many of the culture hero's exploits involve struggles with monsters, such as the giant man-eating animals destroyed by *Saya*. Monsters and malevolent beings of all kinds loom large in Subarctic mythology, reflecting the anxieties of people conscious of their vulnerability in an unpredictable and threatening environment.

Strange noises heard at night were attributed by the Athapaskans to the *Nakhani*, sometimes called the 'bush man' or 'brush man'. This was a monstrous giant who lurked in the undergrowth around summer camps, waiting to kidnap children. Most feared by the Algonquians was the *Windigo*, a man-eating giant with a heart of ice who haunted winter forests and devoured anyone who crossed his path. Other beings included the 'whistlers' who lived in the mountains, the 'tree people' who came out of the trees at night waving their arms, and the 'dog from the earth' which could be heard barking but which was never seen.

Like the culture hero myths, tales of giants and cannibals were also instructional. Mothers used them to frighten their children to prevent them from straying. For adults, too, they contained warnings to be on guard against the dangers of the forest, not only the unseen terrors of the *Nakhani*, but also the very real risks of becoming lost or falling prey to wild animals.

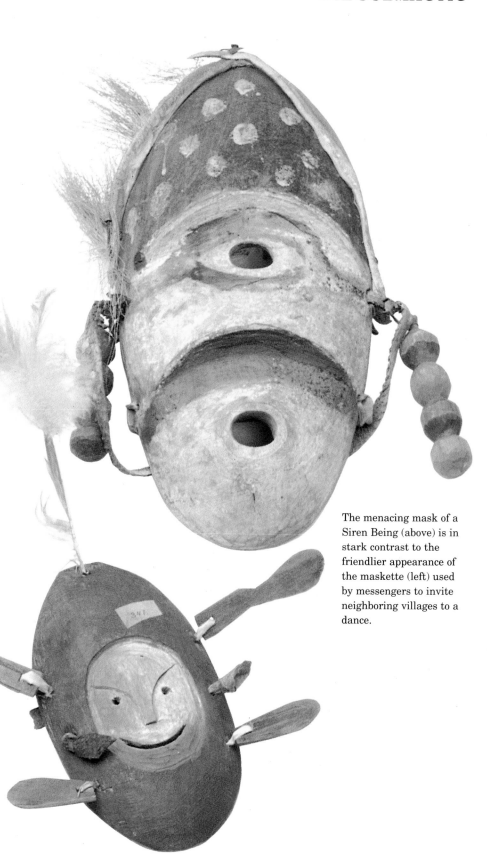

The menacing mask of a Siren Being (above) is in stark contrast to the friendlier appearance of the maskette (left) used by messengers to invite neighboring villages to a dance.

'The country knows. If you do wrong things to it, the country knows. It feels what's happening to it. I guess everything is connected somehow, under the ground.'

KOYUKON HUNTER[6]

Mount McKinley (below) is the highest peak in North America and lies within the traditional territory of the Tanaina, an Athapaskan-speaking group from southwestern Alaska. Their legend cycles are called *sukdu* and contain a tale which tells of Raven being threatened by huge waves. He defended himself by throwing his harpoon at them and turning them into the mountains of the Alaska Range of which Mount McKinley forms part.

For the traditional peoples of the Subarctic, the spirit world and the natural world were inseparable. Spirits were everywhere in the landscape, although not all were possessed of equal power. Certain natural features – waterfalls, lakes and streams, ancient trees, and strangely shaped rocks – might have special powers which needed to be placated or shown deference. Others might have dangerous or hostile presences which needed to be avoided. Iliamna Lake in southwestern Alaska, for example, is said to be home to Big Fish, monsters powerful enough to bite the bottoms out of boats.

Sites with particular historical or mythological associations were also imbued with spiritual power. Abandoned villages and old campsites were places of danger, since the spirits of those who had lived and died there still inhabited them. For this reason, no one would think of remaining in such potentially terrifying places after dark.

The Landscape

Distant Time stories often account for the origin of particular geographical features. Iliamna Lake was created by giants from the north according to Tanaina myth, while Mount McKinley, the highest peak in North America, was created by Raven. The story goes that, while paddling his canoe across a lake, Raven found himself threatened by huge waves sent by his enemies. He threw his harpoon at the waves and they turned into mountains, the largest wave becoming Mount McKinley. Another story explains the presence of large depressions in an area of sand dunes around the upper reaches of the Nulitna River in Alaska. Here, it is said, two giants once fought for possession of the dunes, leaving their footprints in the sand as they wrestled.

The earth itself was a source of power and had to be treated with respect. Digging in the earth was not an action to be taken lightly. Earth had its ceremonial uses. It was used, for example, by shamans as medicine in treating illness, and earth pigments were used for body paint and for decorating clothing and equipment. The several locations along the Yukon and Konukuk rivers where deposits of red ochre occurred were regarded as sacred by the Kutchin and other western Athapaskan groups, and offerings were left when the pigment was extracted.

Ceremonial Shelter

As far as group ceremonialism was concerned, temples as such did not exist. The traditionally nomadic lifestyle of Subarctic peoples meant that most structures were either portable or capable of being erected quickly using readily available materials. It is true that Alaskan groups like the Ingalik did construct substantial wood and turf buildings in their winter villages, where the *kashim*, a large rectangular semi-subterranean

structure, served as a men's meeting house and as an arena for a number of ceremonies.

In general, special shelters and enclosures were built to order for ceremonies, feasts and dances, and were usually destroyed after use. For the widespread Algonquian phenomenon known as the Shaking Tent ritual, for example, a cylindrical open-topped tent was constructed under the direction of the shaman engaged to perform the ritual. During it, the shaman conversed with a number of visiting spirits, whose presence caused the tent to shake violently despite its sturdy construction. The ritual was not associated with a particular site or sites, but was held where an individual or community required the services of a shaman to solve a particular problem.

A number of sacred sites in and around Lake Winnipeg were associated with the ceremonies of the *Midewiwin*, or Grand Medicine Society. The *Midewiwin*, an organization dedicated to curing the sick, was a major religious institution in the traditional culture of the Lake Winnipeg Saulteaux from the 18th century until the early years of the 20th century. Whether the sites were regarded as sacred because of their association with the *Midewiwin*, or whether they were chosen for the *Midewiwin* because of their existing sacred significance, is a moot point.

The name of one site, Dog Head, on the eastern side of the narrows, may be derived from the dog sacrifice which formed part of the *Midewiwin* ceremonies. (Note the similarity to the ceremonies and culture of the adjoining Northeast region.) Another site where the *Midewiwin* was regularly held during the 19th century was Black Island, at the southern end of Lake Winnipeg. The island was regarded as a sacred place on account of the mysterious reverberations or drumming sounds said to be heard there and it may have been for this reason that it was chosen as a spot particularly suited for the performance of the *Midewiwin* Ceremony.

A beautiful landscape of water, rock, trees, and mountains (above left), the Yukon and South Macmillan rivers region (the Mackenzie Range is in the distance) is in the traditional territory of the Kutchin. Their belief system considered it a threatening environment too, with monsters and underwater creatures thought to live in the mountains and waters, and the mysterious *nainah* – 'bushmen' who had been human but had grown odd due to long isolation.

'We have respect for the animals. We don't keep them in cages or torture them, because we know the background of animals from the Distant Time. We know that the animal has a spirit – it used to be human – and we know all the things it did. It's not just an animal; it's lots more than that.'

KOYUKON HUNTER[7]

This otter mask (right) was used in the Ingalik Mask Dance and a similar one would have featured in the ceremony of the Feast of the Animals' Souls. The movement of the otter's feet and tail can be simulated by the jointed appendages at the sides and top of the mask.

The single most consistent feature of northern Athapaskan belief systems was the reciprocal relationship which existed between human beings and the animals on which they depended for their livelihood. There was a widespread belief in reincarnation in animal form which blurred the distinction between men and animals. In addition, animals were thought to retain many of the human characteristics which they had had in Distant Time. They still understood human speech, they had spirits, often very powerful ones, and they had to be treated according to a strict code of moral and social etiquette. Game animals could punish people who breached this code simply by shunning them and thereby condemning them to starvation. People often accounted for the decline in particular species by identifying offenses committed against them in the past. This point is illustrated in the story of a conversation between Bear and Lynx. Bear said that if a human mistreated him, that person would get no more bears until his hair turned grey. But Lynx declared that people who mistreated him would never get another lynx as long as they lived.

The Rules of Respect

Koyukon hunters avoided pointing at animals, because it showed disrespect, 'like pointing or staring at a stranger.' When discussing animals, they chose their words with great care, avoiding boastful talk about hunting or trapping exploits. Bears were so powerful that they were never referred to directly. Hunting therefore involved far more than simply tracking and killing an animal. There were taboos associated with every aspect of hunting – the weapons and equipment used, the approach to the animals hunted, the treatment of the food which they supplied. Nearly all were designed to propitiate the animals' spirits and to ensure that game remained plentiful in the future. There was also a sense that, because of what they gave, animals were inherently deserving of such respect and homage.

There were also a large number of prescribed procedures and rituals for the butchering of game and the disposing of the bones and uneaten or inedible parts. Procedures related not only to animals important for subsistence, such as caribou or salmon, but also to those respected and feared for their power, like the wolf and bear.

The Power of the Bear

Bears commanded particular consideration, and

there were elaborate rules surrounding the way in which they were killed and their carcasses disposed of. Sanction for these rules can be found in such myths as the Inland Tlingit's The Girl Who Married a Bear and the Cree's The Boy Kept By a Bear. Both describe how human beings who have spent some time in the animal world return home bringing with them the knowledge of how bears should be treated after death.

After a bear had been killed, it was laid on its back, thanked by the hunter, and an offering of tobacco placed on its chest. A feast was held to which all the men of the hunting group were invited and small portions of the meat were placed in the fire as offerings to ensure the success of future hunts. The painted skull of the bear and its forelegs, wrapped in birchbark or cloth, were tied to a tree and left as a permanent display when the group moved camp.

Other animal remains were accorded similar treatment. Moose and caribou antlers were often decorated with ribbons and placed on an elevated platform specially built to keep them and other animal bones out of reach of the camp dogs. The bones of water animals, like the beaver and muskrat, were returned to the lake or river with the request, 'Be made again in the water.' Cree hunters in particular often kept parts of certain animals as personal trophies or amulets. These included such items as a bear's chin and the dried and stuffed head of a goose, both decorated and beaded, and ceremonial caribou hides.

Feast of Animals' Souls

The most elaborate rituals were those carried out by the more settled groups of the western Subarctic. The Ingalik held a whole series of animal ceremonies, such as the Mask Dance and the Feast of the Animals' Souls, which were intended to placate the animals and ensure their increase, but which were also great social occasions. During these ceremonies, dancers wearing colorful masks to represent the various animal species, performed to the accompaniment of songs and drumming.

Elaborate animal-deference ceremonies for bears existed among the Naskapi, Montagnais, and the East Cree from whom these bear parts (left) were collected. The skull (top), scapula (center), and lips (bottom) were embellished out of respect for the animal and then carried as hunting charms. In addition, necklaces of bear claws (below) were considered to be powerful medicine and were worn by high-ranking men.

'I also fasted. The spirits came and I bound myself to several. There were good ones who helped me in hunting. There were also maleficent ones, two in particular, who would come, at my call, only if I wanted to do some evil. If someone had offended me, I would make use of these two to avenge myself . . . Thanks to them I have gotten rid of more than one enemy.'

CREE HUNTER[8]

Personal power was a vital element in the religious life of the Subarctic people. Spirits came in dreams or were deliberately sought in visions. As elsewhere in North America, the components of the vision quest were isolation, fasting, and meditation. The vision usually came in the form of an animal or bird, who then became the individual's guardian spirit or spirit helper.

Essential elements for many rituals: the rattle and tobacco. This Cree rattle (above) is rawhide sewn over a hoop with stones inside. The Cree pipe-bag is decorated with typical beadwork (right), while the tobacco in it would probably have been a native mixture known as *kinnikinnik* (bottom).

Shaman Power

Those who acquired greatest power and learned how best to control spirit forces became shamans. Each shaman – who might be male or female – formed special associations with a number of familiar (usually animal) spirits. Some of these were inherited, but most were found through dreams and visions. Shamans summoned their spirit helpers to direct them when they were called upon to exercise their powers. Often, in a trance-like state, they spoke through these spirits and claimed to travel over the world. A Naskapi story tells how, during a famine, a shaman visited the Master of the Caribou at his home inside a hollow mountain in the far north, from where he controls the caribou herds. The shaman persuaded him to release some of the caribou, thus relieving the famine.

The most important shamanistic activity lay in

diagnosing and curing illness and disease. Curing usually involved the extraction, by sucking or blowing, of an object such as a stone, bullet, or piece of string which was considered to be the source of the patient's problem. The prevention of disease involved frightening away the spirit through a shamanistic performance. Apart from curing, the shaman also located game, predicted the weather, and foretold the future.

The accoutrements of shamans included special amulets, representing the various spirits they controlled, skins of their animal helpers, special cups, tubes, and spoons used in curing rituals, and the skin blankets under which they performed. Shamans also 'owned' a number of songs and used drums and rattles for accompaniment when singing them. Tanaina shamans possessed considerable paraphernalia, including an elaborate caribou skin parka decorated with appendages made of beaks and claws which rattled impressively when the wearer danced.

The Shaking Tent

The Shaking Tent ritual was a public performance which took place at dusk and often lasted well into the night. The shaman entered the tent and the arrival of the spirits was signalled by violent movement, strange lights, and cries. The onlookers seated outside could hear conversations and often joined in by shouting questions. The performance had no set form, but depended on the individual shaman and the particular purpose for which the ceremony was being held.

As well as being a form of mediation with the spirits, the ceremony was also a form of community entertainment. In the Cree version of the ceremony, the first spirit to arrive was said to be *Mistaapew*, sometimes described as the 'boss' of the shaking tent, who acts as host or master of ceremonies. He was said to be a great joker who liked to make people, particularly women, laugh. A common feature of the ceremony was the part in which *Mistaapew* had a fight with the spirit of the bears. The presence of the bear inside the tent was revealed by the impression of a claw,

which could be seen through the tent cover by the onlookers. *Mistaapew's* victory indicated that men would be able to kill bears in future.

Divination and Festivals

Scapulimancy was the single most common form of divination and could be done by anyone. It involved heating over a fire a flat bone (such as the shoulder-bone of an animal or the breast-bone of a bird) and interpreting the resulting scorch marks and cracks to determine the whereabouts of game or people. The reading was based on individual interpretations rather than on formalized rules.

Although individual practices predominated, community ceremonials were held by several western Athapaskan groups. The most elaborate were those performed by the Ingalik in their *kashims*. Seven 'great ceremonies' were held, four of which involved invitations to neighboring villages for feasting, dancing, ceremonial exchange, and gift-giving. The Partner's Potlatch was an occasion for fun and could be held at any time of the year. The Death Potlatch was the year's most solemn occasion and was held in midwinter.

Other group activities included trading festivals, winter solstice festivals, feasts, and ceremonies to celebrate events such as a marriage, a boy's first kill, a girl's first menstruation, the first salmon run, or a hunter's killing of a wolf or wolverine. Such occasions also provided opportunities for singing and dancing, racing, gambling, and games of strength and skill.

This stone pipe (above) probably belonged to the Montagnais or Naskapi from the Labrador Peninsula. The woven beadwork suggests it was used in ritual – probably to honor dead game. Such items formed part of a man's equipment and underlined the ethos that religion was a highly personal affair. It was said of individuals 'who lived the right life' that they could acquire greater powers of communication with the spirit world as they grew older.

THE ARCTIC

'Our fathers have inherited from their fathers all the old rules of life which are based on the wisdom of generations. We do not know how, we cannot say why, but we keep those rules in order that we may live untroubled . . . We fear what we see about us and we fear all the invisible things that are about us, all that we have heard of in our forefathers' myths and legends.'

AUA (IGLULIK)[1]

THE 4,000 MILES (6,437 km) of the Arctic coastline from eastern Siberia to Greenland form the very fringes of the habitable world. The landscape varies from the flat coastal plains of Alaska and the Mackenzie Delta to the rocky terrain of the interior barren grounds west of Hudson Bay and the high granite mountains and deeply cut fiords of the eastern islands. The one constant feature is the lack of trees.

During the long cold winter – nine months or more each year – the sea and lakes are frozen solid. Darkness reigns uninterrupted for weeks in midwinter, with only a brief twilight at midday. The brief summer restores life and color to the landscape with varieties of moss, grass, wild flowers, and berries. Days are long, sunny and pleasantly warm with a period near midsummer when the Sun never sets.

The Arctic is home to three separate linguistic groups: the Aleut of the Aleutian Islands, the Yupik, and the Inuit-Inupiaq. The Yupik live on both sides of the Bering Strait, while the Inuit extend from northern Alaska to Greenland, including all of Arctic Canada. Since the 1970s, 'Inuit' (meaning 'people') has come to replace 'Eskimo', which is generally, although probably erroneously, believed to derive from a derogatory Algonquian term meaning 'raw flesh eaters'. However, it should be remembered that not all Eskimos are Inuit. Significant populations of Aleut and Yupik do not use the term in reference to themselves.

Traditional settlements were usually small, consisting of one or two extended families, although at certain times several groups might come together for communal hunting, trading, or religious ceremonies. People depended for survival both on sea creatures, such as seal, walrus, and whale, and on land animals, like caribou and musk ox. Fishing played a major part in the economy of most groups. Birds were also hunted and their eggs collected.

Nevertheless, starvation was an ever-present threat in this desolate environment. The successful food quest required strict observance of taboos and special care had to be taken not to offend game food animals. The belief that the products of land and sea should not be mixed was a widespread one throughout the Arctic. To break this taboo by, for example, cooking seal and caribou meat together, was to risk supernatural retribution in the form of storms or sickness – or even death itself. (In some instances, amulets did offer a degree of personal protection.)

Indeed, the taboo system was the cornerstone of religious life. In a world controlled by supernatural beings – openly dangerous or potentially so – it was only through reference to taboos that the stress and unpredictability of daily life could be made explicable and acceptable. Myths and legends also provided reassurance by validating taboos and by offering structure and meaning to the spirit world.

Labrets piercing below the lips distinguish these as Arctic faces. These Inuit men in 1880 were continuing a tradition that had existed for at least 1,500 years. Their labrets were made of ivory or bone, but some early specimens were jade and even coal. The original meaning is unknown. Despite the rather barren environment distinctive crafts did exist, with hats providing one outlet for artistry. A design from an Aleut conical hat (right and far left) dates from 1868, while the Yupik hat (top left) is painted with a bird design that may well represent a swallow – said to protect hunters - at sea.

'But these are hard things to understand, difficult things to talk about, all this about where something began, where the first people came from. It is sufficient for us to see that they are here and that we are here.'

NALUNGIAQ (NETSILIK)[2]

In the primeval world there was no difference between people and animals. A human being could become an animal at will and vice versa. All spoke the same language and lived in identical fashion. In many other ways this was a world quite different from the present one. It was a world where snow burned, houses flew through the air, tools and weapons moved of their own accord, and forests grew at the bottom of the sea. (This served to explain the presence of driftwood on the sea shore.) As one Iglulik story-teller explained, 'These stories were made when all unbelievable things could happen.'[3]

The Creation of Light

Origin myths relate how present order was created out of this chaotic, topsy-turvy world. In the beginning, for example, there was no light on Earth. Fox argued for the continuance of everlasting darkness, since it provided him with cover under which to raid hunters' caches. Hare, on the other hand, called for the light of day to help him find food. Hare's words proved the more powerful and so it was that day came to alternate with night. According to another myth, it was Raven who won the argument with Fox, and it was Raven's cry of 'qua! qua!' (meaning light or dawn) which brought daylight to mankind.

Origin of Indians and White Men

A widespread myth tells of the origin of Indians and white men and, in its telling, reveals how the Inuit regarded these two groups. The Caribou Inuit version describes how a man, angered by his daughter's refusal to take a husband, forced her to marry his dog and banished the pair to a distant island. Here the woman gave birth to a litter of puppies. To revenge herself on her father, the woman sent her dog-children to drown him by overturning his kayak. The woman then cut the soles from her *kamiks* (boots) and set them at the water's edge. She placed some of her dog-children on one sole, telling them to be skillful in all things. As the dogs drifted away from the island, the sole turned into a ship and they sailed away to the land of the white men. From those dogs, it is said, all the white men came. The woman placed the remaining dogs on the other sole and, reminding them of how they had killed their grandfather, exhorted them to treat all human beings they met in a similarly murderous manner. This sole also drifted out from the island and washed up on a distant shore. The dogs wandered off up country and became the ancestors of the Indians, the traditional enemies of the Inuit.

A mythical bird figure, probably Raven, guards the bowl of this exquisitely crafted ivory pipe (below), carved from a single walrus tusk and elaborately decorated with pictorial engravings showing various animals and aspects of Arctic life.

The Animals

Many myths describe how various animals came to have their present form. Willow grouse, for example, were children who were so frightened by a sudden noise that they grew wings and flew up into the sky. Similarly, gulls were once women who had been abandoned by their traveling companions, whom they continue to seek with their mournful cries.

Other animal myths have a comical quality, like the tale of the raven and the loon. In the days when all the birds were white, these two agreed to tattoo one another using soot. Unfortunately, the loon was so dissatisfied with the pattern produced by the raven that he threw the soot at him, thus causing all the ravens to be black to this day. In his turn, the enraged raven beat the loon so severely that he was unable to walk. That is why loons now walk so awkwardly.

Sun, Moon, Thunder, and Lightning

In several myths, an evil action or breach of taboo is shown as the catalyst by which a human being is transformed into a supernatural being.

A Caribou Inuit tale recounts the story of how *Tatqeq* and his sister *Siqiniq* were surprised in an incestuous relationship. Overwhelmed with shame, they rose up from Earth into the sky. It was winter and dark and both carried flaming torches. *Tatqeq* rushed into the sky with such speed that his torch went out. He became the Moon, giving light but no heat from the embers of his torch. His sister rose more slowly. Her torch remained burning, and she became the Sun, giving out both light and warmth to the world.

Another story tells how there was no theft in the world until a brother and sister stole a caribou skin and a firestone (iron pyrites). No sooner had they done so than they were stricken with guilt. At first they talked of changing into animals to escape retribution, but always they were afraid of being killed. Finally, they decided to turn into thunder and lightning so that people could not catch them. Now when thunder rolls and lightning flashes in the heavens, it is because the brother is rattling the dry caribou skin, while his sister strikes sparks from the firestone.

Carved ivory pipes and other objects were made using various tools, including steel files and needles obtained in early trade with Europeans. The most ingenious, and traditional, method, however, was the bow drill (below). This Bering Strait Inuit artisan is holding one end of the drill with his mouth while he rotates it with the bow, leaving one hand free to hold the ivory.

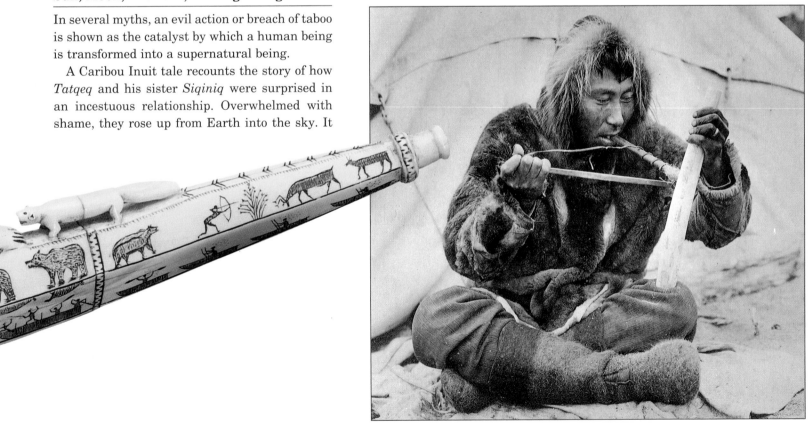

'[Nuliajuk] became the most feared of all spirits, the most powerful and the one who more than any other controls the destiny of men. For that reason almost all taboo is directed against her, though only in the dark period when the sun is low, and it is cold and windy on earth, for then life is most dangerous to live.'

NULUNGIAQ (NETSILIK)[4]

For those who inhabited the inhospitable vastness of the Arctic, supernatural beings were everywhere. The most powerful and dangerous of all was the Sea Spirit, known variously among

different groups from central Canada to east Greenland as *Sedna*, *Nuliajuk*, *Takanaksaluk* ('the terrible one down there'), or *Immap Ukuua* (Mother of the Sea). Her power was based on the fact that, in a region where the struggle for human survival was perhaps more desperate than anywhere else on Earth, she exercised control over the major source of food – the sea.

The Sea Spirit

The myth concerning the Sea Spirit tells of a young woman – sometimes described as a friendless orphan, at others as a rejected daughter –

This Unalit Eskimo mask (right) depicts the Moon goddess and is unusual because the face is modeled on that of a real woman with a labret and facial tattoos. Moon and Sun masks are common among the peoples of the Arctic. The rings may be intended to represent supernatural worlds.

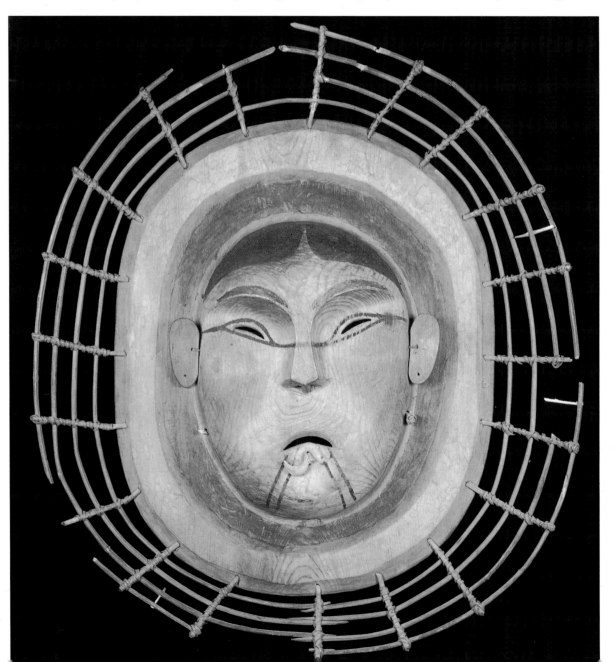

114

who was thrown into the sea by her traveling companions during a storm. As she attempted to climb back into the boat, those on board sought to dislodge her by hacking off the first joints of her fingers. These fell into the sea and turned into seals. Still the woman clung to the side of the boat and this time the rest of her fingers were cut off, becoming walruses. Finally, her hands were struck off at the wrists and became whales. The woman sank to the bottom of the sea, where she became the Sea Spirit.

Because of their cruelty to her, *Sedna* had little love for human beings. In her home at the bottom of the ocean, she jealously guarded the animals which came from her hands. (In some areas she was believed to control the land animals too.) She demanded respect and strict observance of all taboos relating to animals and hunting. Violations enraged her and in revenge she shut the animals away or raised storms to prevent hunting. At such times it was necessary for a shaman, in a trance, to visit *Sedna* to placate her by promising that people would confess and repent their wrongdoings.

A great ceremonial was performed on Baffin Island each summer during which a shaman battled with *Sedna*, harpooning her like a seal and killing her, thus liberating the seals for the coming hunting season. Since *Sedna* subsequently came to life again, the ceremony had to be repeated the following year.

Omnipresent *Pinga*

To some of the inland groups who had no direct contact with the coast, the Sea Spirit had of course no significance. Among the Caribou Inuit, for example, the supreme being was *Pinga*, who corresponded to *Sedna* in many ways but lived in the air. *Pinga* was feared as an omnipresent spirit, watching over people's actions, particularly as regards their treatment of game animals – in this case, of caribou. Although not credited with exercising the same control over caribou as did *Sedna* over seals, she nevertheless demanded that they be treated with respect and dignity.

Master of Weather

Next in power and importance to the Sea Spirit was *Narssuk* or *Sila,* controller of the weather, master of wind, rain, and snow, who could raise a storm at any moment and render hunting impossible. He was envisaged as a giant baby, wrapped in caribou skins tied with thongs. When the thongs were loosened, he was free to move and blizzards swept the country. Then the disembodied spirits of shamans had to fly up in the air and fight to refasten the thongs.

The Moon Spirit

Tatqeq, the Moon Spirit, was generally regarded as better-disposed toward mankind. Through his influence over tides and currents, he was thought to bring good luck to hunters. He was also believed by the Central Inuit to control fertility in women and to enforce the taboos concerning childbirth. In some areas, however, he was greatly feared. Greenlanders believed that he kept a special watch over human behavior and punished disobedience, while around the Bering Strait it was he, and not the Sea Spirit, who ruled the game animals. In this area also it was believed that diseases emanated from the Moon and a lunar eclipse was said to presage an epidemic.

Shaman Summoning *Sedna* by Abraham Anghik, a sculpture in black steatite on stone (below). *Sedna*, the mother and protector of sea mammals, demanded ceremonials to honor the animals' spirits and it was necessary for shamans to visit her and soothe her anger.

'Kivioq *is an* inuk, *a man like ourselves, of our own tribe, but a man with many lives. He is from the time when the ice never laid itself on the sea up here by our coasts . . . from the time when the animals often turned themselves into human beings and human beings into animals and when the wolves had not yet learned to overtake the caribou.'*

KUVLIUTSOQ (NETSILIK)[5]

The adventures of the culture hero *Kivioq* are familiar throughout the Arctic region, from Alaska to Greenland, although often they are told as separate stories, rather than as linked episodes in an epic cycle that would be familiar to readers of the Icelandic Sagas.

Tales of *Kivioq*

Typically, *Kivioq* undertakes a series of long and dangerous journeys to distant lands, where he overcomes fearful obstacles, battles with monsters, and has numerous narrow escapes, before finally achieving great wealth and importance among his people. The stories are set in a primeval time when animals were larger and stronger than they are now and shared the same traits as humans. During the course of his adventures, *Kivioq* takes several animal wives, including a wolf, a fox, and a goose, is attacked by giant caterpillars and mussels, and is carried part of his way on the back of a salmon.

Elements of various forms of myth, in particular origin myths, are contained within the cycle.

This rare mask (right) from the Hooper Bay region portrays the power, grotesqueness, and malevolence of the *Tun-ghat*. These were elemental beings combining human and animal forms who inhabited the Moon and sky lands. The shamans gave them visible form in the carved masks.

However, unlike the actions of culture heroes in other areas, the changes which *Kivioq* is credited with bringing about do not appear to be particularly beneficial to mankind. While living among the wolves, for example, he taught them to run down caribou. Now, thanks to *Kivioq*, all wolves have learned to hunt caribou.

In another adventure, *Kivioq* was pursued by a cannibalistic witch. In an attempt to prevent him escaping in his kayak, the witch hurled her *ulu* (knife) at him. She missed and the *ulu* skimmed over the sea and turned into an ice floe. Until then, according to the myth, the sea had been open all the year round. Now it began to freeze over in winter and people had to learn to hunt seals at their breathing holes in the ice.

Another origin myth, which is also reminiscent of trickster tales, has *Kivioq* hiding in a meat cache in order to catch the thief who has been raiding it. The culprit, a bear in human form, threw *Kivioq* over his shoulder and carried him home, believing him to be a seal carcass. The story describes several comic scenes at the bear's house, with *Kivioq* pretending to be frozen and the bear's wife laying him out to thaw, and the bear-children catching sight of the supposed dead seal opening his eyes. When the bear attempted to cut him up, *Kivioq* hit him with an axe and escaped. He was pursued by the wife in bear form and, in an attempt to throw her off his trail, caused a fast-flowing river to well up between them. The bear-woman attempted to cross the river by drinking it dry and, as a result, burst. All the water in her stomach rose up in the form of a white mist and thus created the first fog.

Finally, in the traditional style of the epic hero, *Kivioq* returns home, rich and powerful. It is interesting to note that, in a Netsilik version recorded in the 1920s, he only finds success by leaving the Inuit and going 'to the land of the white man . . . [who] made him a great man with great possessions. It has been said that he has five ships . . .'[6]

Another form of hero is the orphan boy – poor, friendless, and mistreated – who receives help,

usually from a supernatural source, and thereby becomes strong and powerful. Typical is the story of *Kajjajuk*, who is temporarily transformed into a giant by the sympathetic Moon Spirit and thus able to take revenge on those who had abused and tormented him.

Beings to Fear

Unlike *Tatqeq*, the Moon Spirit, most supernatural beings appear malevolent and dangerous toward human beings. Stories abound of man-eating giants, dwarfs, ghosts, and bloodthirsty monsters of all kinds. Alaskan myths tell of the *Amikuk*, a sea-serpent which dragged unwary hunters from their kayaks, and the *Aziwugum*, a creature like a dog, but with a scaly body and a tail so powerful that one blow from it could kill. The Central Inuit feared the *Amayersuk*, a giant woman who carried children away, and the man-eating *Nakasungnaikut*, who had no leg bones and had to crawl instead of walking.

People lived in great fear of such beings, especially during the long dark winter months. They heard their voices howling in the wind, saw their tracks in the snow, and glimpsed them lurking under the ice. 'Invisible beings, something we cannot see, sometimes murder and kill; it is terrible and almost intolerable.'[7]

An Inuit print from the village of Povungnituk (top left) has taken as its inspirational theme the legend of the eagle who took a human girl to be his wife. Tales of marriage between humans and animals abound in Eskimo mythology.

The people of the Arctic believed that almost everything in the universe had a soul or spirit which could be pleased or angered by the actions of human beings. This belief also extended to inanimate objects and places so that a rock, an island, or a stream was regarded as having a kind of soul or *inua* – a power and vitality of its own. Those crossing dangerous glaciers or stretches of water, where they might encounter treacherous currents or whirlpools, often made a small offering, such as a piece of meat or blubber, in order to pacify the *inua* of that particular locality.

Power in the Landscape

The people of Cumberland Sound left offerings at the places where they quarried steatite for the making of lamps and dishes. Failure to do so, it was believed, would render the stone hard and unworkable. Certain structures were also associated with supernatural beings. A small stone house near Netsilik Lake was said to be the home of the thunder spirits. Those entering it had to exercise great care, for it was believed that if they or their clothing touched the walls they would die within the year.

Most important of all were the places associated with food resources. There were certain spots, for example, which were regarded as sacred simply because they appeared to be particularly attractive to caribou or because they regularly provided good fishing.

The Caribou Inuit, who each summer camped on Sentry Island in Hudson Bay to hunt seals, regarded a certain boulder there as sacred and hung it with gifts of food, tobacco, and trinkets in order to bring good luck in hunting. According to the Netsilik, a similar rock, to which offerings of small stones were made, was originally a woman who turned to stone because she refused to marry. People believed that the stone woman was fond of playing with pebbles and so offered these to her in the hope that she would give them game in return.

Hunting Sites

Taboos and observances which applied to hunting also applied to hunting sites, so that they acquired a kind of holy status. Most Central Inuit observed very strict taboos at fishing weirs and at the river-crossings where caribou were hunted. These related to the important rules separating land and sea animals. Thus it was forbidden to sleep with seal meat in one's tent or to work seal and walrus skins in caribou hunting camps. Indeed the Caribou Inuit made a very sharp distinction between what belonged to the interior and what came from the 'salt-water people.' In their eyes, all trade goods obtained from the coast had to be treated with the utmost caution in the vicinity of caribou crossing places.

Restrictions also applied to all men's and women's work at fishing weirs. Even when a man required to make essential repairs to his fishing gear, it was necessary for him to leave the river bank and hide behind a rock in order to do so.

Part of the sacred character of these hunting places derived from their links with the *Tunrit*, a quasi-mythical, superhuman race of giants who, according to legends told throughout much of the central and eastern Arctic, were the original inhabitants of the area. They were skillful hunters who constructed the stone cairns, which led the caribou herds to the crossing places, as well as the stone fishing weirs. Whatever the historical significance of the *Tunrit* (who can probably be identified with the prehistoric Dorset people), they were regarded by the Inuit as supernatural beings and offerings were made at sites and structures associated with them.

Graves and Cairns

Ancestral graves and memorial cairns could also acquire a sacred character. Offerings and prayers were sometimes made at such places so that the dead could assist the living by bringing fine weather or ensuring good hunting. A poignant Netsilik legend describes the origin of a series of cairns found at Kamigluk on Simpson Strait. They commemorated a group of women who were drowned when the ice from which they were fishing broke up and carried them out to sea. Their grieving husbands set up the cairns on the shore, one for each woman lost, so that their souls could return to dry land instead of remaining in the restless sea.

The harshness of the Arctic terrain, uniformly ice-laden (far left) or with the forbidding vastness of glacial rock and ice (below). The hostile nature of the environment was put to good use by the imaginative and creative story-telling minds of the shamans. They related terrifying journeys through an icy wilderness, viewing it as a spirit land with an external existence. In it dwelt animal helpers who would assist the traveler on their difficult journey.

The Eskimo relied primarily on the seal for food and clothing. These sealskin gauntlets (below) are decorated with the beaks of horned puffins. The shaft of a bird feather has been wedged into each beak. They are meant to be worn in a ceremonial and rattled to enhance the drama. Animal parts were often attached to ceremonial costumes, and generally they invoked the powers of the animal spirits.

'The greatest peril of life lies in the fact that human food consists entirely of souls. All the creatures that we have to kill and eat, all those that we have to strike down and destroy to make clothes for ourselves, have souls like we have, souls that do not perish with the body, and which therefore must be propitiated, lest they should revenge themselves on us . . .'

AUA (IGLULIK)[9]

The concept that animals possessed souls influenced almost every aspect of daily life. Since the regular killing of game animals was essential for human survival, the maintenance of a harmonious relationship between the hunters and the hunted was of paramount importance. To this end, it was necessary for a hunter to show honor and respect to the animal he killed by observing

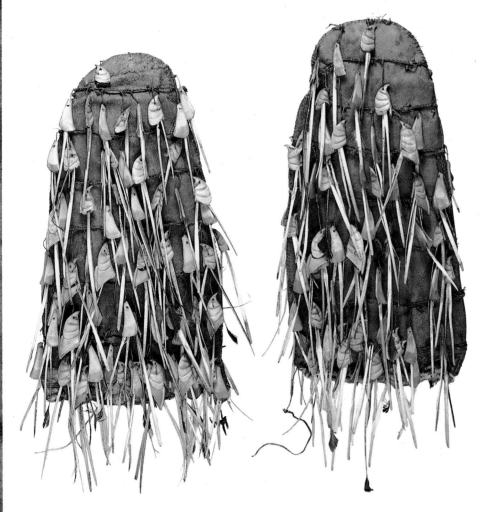

a number of rigorous taboos. One of the most important taboos banned contact between land animals and those of the sea. Thus it was forbidden to eat caribou and seal meat on the same day, or to sew caribou skin clothing while hunting for seal and walrus.

Proper observance of such rules, it was believed, pleased the soul of the dead animal so that it would allow itself to be reincarnated and hunted again. On the other hand, failure to carry out the prescribed procedures could lead to a dearth of game and turn the animal soul into a dangerous spirit. In other words, it was possible for the very food upon which people depended to become a source of evil. The taboo system allowed killing animals to become a safe activity, as well as ensuring successful future hunting.

In that the motivating force in both cases was the conciliation of the departed soul, the treatment accorded to dead animals bore many similarities to the funeral and mourning observances for human beings. For example, just as in the case of a human death, no work was permitted for several days after the capture of a seal, walrus, caribou, or bear.

Another widespread practice was that of offering dead seals and whales a drink by pouring water into the animal's mouth or sprinkling some over its head. On whaling expeditions, Point Barrow Inuit carried a supply of water for this very purpose. Seals and whales were believed to be thirsty creatures and the intention was to provide comfort for the animal's soul.

The Caribou

The souls of caribou were thought to be particularly sensitive and required special care and attention. It was forbidden to do any work on caribou skins while the animal was being hunted. Scraping the skin was considered particularly dangerous since it could offend and drive away the grazing herds before they could be hunted. The Caribou Inuit, who had only the caribou to live on, had to exercise the greatest caution in handling the dead animal. When a caribou was

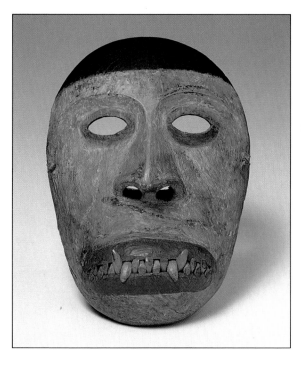

butchered, everything that was not carried home had to be covered up. To fail to do so was regarded as disrespectful to the soul of the caribou and could incur the anger of *Pinga*.

The Seal

As perhaps the most important food animal, seals were also treated with great respect. If a seal carcass was brought indoors for butchering, it was never placed directly on the floor, since it was thought to be offensive to the seal to lie where women had been walking. When people moved camp in winter, the skulls of the seals caught at the old site were laid out facing in the direction of the new one so that their souls could accompany the hunters on their way.

The Bear

The bear's soul was regarded as most powerful and dangerous of all. It was believed that after a bear had been killed, its soul remained on the tip of the hunter's spear for four or five days. During this period, certain procedures had to be followed if the bear was not to turn into an evil spirit. All

work in the house was forbidden. The bear's skin was hung outside and surrounded by tools (women's tools for a female bear, men's tools for a male). In addition, gifts and offerings to the soul of the bear were placed on the skin.

Feasts and Festivals

The most elaborate rites were those held by the Yupik-speaking people of the western Arctic. The Inviting-In Feast was a masked ceremonial held in January to appeal to the spirits for success in hunting during the coming year. The Bladder Festival, held in November and December, was intended to placate the animals slain during the previous year. At the start of the five-day ceremony, each hunter hung up in the *kashim*, or meeting house, the inflated bladders of all the seals, walruses, whales, and bears which he had killed. Food and drink were offered to the bladders, which represented the souls of the animals. After several days of ceremonies and dancing, the bladders were taken down, burst, and thrust into holes in the ice. In this way the animals' souls were returned to the sea to enter the unborn.

Amulets or charms were very important among the peoples of the Arctic. Usually designed to be hung, they ranged in size and might consist of an entire bird (above right) wrapped in caribou skin. Bird amulets were invariably used when appealing for speed.

Masks were worn in Totem dances when men took the floor to depict the life of the animal represented by their spirit masks. It might be a walrus, a fox, a raven, or, as shown here (above left), a wolf.

'We will sing a song.
We will go down the current.
The waves will rise;
The waves will fall.
The dogs will growl at us.'

GREAT FEAST OF THE DEAD (YUPIK)[10]

In addition to the taboos and practices governing hunting, there was also a series of equally exacting observances relating to the critical phases of human life, such as birth, puberty, and, of course, death.

Mourning the Dead

Those relating to death were particularly important. A death was normally followed by a mourning period of four or five days, during which time all work in the household ceased. Everyone within the camp was banned from cutting their nails or combing their hair, eating certain foods or undertaking certain activities, such as cleaning lamps or gathering fuel. After the funeral, the camp was moved to a new site. If these things were not done correctly, there was a danger that the soul of the deceased might become an evil spirit, as happened to *Qubliusaq* in this Netsilik story:

'. . . And when they came to the snow hut where the body had been left, they found *Qubliusaq* all alive . . . they could just see her on the platform, where she was already turning ugly, unrecognisable and terrible as a ghost. She was sitting at her lamp boiling blood . . . People were stricken with terror and now, too late, repented that they had not given her the full death taboo. Happily, among the men there was a great shaman who was accustomed to overcoming ghosts . . . If she had not been killed in time she would certainly have persecuted her old neighbours and either stricken them with disease or frightened them all to death.'[11]

In Alaska, where ceremonial life was most devel-

A Shaman's Helping Spirits by Inuit artist Jessie Oonark gives a glimpse of the spirit world of the Inuit people. Here, the shaman is depicted in rapport with the animal spirits who the myths say can speak as human beings. The souls of animals and their reincarnation were matters of great importance to the peoples of the Arctic. The shaman might 'travel' to the animal villages to request that some of the young animals be sent to the hunters.

oped, an annual Feast of the Dead was held to which the spirits of the dead were invited and offered gifts of food, drink, and clothing.

A more elaborate version of this ceremony, the Great Feast of the Dead, was held every 10 or 15 years, depending on the ability of the surviving relatives to accumulate sufficient property to honor the dead. The ceremony was similar to a potlatch. During several days of singing, dancing, and drumming, vast quantities of food, clothing, skins, and other valuables were distributed to those present.

Amulets

Personal protection from ghosts and evil spirits was provided by amulets. Most men and women

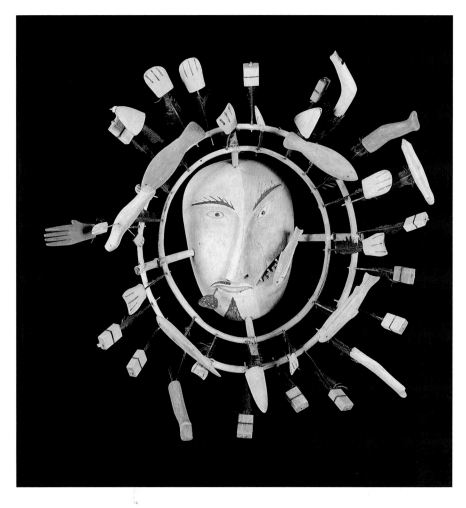

carried several, stitched into their clothing or hung on a special belt. Almost any small object could serve as an amulet, since its power derived from the spirit resident within rather than from any physical property. Children were given amulets as soon as they were born and one Netsilik child was found to have as many as 80 sewn up in various parts of his clothing.

Each amulet generally had a specific purpose. *Pilarqaq,* a young Netsilik hunter, had six amulets stitched into his coat. These consisted of seal teeth to bring him luck in sealing, the head of a tern to bring him luck in fishing, an ermine skin to make him a good runner, two miniature snow beaters to protect him from evil spirits, and a small kayak cleaner intended to help him to paddle faster.

The Shaman

The *angatok,* or shaman, occupied an extremely important position in society. Shamans, both male and female, provided protection, both for the individual and the community as a whole, by acting as mediators between human beings and the spirit world.

They used their powers to cure sickness, attract game, control the weather, and locate lost people or property. Sickness, for example, was always regarded as having been caused by evil ghosts and spirits. It was for the shaman to iden-

tify the reason for the sickness (usually a breach of taboo) and then, with the aid of his spirit helpers, to drive the evil spirits from the patient's body and kill them.

In public performances or seances the shaman fell into a trance, communicating with his audience through his spirit helpers, usually in an archaic or incomprehensible language. At such times his disembodied spirit travelled to the spirit world, to the Moon or below the sea, in order to discover the causes of people's misfortunes and to intercede with the spirits on their behalf.

Shamanism thus operated as a form of social control, enforcing taboos and thereby establishing harmony and balance between the physical and spiritual worlds.

When a feast was decided upon, the people gathered nightly in the *kazgi,* or communal house, to rehearse the songs. This dancer (above left) is imitating an animal, but more often than not imaginative masks were worn such as this Aleut shaman's mask (above) with rings representing Earth and heaven, and wood carvings representing spirit helpers.

THE NORTHEAST

'The Sun is my father, and the Earth is my mother. I will repose upon her bosom.'

TECUMSEH (SHAWNEE)[1]

Iₙ overtly simple terms, this quote reveals the very essence of native philosophy and cosmology among the tribes of the Northeast Woodlands and Great Lakes. The mythological origins of the people, arising as they did from the union of Sun and Earth, had, and continues to have, a profound effect on their lives.

The diverse Northeast Woodlands and Great Lakes area was united by a number of common cosmological beliefs. Central to these beliefs was a reverence for the three cosmic zones of Upper World (sky and Sun), Earth, and Under World (water or beneath the earth), and the recognition of a continuum that encompasses human persons to other-than-human persons. Included, too, was the understanding that features of the landscape and the forces of nature, as well as animals and vegetation, possessed spiritual power in the form of *Orenda* for the Iroquoians, *Manitou* for the Algonquians, and *Wakan* for the Siouans. Paramount was the gaining of personal power through dreams, visions, and the acquisition of spirit helpers. Shamans, as individuals with great personal power and numerous spirit helpers, were efficacious in curing and concerns effecting group well-being. Common to all were ritual obligations of propitiation to these powers, often in the form of tobacco offerings and prayers.

Evidence of their cosmological beliefs has been made manifest in a number of material forms. At times the human body itself has been the canvas for ritual painting and permanent tattooing. Sacred items range from clothing and personal adornment to items such as drums, rattles, and wands used in ceremonies and weapons used in war. Vision quests, shamanic experience, and guidelines for the litany of certain healing ceremonies are recorded in pictographic form on rock formations, wooden prayer sticks, and birch bark scrolls. For each society these tangible items metonymically revealed the depth of their being.

Within the culture area, three cultural 'zones' based on language affiliation, geographic distribution, and subsistence are apparent. A Coastal Zone that included the eastern Algonquian tribes of Micmac, Maliseet-Passamaquoddy, Abenaki, Delaware, Nanticoke, and Powhatan followed a maritime foraging subsistence with agriculture in the southern portion. In the Saint Lawrence Lowlands and below the Great Lakes, the northern Iroquoian speakers were represented by the Saint Lawrence Iroquoians, Mohawk, Oneida, Onondaga, Cayuga, Seneca, Tuscarora, Huron, Erie, and Susquehannock. The practice of intensive horticulture augmented by fishing and hunting permitted increased social complexity. In the third zone the central Algonquian linguistic group of the Great Lakes-Riverine region embraced the Chippewa (Ojibwa in Canada), Ottawa, Potawatomi, Menominee, Sauk and Fox, Kickapoo, Miami, Illinois, and Shawnee. Contiguous with these Algonquian tribes were the Siouan-speaking Winnebago. Their culture resembled that of their Algonquian neighbors.

The famous Sauk chief *Keokuk* (far left), pictured in 1846, wears regalia typical of his tribe – a turban, bearclaw necklace, and earrings. The Sauk were one of the tribes which constituted the central Algonquian linguistic group of the Great Lakes-Riverine region whose main subsistence depended on wild rice harvesting and horticulture.
Much of the sewn artwork of the Northeast reflected their environment, most notably the distinctive floral motifs used on Micmac garters (right and far left). Another material craft related to the environment was the carving of wood from the abundant forests. Masks, such as this unpainted Seneca example (left), depicted beings seen in the forest or in dreams and were used in the cure and prevention of illness.

125

A clay sculpture of the Tree of Peace by Diane Schenandoah, an Oneida artist. The inspiration for it comes from the dream of *Deganawidah* who saw a great tree on the back of a turtle being used to shelter the tribes in a just world.

'On long winter evenings the Indian hunters gathered around their fireside, to listen to the historical traditions, legends . . . and fairy tales which had been handed down through their fathers and father's fathers . . .'

CHIEF ELIAS JOHNSON (TUSCARORA)[2]

The strength of origin stories in the form of myths and legends that continue to be passed down from generation to generation serve to preserve traditions and instill cultural values.

The Origin of Stories

This myth reveals how the Senecas acquired their knowledge of the world before this one. It all began with young Orphan Boy who had become very successful at hunting birds. One day when deep in the woods pursuing birds, he sat down on a flat-topped round stone. As he began to repair his arrow, a voice near him asked, 'Shall I tell you stories?' Looking around he saw no one. However, when the voice repeated the question, Orphan Boy asked, 'What is that? What does it mean to tell stories?' The stone responded that it meant telling what happened a long time ago. In exchange for the boy's birds, the stone told story after story about the world before the present. Each day Orphan Boy would bring birds in exchange for more stories. One day he was joined by an older boy, then by two men, all of whom listened to the origin stories related by the stone. Eventually the stone requested that all the villagers should come to listen. Each person brought a gift of food in exchange for the stories. And from then on, following the instructions of the rock, these stories were to be told to generation after generation as long as the world lasts.

The World on the Turtle's Back

This tale relates the origins of the Iroquoians which began in the sky with the uprooting of the Celestial Tree of Light. *Ataentsic*, or Sky Woman, slipped through the hole and began to fall through the air to the ocean below. As she fell, the geese spread out their wings to catch her. Seeing this, Great Turtle entreated the other aquatic creatures to dive to the bottom of the sea to gather earth to place on his back. One by one the diving birds and animals tried without success until finally Muskrat, more dead than alive, returned to the surface clutching some soil in his paw. Placing it on the turtle's back, the soil expanded to form an island, and Sky Woman was placed upon it. And so the Earth came into being.

Children of the Rising Sun

The Wabenaki, living on the shores of the Atlantic Ocean, considered themselves to be the children of the rising sun. According to an early myth, the Sun first created the entire universe and then, with the power of his penetrating rays, impregnated Mother Earth, and the people were brought forth into this world. At the dawn of each new day, the Wabenaki directed their prayers of respect and adoration to their father, the Rising Sun, and invoked his blessings. At sunset these rituals were repeated.

Great Tree of Peace

This signifies the legendary founding of the Confederacy or League of the Five Nations of the Iroquois. The vision of bringing together the warring Iroquoian tribes into a peaceful alliance is attributed to *Deganawidah*, culture hero and prophet, and was brought to fruition by the eloquent and persuasive speech-making of his co-worker, *Hiawatha*. Initial efforts were obstructed by Onondaga chief *Thadodaho*, who represented all that was repugnant, anti-social, and profane to the ideals of the proposed Iroquois League. By combing out these snakes, *Hiawatha* brought about a transformation from repulsive creature to the epitome of ideal leader, holder of the prestigious position of Keeper of the League's Sacred Fire. To symbolize the formation of the League, *Deganawidah* planted the Tree of Peace in Onondaga territory as the center of the League, its roots of peace reaching to the four corners of the Earth, its branches reaching into the sky. Placed on the top of the tree was the 'Eagle who Sees Afar', and in a cavity below the roots were buried all the weapons of strife.

Origin of the Medicine Society

The rituals of the Medicine Society were given to the Great Lakes people by the culture hero *Manabus*, or *Nanabojo*, to save them from certain extinction by a deadly disease. In the Upper World, the Upper and Lower powers worked together to make a lodge for *Manabus*. It was in this specially constructed lodge that he received instructions for curing. Here he was taught the use of medicines found on Earth, the specific rites to be performed, and to revere the Earthly forms of the Sacred Otter, the Bear, and the Megis shells as powerful medicines. Descending to Earth with his medicine bag, *Manabus* instructed the people and initiated them into the society's mysteries.

The legendary figure *Thadodaho* (left, painted by Jack Unruh) was an evil shaman of the Onondaga whose powerful medicine was believed to kill people, He was so badly infected with evil that snakes writhed from his head. It was *Thadodaho* who opposed *Hiawatha* in his attempt to get the Onondaga to join the League of the Iroquois. *Hiawatha*, however, won him over and can be seen in this painting using a typical Iroquois carved bone comb to remove the snakes from *Thadodaho*'s hair and thereby calming his mind. *Thadodaho* ultimately became Keeper of the Sacred Fire and a distinguished Iroquois leader.

'The skies were filled with deities . . . The constellations of stars were council gatherings of the gods . . . The earth teemed with all sorts of spirits, good and bad . . . '

CHIEF KAH-GE-GA-GAH-BOWH (CHIPPEWA/OJIBWA)[3]

It is no surprise to find the Sun with an important position in regional culture, a feature of so many belief systems. Another common but more intriguing concept is that of the duality of good and bad and their constant struggles against each other for supremacy.

The Sun

In his various guises as Grandfather, Elder Brother, Good Twin, Honored Chief, Great Warrior, and War God, the Sun played a paramount role in the early times for all groups. Certainly, the Sun was regarded as eternal, all-seeing and all-penetrating, source of growth and vigor, father and master of all life, and bringer of daylight. The extent and variety of this Sun veneration (including his Earthly representation as fire) acknowledges the antiquity and importance of the Sun's role.[4]

The Great Lakes peoples (as did the ancient Micmacs) also associated the Sun with war. In his guise as Great Warrior and Patron of War, the Sun was honored with scalp-taking, ritual torture, and sacrificial burning of war captives. Those Menominee warriors who dreamed of the Sun were believed to benefit from his protection in war, and they signified this power by roaching their hair and suspending an amulet-like figure of the Sun over their chests.

Manabus

This semi-divine culture hero of the Algonquians (also known as *Nanabojo*) has a lively and somewhat enigmatic personality. The old stories cast him as the endower and master of life, and as introducer of technological inventions – the making of fire, clothing, snares, traps, nets – who instructed the people in their use. His teachings also provided each of the floral and faunal species with ways to protect themselves from enemies. And in his capacity as intermediary between the Creator and the people, *Manabus* brought the life-prolonging powers of the *Midewiwin* to the Earth world.

However, *Manabus* has become renowned as a trickster, deceiving and playing pranks on humans. Coupled with this is his ability to transform into a number of corporal forms, including that of a hare. These numerous impersonations of diverse personalities strongly suggest that *Manabus* is the quintessential embodiment of the concept of Life.

Earthmaker

The Creator or Great Spirit of the Winnebago

The Creation's Battle (right) by John Fadden, a Mohawk artist, shows the Twin Brothers of Iroquois mythology, *Iouskeha* representing good, and *Tawiscaron* representing evil. The exploits of these twins mirrors much of Iroquois culture, referred to repeatedly in their myths and art, with frequent reference to opposites such as creative and destructive forces, lightness and darkness, good and evil.

created the spirits who live above the earth, those who live on the earth, and those who live below the earth and in the water. Thus, it was he who created the world and all that exists in it and who sent their great transformer heroes, Trickster, Turtle, and Hare. In this Winnebago pantheon, Earthmaker, as a deity of peace, serves as the antithesis to the violence and force pre-eminent in ceremonies devoted to enhancing warriors and warfare.

After creating tobacco, Earthmaker entrusted its power to the people so they would have a desirous item to exchange with the spirits in return for their favors. Often described as being anthropomorphic, Earthmaker was symbolized by a cross representative of the four cardinal points.

Glooskap

Similar to *Manabus*, *Glooskap*'s position in the cast of pantheonic characters of the eastern Algonquians was paradoxical. His divinity, established in some accounts as being the creation of the Great Spirit, was recognized in *Glooskap*'s special spiritual and physical powers. It is *Glooskap*, as protagonist, who competed with the Creator in a power of wills to give existence to things. At other times he was portrayed as the Good Twin constantly thwarting the destructive powers of his evil brother, *Malsum*. Even in his capacity as a trickster, *Glooskap* continues to exude benevolence.

The Theme of Twins

According to Iroquoian mythology, Sky Woman (or, variously, her daughter) gave birth to twin boys named *Iouskeha*, the Good-minded Twin, and *Tawiscaron*, the Evil-minded Twin. The Good-minded Twin was born in the normal manner while his twin brother burst forth from their mother's armpit, killing her in the process.

Iouskeha, possessing the ability to create constructively, made the plants, animals, birds, and mankind, while *Tawiscaron*, controlling the destructive forces, tried to destroy his brother's

work. Together they established a world simultaneously divided and yet balanced. However, a last relentless contest left the Evil-minded Twin dead and sent the Good-minded Twin to the Sky World or Upper World as the Master of Life.

This motif of twins, giving corporal form to the powers of good and bad, is prevalent among other Northeast groups, and in other regions too. In the eastern regions *Glooskap* and his twin brother, *Malsum* or Wolf, entered the world in the same way with similar results as the Iroquoian twins. Tales of their escapades reinforce the concept of an inherent dualism in the structuring of the cultures and the on-going battle between good and evil principles. This also holds true among the Chippewa/Ojibwa, Potawatomi, and Ottawa who provide *Nanabojo* with a brother. In these alternative versions, it is the brother who is represented as a hare.

Grandmother Moon (above), a clay sculpture by Tammy Tarbell, a Mohawk artist. The metaphor of light was central to the thought of the Woodlands Indian. The use of reflective and shiny materials was widespread, being associated with supernatural beings. Foremost was the use of Sun motifs underlining the importance of the sky powers, which included the Moon – the consort of the Sun. Mohawks favored tattooing and painting, and the hand and stripe on this face emphasize that custom.

A Man's Vision of the False Face Society by Ernest Smith (below). Sleeping within an elm bark covered longhouse, clay pots and maize on a platform above, tanned bearskin across the doorway and central fire, this imaginative painting tells us much regarding Iroquois culture. Central to the ethos of these people was the complex False Face Society. Members of the society were credited with special powers when they donned fantastical face masks carved from wood – an Onondaga mask (right) shows the visual impact they had – with some wearers carrying turtle rattles.

'The Great Spirit made the birds, big birds and small birds. The big birds, God gave them lots of power; like these Thunderbirds and eagles . . . And he put one in the sky; that's the one that's looking after the Indians.'

JOHNNY MATCHOKAMOW (MENOMINEE)[5]

Many of the Northeast's themes are familiar from other regions - serpents, underwater monsters, and so on – and draw from the diversity of nature. Familiar, too, are feared anthropomorphic beings – cannibals, little people, and disembodied heads – that become sources of power and medicine. A more novel concept is that of the Iroquoian False Faces, although even they have some parallels elsewhere.

Thunderbird

A super-eagle (Winnebago) or hawk (Chippewa/Ojibwa) with lightning flashing from its eyes and thunder rumbling with the beat of its wings, lived in the Upper World. It was customary to give the Thunderbird and his assistants a ceremonial smoke directed to the four directions whenever they were heard to cry. As an ally and protector of the people, Thunderbird aided cultivation by watering the land with rain, and rendered the Earth safer by terrorizing and ultimately consuming the much-feared Horned Water Snake of the Under World. Seeking the benevolent power of the Thunderbird as guardian spirit was a common visionary quest of youths and men. Those who received such visions were blessed with victory in war and protection in life. Capable of transforming into human form with a large beak, the Thunderbird was often depicted in either manifestation in native art.

Underwater Monster

Among the Great Lakes tribes, this was a widespread supernatural force appearing in variations of two major forms, mammalian and serpentine. In mammalian form, the monster occurred as an underwater panther, lynx, or bear, with such anomalous characteristics as horns, dragon-like spikes, scales, orcopper tails. In its serpentine form, its flesh was pure copper and it possessed horns, a hairy body and, occasionally, legs. This evil force continually sought to destroy man both in the water and on the earth. Success was rare due to the unrelenting efforts of the Thunderbird. A single clap of thunder was sufficient to send the monster to seek the depths of the Under World.

False Faces

These supernatural beings of the Iroquois were bodiless flying heads with long streaming hair and huge eyes who sought to frighten the unwary. Manifested in masks carved from living trees by the Iroquois, the False Faces were used in curing rites performed by the False Face Society. Each class of mask has its own origin story, the most important of these being Old Broken Nose whose twisted features resulted when he dared to contest the supremacy of the Creator. As a consequence of this confrontation, he became known as the Great Doctor destined to wander the rim of the Earth healing and curing the people. The power of all False Faces to cure is acquired and renewed through the performance of the society's rites and the masks' ritual association with the sacred fire, the turtle rattle, and the Cosmic Tree. When not in use, their spiritual power must be kept alive with frequent feedings of tobacco.

Little People

The Algonquian *May-may-gway-shi* were the Little People who lived in caves or crevices in waterside rock faces. Exceedingly fond of fish, they resorted to stealing them from Indian nets. If sighted or pursued, these hairy-faced little men would paddle their stone canoes straight into the rock face and disappear. *May-may-gway-shi* are credited with carving and painting the petroglyphs and pictographs, and in some places reaching their hands out of the water to leave red hand prints on the rock. They were thought to have strong spirit power but only the most gifted shamans were able to enter the rock to exchange tobacco for this extremely potent rock medicine.

Giants

These loom large in myths and legends. Among the Iroquois and Chippewa/Ojibwa, giants were fearsome creatures displaying undesirable traits, the foremost being the consumption of human flesh. The Stone Giants of the Iroquois, man-like and covered with coats of flint, were ravenous cannibals who devoured all they encountered on their journey from the west.[6] The cannibal giant of the Chippewa/Ojibwa came from the north, killing and consuming all those who showed him kindness. In one village along the way, one little boy escaped and when he grew into manhood he sought revenge. He appealed to the spirits for power and they sent 100 winged men to assist him. The ploy they devised was to entice the cannibal giant with a feast of his favorite white bear meat. Eagerly succumbing to this invitation, he afterward became lethargic and the winged spirit people clubbed him to death. His body was then devoured by a host of small animals and his bones consumed by fire. The ashes, scattered by the four winds, became the birds of the air.

'When I see one of those marks, I know what it is right away. But there's more meaning to it. It's like shorthand. You have to dream about it. It's an effort on your soul by the spirits.'

SUN RISING OVER THE MOUNTAIN (CHIPPEWA/OJIBWA)[7]

While these words are a Chippewa/Ojibwa shaman's reference to the visual images depicted in pictographs and petroglyphs on rock faces in the Upper Great Lakes area, this form of visual expression is found in many locations throughout the entire culture area. Located on dramatic rock formations, vertical cliffs rising out of the water, or hidden in rocky caverns, the red ochre paintings and carved glyphs serve as both testimony and supplication to the spirits. Revered as sacred sites by shamans and vision-seekers as well as for individual rites and group ceremonials, it is here that communion with the supernatural occurs. The presence of tobacco and other offerings attests to their continued sanctity.

Lake Superior

At the Agawa Rock site on the northeastern shore of Lake Superior, the soaring cliff provides a dramatic contrast to the surrounding landscape.

In Iroquoian myths, the Niagara Falls were created after a conflict between sky and earth powers. Such powers were epitomized by the concepts associated with the Great Tree of Peace which, with its branches piercing the sky and its roots the earth, connected the cosmic regions of the Iroquoian domain.

With the mythological *Michipeshu* housed in the watery depths of Lake Superior and Thunderbird nests on its highest reaches, this stone shrine is the uniting force between the cosmic powers of the Under World and the Upper World.

At Agawa Rock over 100 images of indeterminate age record the supernatural and natural worlds of the Great Lakes Algonquians. Of especial significance are the pictographs of *Michipeshu* with lynx-like tufts of cheek fur, incurving horns on his head, and spiny protrusions on his back and tail. Always depicted with serpents, fish, and canoes as evidence of *Michipeshu's* Under World powers, at this particular site the association becomes an apt metaphor for the unpredictable and dangerously powerful tempests of Lake Superior.

Some miles to the east there are over 900 glyphs engraved into the white crystalline limestone of the Peterborough Petroglyphs site.

Niagara Falls

These were created following a conflict between the Thunderer and the Great Snake Monster. Long, long ago a beautiful Seneca maiden, escaping from an undesirable marriage, launched her canoe into the swift-flowing Niagara River. From his cave behind the rushing waters the Thunderer spotted the maiden's impending peril as her canoe was dashed against the rocks. Spreading out his wings, he caught her just as her canoe splintered into innumerable pieces.

During the following weeks, the Thunderer taught the girl many things. For one, the source of illness among her people was caused by the Snake Monster coiled beneath their village. However, a move to a new village site closer to the great lake was soon discovered by the snake. Once again coming to the assistance of the Seneca, the Thunderer hurled lightning bolts at the monster until its enormous dead body lay wedged in the rocks. The Niagara River was forced to rise above it and then fall in a magnificent cascade, a permanent reminder to mankind of the victorious contest of good over evil.

The Longhouse

In contrast to the permanency of sacred rocks, microcosmic structures were erected and dissembled in response to a society's needs. Wherever built, these structures replicated the cosmology in material form.

After the formation of the League of Five Nations, the Iroquois Confederacy was referred to as a Longhouse. The Mohawks guarded the eastern door while the Senecas became the keepers of the western door. In the center of the Longhouse was the territory of the Onondagas who, as keepers of the fire, were said to stand directly beneath the Longhouse's central smokehole. Inside the northern and southern walls, respectively, lived the Cayugas and Oneidas. Clan leaders were the supporting braces and the tribal chiefs served as posts. Communication and mutual defense were hastened by means of the Iroquois Trail, the symbolic central aisle. As a collective symbol, the Longhouse retains its potency as an Iroquois institution to this day.

The Big House

This sacred structure of the Delawares symbolized their universe. A gable-ended log structure, the dirt floor represented the earth, the roof the sky, the four walls the four sides of the horizon. Painted carved faces on the supporting posts and sacred center pole represented the *Manitous* of the 12 layers of the Delaware cosmos.

Midewigan

The *midewigan* of the *Midewiwin* (Medicine Lodge Society), was a long bower-like enclosure formed from ritually harvested saplings. Within this structure, members of the Great Lakes tribes followed rites inscribed in pictographs on sacred birch bark scrolls. Once the ceremonies were completed, the *midewigan* was left to decay.

The Tree of Life

Common to all groups was the Tree of Life or World Tree, further recognized as the Cosmic Axis, located at the center of the world and serv-

ing as the pathway connecting the various layers of the cosmos. For the Great Lakes tribes and the Delaware, the Tree of Life and Cosmic Axis are symbolized by the ceremonial posts in their respective sacred structures. For the Iroquoians, this Tree of Life encompasses many levels of meaning. Integrated with the concept of Cosmic Axis is the Great Tree of Peace arising from the back of the primal turtle, its branches piercing the sky, its top surmounted by an eagle, and its roots spreading to the four directions serves to connect the cosmic regions.

Pictured Rocks Caves in Michigan (above). The permanency of rock and its often weird formations gave it a sacred character and power.

A *Midewiwin* Medicine Lodge (below) erected on the White Earth Reservation in 1910. The curative rituals were performed within this enclosure.

Of all the other-than-human persons, animals play an enormous role in native spiritual life. As *Manitous*, mediators, and protagonists animals do indeed 'tell the grand story.'

The Turtle

As Earth-holder Turtle bears the colossal weight of Iroquoian creation on his back and serves to both separate and mediate between the Sky and the Under worlds. This protective role of the turtle continues with the healing powers of the snapping turtle rattle used by the Great Doctor, its powers renewed by rubbing it on pine tree trunks. Turtle's strengths were such that he presided over one of the four worlds of the Winnebago and in his land-turtle form he supported the four sacred poles of each Medicine Lodge member's *tipi* on his paws. Acting as a messenger to the spirits, Turtle often appeared as one of the many *Midewiwin* patrons. To both Iroquoians and Algonquians the turtle was one of the most important *Manitous*, a metaphoric symbol for the Earth and, by extension, a symbol of fertility. Among the Ottawa it is believed that Mackinac Island, between Lake Huron and Lake Michigan, was formed when the Great Turtle froze to death on his pilgrimage northward.

The Bear

Bear, in his many guises and on each of the cosmic levels, was revered as the embodied source of shamanic medicine. Human-like in his Earthly form, Bear was treated as a wise and honored guest, powerful in his curative abilities and Grandfather to all. These curative powers, including success in hunting, were bound up in a form of complex ceremonialism designed to honor and propitiate the revered spirit of the bear.

In the Sky World of the Micmac, the Great Bear (Ursa Major) exemplified cyclic renewal, replicating the winter hibernation and spring awakening of the bear's Earthly form. In the world above, Bear is chased by three avian hunters who finally succeed in mid-autumn. Once the flesh is consumed, the skeleton lies on its back in the winter sky to be revitalized once again each spring. And the cycle continues.

The White Bear of the Great Lakes, intimate with the Great Spirit and assistant to Shell, brought forth the *Midewiwin* from Below, along the Cosmic Axis to the people on the Earth. As guardian of the *Mide* Ceremony, Bear opens the eastern door of the *Mide* Lodge admitting only those who are ritually prepared. Partial preparation entailed purification rites within the sanctity and protection of Grandfather Bear's sweat lodge constructed from his ribs (bent branches) and covered with his skin.

Turtle rattles, such as this Seneca example (above), were used in the shamanistic music of the Iroquois. Traditionally, they were made from a snapping turtle's shell with a hickory handle wrapped with bark and used by most of the participants in both the Feather Dance and False Face Society ceremonials to frighten away the evil spirits. In contrast (right) is this single Chippewa drummer who is regaled for the dances of the *Midewiwin* Society. His drum is made of rawhide stretched over a hoop and turtle power is represented by the painted motif at the center.

Eagle

Revered as chief of the birds, Eagle soars the highest, is the bravest, possesses keen sight, looks straight into the eye of the Sun, and serves as mediator between Earth and Sun. The mythological Dew Eagle of Iroquoian tradition was believed to inhabit the uppermost level in the sky, was suffused with *Orenda*, and held restorative powers to cure illness. It was further believed that the Dew Eagle, as the Thunderbird, was capable of transforming from bird to human at will. In his role as the 'Eagle who Sees Afar' perched on the topmost branch of the Tree of Peace, the eagle was the terrestrial counterpart of the orb or ball of light on the topmost branch of the celestial Tree of Light. Algonquian speakers held similar concepts emphasizing the eagle's superior strengths as a fighter.

Animals as Mediators

Certain birds, animals, and serpents are venerated for their mastery of more than one cosmic zone, and the additional powers thus gained by communication with the supernatural. This ability to cross cosmic thresholds is best exemplified by waterfowl as they move from water to land to air, or directly from the Under World to the Sky World. As mediators between these zones, the waterfowl played a significant role in Iroquoian mythology by intercepting Sky Woman's precipitous fall into the watery Under World until the Earth could be formed

Otter's role as mediator is revealed in the origin myth of the *Mide* Ceremony. When the *Mide* Lodge was finished the Upper World Powers, or Grandfathers, sent a hawk with the message for *Manabus* to enter. Only when Otter, as representative of the Under World Powers, delivered the message would *Manabus* accept the invitation. During the Grandfathers' ensuing presentations of protective powers and medicines, *Manabus* was given an otter skin medicine bag with its own song. Otter, as embodied by the skin bag, dispenses medicine and symbolically restores the life of initiates during the ceremony.

Similar beliefs in the mediating and curing abilities of the otter were demonstrated by the Otter Society. The otter, chief of the small water animals, was a powerful medicine animal controlling the health, fortunes, and destinies of the people. The Otter Society possessed no songs or dances, but was organized to retain the favors of the water animals. Failure to express gratitude would result in illness.

Also mediating between the Under World and the Earth, snakes carry messages from one cosmic zone to another by entering and emerging through holes in the ground, and by transporting souls to the world beyond. While connections with the Under World were reflected by their relationship with powers of darkness and evil, snakes also signified regeneration through both their winter dormancy and spring rejuvenation, and the shedding of their old skin. These features meant that reptiles were abhorred yet widely accepted as powerful *Manitous*.

Animal clan crests were recorded among the Seneca as early as 1666, and as with other Iroquois tribes turtle and wolf motifs were given prominence. The wolf's head and the turtle incised on the handle of this war club (above) probably state clan membership, while the wolf spirit mask (left) invokes the powers of a mythical giant and combines them with those of the wolf for healing rituals.

RITUALS AND CEREMONIES

*'The Drums shall beat, so my heart shall beat,
And I shall live a hundred thousand years.'*

SHIRLEY DANIELS (CHIPPEWA/OJIBWA)[9]

Drumbeats are the heartbeats of the people summoning the *Manitous* to participate in the ceremonies. For centuries the drum has been identified with the spiritual and cultural lives of the Indians, its very rhythm profoundly affecting all ceremonial activity. The importance of drums and drumming to the Chippewa identity is instilled in young babies before they are able to walk. Ceremonies may involve a single shaman drumming in his conjuring tent for a few hours, or the ritual drumming in the *Mide* Lodge, or the four-day ceremony of the Drum Dance[10] with several drums following the *Midewiwin*.

The Midwinter Festival

Held in the Iroquoian longhouse this was considered to be the most important of the calendric ceremonies. In ancient times this ceremonial had been a

winter solstice rite whose purpose was to bring back the Sun from its nadir. Handsome Lake's addition of the Four Sacred Rituals in the early 1800s had little effect on the earlier Sun veneration, for many of the rituals continued to focus on the power of the Sun. For instance, the ceremonial climax, the Creator's own Feather Dance, symbolized the diurnal journey of the Sun. Similarly, the Bowl Game dedicated to the Great Warrior, the Sun, who determined the results of the game, supported the theme of renewal. In earlier times, arrows had been shot at the Sun, each volley accompanied by a chorus of war cries to call back the Sun. More recently, participants attired in their finery carried wooden Sun disc wands painted with Sun motifs surrounded with down and eagle feathers signifying the Sun's corona as metonymic reminders to ensure the Sun's return.

The White Dog Sacrifice

At one time throughout the entire Woodlands and Great Lakes area, this sacrificial rite had

Rattles, such as this Seneca example (below), were an essential accompaniment to singers and dancers such as those Chippewa (below right) recreating a Scalp Dance from bygone days. A triple drum rhythm was pounded and the scalps were held up on poles. Afterward the honored youth could walk with the men and wear an eagle feather in his hair.

136

taken place throughout the year. By the 1800s it, too, had become one of the rituals of the Iroquoian Midwinter Ceremony. This ritual necessitated the selection of a pure white dog free of blemishes and imperfections. Ritually prepared, its hair was combed, its face painted to represent *Teharonhiawagon* (Sky God or Sun), and its legs wound spirally with red ribbon. Strangled without shedding blood, the dog was sacrificed to *Areskoue*, the Sun in his guise as God of War. Designed to secure the continued protection of the Sun and to sustain the cycle of life for another year, it was the most sacred and emotional moment of the entire Midwinter Ceremony.

Initiation

For all the tribes scalp-taking was recognized as a rite of passage marking social puberty and the incorporation of youths into the warrior status. Following a regime of ritual purification and the sanctification of their weapons by dancing, the youth and his sponsors undertook a foray. With the acquisition of a scalp, the youth was given instructions for its ritual preparation. Offered first to the Sun for its blessing, the flesh was then removed, the skin and hair were sewn on to a hoop and the inner side painted with motifs associated with the Sun, a face, a sunburst, or concentric circles. Mounted on a slender pole, the scalp was carried home where a Scalp Dance formally incorporated the youth into the society.

Acquiring Power

According to Menominee elders, power is an invisible force that emits bright light. The much-desired acquisition of power began in early childhood with short periods of fasting and instructions on the appropriateness of humble behavior. Puberty was marked by the Great Fast when a boy or girl blackened his or her face and retreated into the woods. There, in seclusion, the power-seeker remained alone without food for periods up to 10 days, all the while focusing on receiving a vision, and through that the source of power.

Appearance of the Golden Eagle, White Bear or any other of the Upper World spirits indicated success, while visions of Under World creatures such as the Horned Snake marked an unsuccessful attempt. If success was not attained after four tries, the power-seeker was doomed to life thereafter as a witch.

The Arrival of Strangers

Many of these traditions changed with the coming of the Europeans. It is fitting, therefore, to conclude with the Micmac legend relating the arrival of these strange beings. While *Glooskap* is the protagonist in some versions and in others it is a young woman who dreams about the event, the details are similar. A small island was seen to be drifting toward the land. It was covered with tall trees with a number of bear-like creatures climbing in the branches. As the floating island came closer it was seen that these bears were men with white skins and hair on their faces. These strangers brought items of great curiosity that excited the people. And changes began to take place . . .

The spiritual life of the Chippewa/Ojibwa was centered around the *Midewiwin* Ceremony. That seen here (below) took place on the Mille Lac Reservation in 1910. The society met once a year in a special mat lodge, of the type seen here, to perform healing and initiatory rites. Each member had to pass the order's eight degrees.

BIBLIOGRAPHY

INTRODUCTION

Kroeber, A. L. 'Handbook of the Indians of California' in *Bureau of American Ethnology*, Bulletin 78, Washington D. C., 1925.

Lowie, R. H. 'Myths and Traditions of the Crow Indians' in *Anthropological Papers of the American Museum of Natural History* Vol. XXV, Part 1, New York, 1918.

THE SOUTHEAST

Books

Adair, J. *The History of the American Indians*, New York, 1775.

Barbour, P. *The Three Worlds of Captain John Smith*, Boston, 1964.

Feldman, S. (ed.) *The Storytelling Stone: Traditional Native American Myths and Tales*, New York, 1965.

Foreman, G. *Indian Removal: The Emigration of the Five Civilized Tribes of Indians*, Norman, Oklahoma, 1932.

Henri, F. *The Southern Indians and Benjamin Hawkins: 1796-1816*, Norman, Oklahoma, 1986.

Hudson, C. *The Southeastern Tribes*, Knoxville, Tennessee, 1976.

Lankford, G. E. (ed.) *Southeastern Legends: Tales from the Natchez, Caddo, Biloxi, Chickasaw, and Other Nations*, Little Rock, Arkansas, 1987.

Larson, J. *A New Voyage to Carolina*, Chapel Hill, North Carolina, 1967.

Lewis, T. M. N. and Kneberg, M. *Tribes That Slumber*, Knoxville, Tennessee, 1958.

McLoughlin, W. G. *The Cherokee Ghost Dance: Essays on the Southeastern Indians*, Mercer, West Virginia, 1984.

McLuhan, T. C. (ed.) *Touch the Earth*, London, 1971.

Matthiessen, P. *Indian Country*, London, 1986.

Mooney, J. *Myths of the Cherokees and Sacred Formulas of the Cherokees*, Nashville, 1972.

Moore-Willson, M. *The Seminoles of Florida*, New York, 1910.

Speck, F. G. and Broom, L. *Cherokee Dance and Drama*, Norman, Oklahoma, 1951.

Thurston, G. P. *Antiquities of Tennessee and the Adjacent States*, Cincinatti, 1987.

Timberlake, H. *Memoirs: 1756-1765*. Edited by Williams, S. C., Marietta, Georgia, 1948.

Weisman, B. R. *Like a String of Beads: A Cultural History of the Seminole Indians in North Peninsular Florida*, London, 1989.

Other

Mooney, J. 'Myths of the Cherokee' in *Annual Report of the Bureau of American Ethnology, 1897-98*, Part I, Washington D. C., 1900.

THE SOUTHWEST

Books

Bahti, M. *Pueblo Stories and Storytellers*, Tucson, 1988.

Baldwin, G. C. *The Apache Indians: Raiders of the South-West*, New York, 1978.

Barrett, S. M. (ed.) *Geronimo: His Own Story*, New York, 1970.

Benedict, R. *Zuni Mythology: Vols. I-II*, New York, 1935.

Burland, C. *North American Indian Mythology*, Northampton, 1965.

Courlander, H. *Hopi Voices: Recollections, Traditions and Narratives of the Hopi Indians*, Albuquerque, 1982.

Dutton, B. and Olin, C. *Myths and Legends of the Indians of the Southwest: Navajo, Pima, Apache: Book I*, Santa Barbara, California, 1991.

Dutton, B. and Olin, C. *Myths and Legends of the Indians of the Southwest: Hopi, Acoma, Tewa, Zuni: Book II*, Santa Barbara, California, 1991.

Eagle Walking Turtle. *Indian America: A Traveller's Companion*, Santa Fe, New Mexico, 1991.

Erdoes, R. and Ortiz, A. *American Indian Myths and Legends*, New York, 1984.

Evers, L. (ed.) *The South Corner of Time: Hopi, Navajo, Papago, Yaqui Tribal Literature*, Tucson, 1983.

Ferguson, T. J. and Hart, R. E. *A Zuni Atlas*, Norman, Oklahoma, 1985.

Gill, S. D. 'Navajo View of Their Origin' in Ortiz, A. and Sturtevant, W. C. (eds.) *Handbook of North American Indians: Vol. 10*, Washington D. C., 1979.

Hieb, L. A. 'Hopi World View' in Ortiz, A. and Sturtevant, W. C. (eds.) *Handbook of North American Indians: Vol. 9*, Washington D. C, 1979.

Mackenzie, D. A. *Myths of Pre-Columbian America*, London, no date.

McLuhan, T. C. (ed.) *Touch the Earth*, London, 1971.

Matthiessen, P. *Indian Country*, London, 1986.

Moon, S. *A Magic Dwells: A Poetic and Psychological Study of the Navajo Emergence Myth*, Middletown, Connecticut, 1970.

Mullet, G. M. *Spider Woman Stories: Legends of the Hopi Indians*, Tucson, 1979.

Rock Point Community School, *Between Sacred Mountains: Navajo Stories and Lessons from the Land*, Tucson, 1984.

Tedlock, D. 'Zuni Religion and World View' in Ortiz, A. and Sturtevant, W. C. (eds.) *Handbook of North American Indians: Vol. 9*, Washington D. C., 1979.

Wright, B. *Kachinas of the Zuni*, Flagstaff, 1985.

Underhill, R. M. *Red Man's Religion: Belief and Practices of the Indians North of Mexico*, Chicago, 1965.

Yazzie, R. *Between Sacred Mountains: Navajo Stories and Lessons from the Land*, Tucson, 1984.

Other

Benedict, R. 'Tales of the Cochiti Indians' in *Bureau of American Ethnology*, Bulletin 98, Washington D. C., 1931.

Bunzel, R. L. 'Zuni Texts' in *American Ethnological Society* Vol. XV, New York, 1933.

Goodwin, G. 'Myths and Tales of the White Mountain Apache' in *Memoirs of the American Folk-Lore Society*, Vol. XXXIII, New York, 1939.

Opler, M. E. 'Myths and Tales of the Jicarilla Apache Indians' in *Memoirs of the American Folk-Lore Society*, Vol. XXXI, New York, 1938.

Parsons, E. C. 'Hopi and Zuni Ceremonialism' in *Memoirs of the American Anthropological Association*, No. 39, Menasha, Wisconsin, 1933.

Parsons, E. C. 'Tewa Tales' in *Memoirs of the American Folk-Lore Society* Vol. XIX, New York, 1926.

THE PLAINS

Books

Ben Calf Robe, *Siksika: A Blackfoot Legacy*, Invermore, British Columbia, 1979.

Bowers, A. *Mandan Social and Ceremonial Organization*, Chicago, 1950.

Chamberlain, V. D. *When Stars Came Down to Earth: Cosmology of the Skidi Pawnee Indians of North America*, Maryland, 1982.

DeMallie, R. J. and Lavenda, R. H. 'Wakan: Plains Siouan Concepts of Power' in Fogelson and Adams (eds). *The Anthropology of Power*, New York, 1977.

Dodge, R. Col. *The Hunting Grounds of the Great West*, London, 1877.

Dooling, D. M. (ed.) *The Sons of the Wind*, New York, 1992.

Eppridge, T. 'The Star Image and Plains Indian Star Legends' in Ball, G. and George P. Horse Capture (eds.) *Plains Indian Design Symbology and Decoration*, Cody, Wyoming, 1980.

Ewers, J. C. *Plains Indian Sculpture: A Traditional Art from America's Heartland*, Washington D. C., 1986.

Grinnell, G. B. *Blackfoot Lodge Tales*, New York, 1920.

Grinnell, G. B. *The Cheyenne Indians: Their History and Ways of Life: Vols. I-II*, New Haven, 1923.

Guthrie, A. B. Jr. *The Big Sky*, New York, 1947.

Jones, D. E. *Sanapia, Comanche Medicine Woman*, New York, 1972.

Linderman, F. B. *The Sacrifice to the Morning Star by the Skidi Pawnee*, Chicago, 1922.

Linderman, F. B. *Annual Ceremony of the Pawnee Medicine Men*, Chicago, 1923.

Linderman, F. B. *Plenty Coups: Chief of the Crows*, London, 1930.

Loendorf, L. L. 'Remnants of the Mountain Crow in Montana and Wyoming' in Tobias, M. (ed.) *Mountain People*, Norman, Oklahoma, 1986.

Lowie, R. H. *Myths and Traditions of the Crow Indians*, Lincoln, Nebraska, 1993.

Nabakov, P. *Two Leggings: The Making of a Crow Warrior*, New York, 1967.

Neihardt, J. G. *Black Elk Speaks*, New York, 1932.

Petersen, K. D. *American Pictographic Images*, New York, 1988.

Sturtevant, W. C. and Taylor, C. F. (eds.) *The Native Americans*, London & New York, 1991.

Taylor, C. F. *Saam: The Symbolic Content of Early Northern Plains Ceremonial Regalia*, Wyk auf Foehr, Germany, 1993.

Turner, F. (ed.) *The Portable North American Indian Reader*, London, 1977.

Walker, J. R. *Lakota Belief and Ritual*. Edited by DeMallie, R. J. and Jahner, E. A., Lincoln, Nebraska, 1980.

Walker, J. R. *Lakota Society*. Edited by DeMallie, R. J., Lincoln, Nebraska, 1982.

Walker, J. R. *Lakota Myth*. Edited by Jahner, E. A., Lincoln, Nebraska, 1983.

Wildschut, W. *Crow Indian Medicine Bundles*. Edited by Ewers, J. C., New York, 1960.

Other

Brasser, T. J. 'Backrest Banners Among the Plains Cree and Plains Ojibwa' in *American Indian Art Magazine*, Vol. 10, No. 1, Winter, Scottsdale, Arizona, 1984.

Conner, S. W. 'Archaeology of the Crow Indian Vision Quest' in *Archaeology in Montana*, Vol. 23, No. 3, Butte, Montana, 1982.

Dorsey, J. O. 'A Study of Siouan Cults', *11th Annual Report of the Bureau of American Ethnology*, Washington D. C., 1894.

Ewers, J. C. 'The White Man's Strongest Medicine,' reprint in *Bulletin of the Missouri Historical Society*, St Louis, 1967.

Ewers, J. C. 'A Unique Pictorial Interpretation of Blackfoot Indian Religion in 1846-1847' in *Ethnohistory*, Vol. 18, No. 3, Summer, Tempe, Arizona, 1971.

Fletcher, Alice C. 'The Sun Dance of the Ogallala Sioux' in *American Association for the Advancement of Science Proceedings*, Washington D. C., 1883.

Fletcher, Alice C. 'The Religious Ceremony of the Four Winds or Quarters, as Observed by the Santee Sioux' in *Sixteenth Report Vol. III, Peabody Museum of American Archaelogy and Ethnology*, Harvard University, Cambridge, Massachusetts, 1887.

Fletcher, Alice C. 'The Elk Mystery or Festival. Ogallala Sioux' in *Sixteenth Report Vol. III, Peabody Museum of American Archaelogy and Ethnology*, Harvard University, Cambridge, Massachusetts, 1887.

Fletcher, Alice C. 'The White Buffalo Festival of the Uncpapas' in *Sixteenth Report Vol. III, Peabody Museum of American Archaelogy and Ethnology*, Harvard University, Cambridge, Massachusetts, 1887.

Fletcher, Alice C. 'The Shadow or Ghost Lodge: A Ceremony of the Ogallala Sioux' in *Sixteenth Report Vol. III, Peabody Museum of American Archaelogy and Ethnology*, Harvard University, Cambridge, Massachusetts, 1887.

Fletcher, A. C. and La Flesche, F. 'The Omaha Tribe' in *27th Annual Report of the Bureau of American Ethnology*, Washington D. C., 1911.

Howard, J. H. 'The Arikara Buffalo Society Medicine Bundle' in *Plains Anthropologist*, Vol. 19, No. 66, Part I, Lincoln, Nebraska, 1974.

Pepper, G. H. and Wilson, G. L. 'An Hidatsa Shrine and the Beliefs Respecting It' in *Memoirs of the American Anthropological Association*, Vol. II, Part 4, New York, 1974.

Simms, S. C. 'Traditions of the Crows' in *American Anthropology*, Vol. II, Chicago, 1903.

Taylor, C. F. 'Wakanyan: Symbols of Power and Ritual of the Teton Sioux' in *Amerindian Cosmology*, Brandon, Manitoba, 1989.

Walker, J. R. 'The Sun Dance and other Ceremonies of the Oglala Division of the Teton Dakota' in *Anthropology Papers of the American Museum of Natural History*, Vol. XVI, Part II, New York, 1917.

Wissler, C. *Field Notes on the Dakota Indians: Collected on Museum Expedition of 1902*, unpublished manuscript from the library of the American Museum of Natural History, New York, 1902.

Wissler, C. 'The Whirlwind and the Elk in the Mythology of the Dakota' in *The Journal of American Folk-Lore*, Vol. XVIII, No. LXXI, Washington D. C., 1905.

Wissler, C. 'Some Protective Designs of the Dakota' in *Anthropology Papers of the American Museum of Natural History*, Vol. I, Part II, New York, 1907.

Wissler, C. 'Social Organization and Ritualistic Ceremonies of the Blackfoot Indians. Part II: Ceremonial Bundles of the Blackfoot Indians' in *Anthropology Papers of the American Museum of Natural History*, Vol. VIII, New York, 1912.

Wissler, C. 'Societies and Ceremonial Associations in the Oglala Division of the Teton-Dakota' in *Anthropology Papers of the American Museum of Natural History*, Vol. XI, New York, 1912.

Wissler, C. 'The Sun Dance of the Blackfoot Indians' in *Anthropology Papers of the American Museum of Natural History*, Vol. XVI, New York, 1918.

Wissler, C. and Duvall, D. C. 'Mythology of the Blackfoot Indians' in *Anthropology Papers of the American Museum of Natural History*, Vol. II, New York, 1908.

PLATEAU AND BASIN

Books

Clark, E. E. *Indian Legends from the Rockies*, Norman, Oklahoma, 1988.

Curtis, E. S. *The North American Indian: Vols. 7-8*, Norwood, Connecticut, 1911.

D'Azevedo, W. L. (ed.) *Handbook of North American Indians: Vol. II*, Washington D. C., 1986.

Eliade, M. *Shamanism: Archaic Techniques of Ecstacy*, London, 1989. (Translated from the French by Willard P. Trask.)

Farb, P. *Man's Rise to Civilization as Shown by the Indians of North America from Primeval Times to the Coming of the Industrial State*, London, 1969.

Gidley, M. *Kopet: A Documentary Narrative of Chief Joseph's Last Years*, Seattle, 1981.

Hultkrantz, A. 'Mythology and Religious Concepts' in D'Azevedo, W. L. (ed.) *Handbook of North American Indians: Vol. II*, Washington D. C., 1986.

La Barre, W. *The Peyote Cult*, New York, 1975.

Liljeblad, S. 'Oral Tradition: Content and Style of Verbal Arts' in D'Azevedo, W. L. (ed.) *Handbook of North American Indians: Vol. II*, Washington D. C., 1986.

Lopez, B. H. *Giving Birth to Thunder, Sleeping with His Daughter: Coyote Builds North America*, New York, 1977.

McLuhan, T. C. (ed.) *Touch the Earth*, London, 1973.

Miller, H. and Harrison, E. *Coyote Tales of the Montana Salish*, Rapid City, South Dakota, 1974.

Mooney, J. *The Ghost Dance Religion and the Sioux Outbreak of 1890*, Chicago, 1986.

Ramsey, J. *Coyote Was Going There: Indian Literature of the Oregon Country*, Seattle, 1977.

Stewart, O. C. 'The Peyote Religion' in D'Azevedo, W. L. (ed.) *Handbook of North American Indians: Vol. II*, Washington D. C., 1986.

Vanderweth, W. C. *Indian Oratory: Famous Speeches by Noted Indian Chiefs*, Norman, Oklahoma, 1971.

Other

Hultkrantz, A. 'Diversity in Cosmology: the Case of the Wind River Shoshone' in *Amerindian Cosmology*, special edition of *Cosmos*, No. 4, Edinburgh, 1988.

Teit, J. A. 'The Salishan Tribes of the Western Plateaus' in Boas (ed.) *45th Annual Report of the Bureau of American Ethnology*, Washington D. C., 1930.

CALIFORNIA

Books

Barrett, S. A. 'Myths of the Southern Sierra Miwok' in *University of California Publications in America Archaeology and Ethnology*, Berkeley, California, 1919.

Bates, C. D. and Martha J. L. *Tradition and Innovation: A Basket History of the Indians of the Yosemite-Mono Lake Area*, Yosemite, California, 1990.

Densmore, F. *Music of the Maidu Indians*, Los Angeles, 1958.

Gifford, E. W. and Block, G. H. *California Indian Nights Entertainments: Stories of the Creation of the World, of Man, of Fire of the Sun, of Thunder*, Glendale, California, 1930.

Gifford, E. W. and Block, G. H. *California Indian Nights Entertainments: Stories of Coyote, the Land of the Dead, the Sky Monsters, Animal People*, Glendale, California, 1930.

Heizer, R. F. (ed.). *Handbook of North American Indians: Vol. 8*, Washington D. C., 1978.

LaPena, F. R., Bates, C. D., and Medley, S. P. *Legends of the Yosemite Miwok*, Yosemite, California, 1993.

LaPena, F. R. and Driesbach, J. T. (eds.) *The Extension of Tradition: Contemporary Native American Art in Cultural Perspective*, Sacramento, California, 1985.

Latta, F. F. *California Indian Folklore*, Shafter, California, 1936.

Other

Bean, L. J. and Brakke Vane, S. (eds.) 'California Indian Shamanism' in *Ballena Press Anthropological Papers*, No. 39, Menlo Park, California, 1992.

Gayton, A. H. 'Areal Affiliations of California Folktales' in *American Anthropologist*, No. 37 (4), New York, 1935.

Spott, R. and Kroeber, A. L. 'Yurok Narratives' in *American Archaeology and Ethnology*, No. 35 (9), Berkeley, California, 1942.

THE NORTHWEST COAST

Books

Barbeau, M. *Totem Poles: Vols. 1-2*, Hull, Quebec, 1990.

Barbeau, M. and Benyon, W. *Tricksters, Shamans and Heroes: Tsimshian Narratives*, Ottawa, 1987.

Barnett, H. G. *The Coast Salish*, Eugene, Oregon, 1955.

Boas, F. *Primitive Art*, New York, 1951.

Boas, F. *Kwakiutl Ethnography*, Chicago, 1966.

Boas, F. *Tsimshian Mythology*, New York, 1970.

Boas, F. *Bella Bella Tales*, New York, 1973.

Curtis, E. S. *The North American Indian: Vol. II*, New York, 1916.

De Laguna, F. 'Under Mount Saint Elias: The History and Culture of The Yakutat Tlingit' (Parts One and Two) in *Smithsonian Contributions to Anthropology*, Vol. 7, Washington D. C., 1972.

Hall, E. S. Jr., Blackman, M. B. and Rickard, V. *Northwest Coast Indian Graphics: An Introduction to Silk Screen Prints*, Vancouver, 1981.

Halpin, M. M. 'Seeing in Stone: Tsimshian Masking and the Twin Stone Masks' in Abbot, D. N. (ed.) *The World is as Sharp as a Knife*, Vancouver, 1981.

Holm, B. and Reid, B. *Indian Art of the Northwest Coast: A Dialogue on Craftsmanship and Aesthetics*, Seattle, 1975.

Inverarity, R. B. *Art of the Northwest Coast Indians*, Berkeley, California, 1950.

Sheehan, C. *Pipes That Won't Smoke; Coal That Won't Burn*, Calgary, Alberta, 1981.

Sheehan (McLaren), C. *Unmasking Frontlet Headdresses: An Iconographic Study of Images in Northern Northwest Coast Ceremonial Headdresses*, Vancouver, 1977.

Stewart, H. *Looking at Indian Art of the Northwest Coast*, Vancouver, 1979.

Swanton, J. R. *Social Conditions, Beliefs, and Linguistic Relationships of the Tlingit Indians*, New York, 1970.

The Book Builders of 'Ksan. *We-Get Wanders On*, Saanichton, British Columbia, 1977.

The Suquamish Museum. *The Eyes of Chief Seattle*, Suquamish, Washington, 1985.

Other

Boas, F. 'The Bilqula' in the *British Association for the Advancement of Science*, Vol. 17, London, 1891.

Boas, F. 'The Social Organization and Secret Societies of the Kwakiutl Indians' in *Report of the U.S. National Museum*, New York, 1895.

Boas, F. 'Tsimshian Texts' in *Bureau of American Ethnology*, Bulletin 27, Washington D. C., 1902.

Boas, F. 'Kwakiutl Tales' in *Columbia University Contributions to Anthropology*, Vol. 2, New York, 1910.

Boas, F. 'Folk-Tales of Salishan and Sahaptin Tribes' in *Memoirs of the American Folk-Lore Society*, New York, 1917.

Boas, F. 'Ethnology of the Kwakiutl' in *35th Annual Report of the Bureau of American Ethnology*, Washington D. C., 1921.

Boas, F. 'Contributions to the Ethnology of the Kwakiutl' in *Columbia University Contributions to Anthropology*, Vol. 3, New York, 1925.

Boas, F. 'Religion of the Kwakiutl Indians. Part 2.' in *Columbia University Contributions to Anthropology*, Vol. 10, New York, 1930.

Boas, F. 'Kwakiutl Tales' in *Columbia University Contributions to Anthropology*, Vol. XXVI, New York, 1935(a).

Boas, F. 'Kwakiutl Culture as Reflected in Mythology' in *Memoirs of the American Folk-Lore Society*, New York, 1935 (b).

Emmons, G. T. 'The Chilkat Blanket' in *American Museum of Natural History, Memoirs*, Vol. III, New York, 1907.

Gould, J. C. 'Iconography of the Northwest Coast Raven Rattle,' unpublished MA thesis, University of British Columbia, Vancouver, 1973.

Kennedy, D. and Bouchard, R. 'The Bella Coola Indians,' manuscript of the British Columbia Indian Language Project, 1977.

Sheehan (McLaren), C. 'Moments of Death: Gift of Life. A Reinterpretation of the Northwest Coast Image Hawk' in *Anthropologica*, Vol. XX, New York, 1978.

Swanton, J. R. 'Contributions to the Ethnology of the Haida' in *American Museum of Natural History, Memoirs*, Vol. VIII, New York, 1905 (a).

Swanton, J. R. 'Haida Texts and Myths: Skidegate Dialect' in *Bureau of American Ethnology*, Bulletin 29, Washington D. C., 1905. (b).

Swanton, J. R. 'Haida Texts and Myths: Masset Dialect' in *American Museum of Natural History, Memoirs 14, Part 1*, New York, 1908.

Swanton, J. R. 'Tlingit Myths and Texts, *Bureau of American Ethnology*, Bulletin 39, Washington D. C., 1909.

Waterman, T. T. 'Some Conundrums in Northwest Coast Art' in *American Anthropologist*, No. 25, New York, 1923.

THE SUBARCTIC

Books

Boudreau, N. J. (ed) *The Athapaskans: Strangers of the North*, Ottawa, 1974.

Dunning, R. W. *Social and Economic Change Among the Northern Ojibwa*, Toronto, 1959.

Helm, J. (ed.) *Handbook of North American Indians: Vol. 6*, Washington D. C., 1981.

Martin, C. *Keepers of the Game: Indian-Animal Relationships and the Fur Trade*, Berkeley, California, 1978.

McMillan, A. D. *The Native Peoples and Cultures of Canada*, Vancouver, 1988.

Nelson, R. K. *Make Prayers to the Raven: A Koyukon View of the Northern Forest*, Chicago, 1983.

Tanner, A. *Bringing Home Animals: Religious Ideology and Mode of Production of the Mistassini Cree Hunters*, New York, 1979.

Vanstone, J. W. *Athapaskan Adaptations: Hunters and Fishermen of the Subarctic Forests*, Chicago, 1974.

Other

Cooper, J. M. 'The Northern Algonquian Supreme Being' in *Primitive Man*, Vol. 6, 1933.

De Laguna, F. 'Indian Masks from the Lower Yukon' in *American Anthropologist*, No. 38 (4), New York, 1936.

Hallowell, A. I. 'Some Empirical Aspects of Northern Salteaux Religion' in *American Anthropologist*, No. 36 (3), New York, 1934.

Hallowell, A. I. 'The Passing of the Midewiwin in the Lake Winnipeg Region' in *American Anthropologist*, No. 38 (1), New York, 1936.

Jarvenpa, R. 'Symbolism and Inter-Ethnic Relations Among Hunter-Gatherers: Chipewyan Conflict Lore' in *Anthropologica*, Vol. XXIV, New York, 1982.

Rossignol, M. 'Cross-Cousin Marriage Among the Saskatchewan Cree' in *Primitive Man*, Vol. XI, 1938.

THE ARCTIC

Books

Balikci, A. *The Netsilik Eskimo*, New York, 1970.

Birket-Smith, K. *The Eskimos*, London, 1959.

Damas, D. (ed.) *Handbook of North American Indians: Vol. 5*, Washington D. C., 1984.

McMillan, A. D. *The Native Peoples and Cultures of Canada*, Vancouver, 1988.

Weyer, E. M. *The Eskimos: Their Environment and Folkways*, New Haven, Connecticut, 1932.

Other

Nelson, E. W. 'The Eskimo About Bering Strait' in *18th Annual Report of the Bureau of American Ethnology*, Washington D. C., 1899.

Rasmussen, K. 'Intellectual Culture of the Iglulik Eskimos' in *Report of the Fifth Thule Expedition 1921-24*, Vol. 7, Part 1, 1929.

Rasmussen, K. 'Observations on the Intellectual Culture of the Caribou Eskimos' in *Report of the Fifth Thule Expedition 1921-24*, Vol. 7, Part 2, 1930.

Rasmussen, K. 'The Netsilik Eskimos: Social Life and Spiritual Culture' in *Report of the Fifth Thule Expedition 1921-24*, Vol. 8, Parts 1-2, 1931.

Turner, L. M. 'Ethnology of the Ungava District, Hudson Bay Territory' in *11th Annual Report of the Bureau of American Ethnology*, Washington D. C., 1894.

THE NORTHEAST

Books

Axtell, J. (ed.) *The Indian Peoples of Eastern America*, New York, 1981.

Clark, E. A. *Indian Legends of Canada*, Toronto, 1960.

Conway, T. and Conway, J. *Spirits on Stone: The Agawa Pictographs*, San Luis Obispo, California, 1990.

Dewdney, S. and Kidd, K. E. *Indian Rock Paintings of the Great Lakes*, Toronto, 1962.

Fenton, N. (ed.) *Parker on the Iroquois*, New York, 1968.

Gooderham, K. (ed.) *I Am An Indian*, Toronto, 1969.

Hallowell, A. I. *The Ojibwa of Berens River, Manitoba*. Edited by Jennifer S. H. Brown. 1992.

Hamilton, C. *Cry of the Thunderbird: The American Indian's Own Story*, Norman, Oklahoma, 1972.

Helbig, A. (ed.) *Nanabozho: Giver of Life*, Brighton, Michigan, 1987.

Adolf Hungry Wolf and Beverley Hungry Wolf. *Children of the Sun: Stories By and About Indian Kids*, New York, 1987.

Johnson, Chief E. *Legends, Traditions, and Laws of the Iroquois or Six Nations and History of the Tuscarora Indians*, New York, 1881.

Johnston, B. *Ojibway Ceremonies*, Toronto, 1982.

Kah-ge-ga-gah-bowh. *(Chief George Copway) Traditional History and Characteristic Sketches of the Ojibway Nation*, Boston, 1851.

Landes, R. *Ojibwa Religion and the Midewiwin*, Madison, Milwaukee, 1968.

Morgan, L. H. *League of the Iroquois*, Secaucus, New Jersey, 1851.

Morriseau, N. *The Legends of my People The Great Ojibway*, Toronto, 1965.

Radin, P. *Some Myths and Tales of the Ojibwa of Southeastern Ontario*, Ottawa, 1914.

Radin, P. *The Trickster*, New York, 1956.

Radin, P. *The Winnebago Tribe*, Lincoln, Nebraska, 1923.

Ritzenthaler, R. E. and Ritzenthaler, P. *The Woodland Indians of the Western Great Lakes*, Milwaukee, 1970.

Robertson, M. *Rock Drawings of the Micmac Indians*, Halifax, Nova Scotia, 1973.

Skinner, A. *The Indians of Greater New York*, Cedar Rapids, Iowa, 1915.

Speck, F. G. *Delaware Indian Big House Ceremony*, Harrisburg, Pennsylvania, 1931.

Speck, F. G. *The Celestial Bear Comes Down to Earth*, Reading, Pennsylvania, 1945.

Speck, F. G. *The Iroquois: A Study in Cultural Evolution*, Michigan, 1945.

Speck, F. G. *Midwinter Rites of the Cayuga Longhouse*, Philadelphia, 1949.

Spindler, G. and Spindler, L. *Dreamers Without Power: The Menomini Indians*, New York, 1971.

Vastokas, J. M. 'The Shamanic Tree of Life' in *Stones, bones and skin: ritual and Shamanic Art* (Edited by Brodzky, A. T., Daneswich, R. and Johnson, N.), Toronto, 1973.

Vastokas, J. M. and Vastokas, R. *Sacred Art of the Algonkians: A Study of the Peterborough Petroglyphs*, Peterborough, Ontario, 1973.

Wallis, W. D. and Wallis R. S. *The Micmac Indians of Eastern Canada*, Minneapolis, 1955.

Vennum, T. Jr. *The Ojibwa Dance Drum*, Washington D. C., 1982.

Whitehead, R. H. 'I have Lived Here Since the World Began' in *The Spirits Sings* by Glenbow-Alberta Institute, Toronto, 1987.

Whitehead, R. H. *Stories from the Six Worlds: Micmac Legends*, Halifax, Nova Scotia, 1988.

Other

Axtell, J. 'Who Invented Scalping?' in *American Heritage*, No. 28 (3), New York, 1977.

Densmore, F. 'Chippewa Customs' in *Bureau of American Ethnology*, Bulletin 86, Washington D. C., 1929.

Fenton, W. N. 'Masked Medicine Societies of the Iroquois' in *Smithsonian Institution Annual Report*, Washington D. C., 1940.

Fenton, W. N. 'This Island, the World on the Turtle's Back' in *The Journal of American Folk-Lore*, No.75, Washington D. C., 1962.

Friederici, G. 'Scalping in America' in *Smithsonian Institution Annual Report*, Washington D. C., 1907.

Harrington, M. R. 'Religion and Ceremonies of the Lenape' in *Indian Notes and Monographs, Museum of the American Indian Heye Foundation 19*, New York, 1921.

Hewit, J. N. B. 'Iroquoian Cosmology' in *43rd Annual Report of the Bureau of American Ethnology, 1925-26*, Washington D. C., 1928.

Hoffman, W. J. 'The Midewiwin or "Grand Medicine Society" of the Ojibwa' in the *7th Annual Report of the Bureau of American Ethnology*, Washington D. C., 1891.

Morrison, A. H. 'Dawnland Dog-Feast: Wabanaki Warfare, c.1600-1760' in *Proceedings of the Twenty-first Algonquian Conference*. Edited by William A. Cowan. Ottawa, 1990.

Parsons, E. C. 'Micmac Folklore' in *The Journal of American Folk-Lore*, No. 38, Washington D. C., 1925.

Skinner, A. 'Medicine Ceremony of the Menomini, Iowa, and Wahpeton Dakota, With Notes on the Ceremony Among the Ponca, Bungi, Ojibwa, and Potawatomi' in *Indian Notes and Monographs, Museum of the American Indian Heye Foundation Vol. IV*, New York, 1920.

Vecsey, C. 'Midiwiwin Myths of Origin' in *Papers of the Fifteenth Algonquian Conference*. Edited by William A. Cowan. Ottawa, 1984.

REFERENCES

INTRODUCTION

1 Lowie, 1918:13
2 In central California – and this is of considerable interest in the light of recent disasters – several myths refer to the idea of a succession of world destructions by flood and fire (Kroeber, 1925:206).
3 Even within the cultural areas there is evidence of considerable variation in myth structure. Lowie found, for example, that the tendency toward abstract thought in mythology, which was so characteristic of the Sioux, was 'strangely lacking' in Crow mythology and there was an aversion to systemization (Lowie, 1918:7).
4 For this reason, thunder is heard in different parts of the sky at once – being the noise from each wing. Nootka basketry repeatedly shows Thunderbird and whale figures.

THE SOUTHEAST

1 Hudson, 1976:3
2 Hudson, 1976:4
3 This fatalistic theme bears a marked similarity to the attitude reflected in Norse and Germanic mythologies in which the world hangs in the limbs of a dying tree. Eventually, the tree will fall and the world will be destroyed.
4 Henri, 1986:11
5 Mooney, 1972:239-40
6 The number seven is undoubtedly the most significant in Cherokee culture. This significance is related directly to Cherokee cosmology and arises from the identification of seven directions: east, west, north, south, up, down, and here (where the speaker is standing).
7 Mooney, 1972:241
8 It is interesting that in Cherokee mythology, the creation of man and woman comes *after* the creation of animals. Consequently, the Middle Earth was a paradise inhabited by divinities until mankind appeared and despoiled it.
9 George Lankford, editor of *Southeastern Legends*, notes that there is considerable evidence that the mythology of some southeastern tribes was influenced by the 'emergence' tradition of the southwest. Specifically, these are myths that explain the origin of tribes by their having emerged from a hole in the Earth. Variations of this myth are common among the Creeks, but unknown to the Cherokees and Yuchi. Lankford, 1987:112
10 Adair, 1775:20
11 According to a popular (non-Indian) story, a gathering of little peoples was witnessed atop Chimney Rock in 1806 by a number of witnesses who later signed sworn statements. They were dressed in white and flew to and from the mountain crest in large numbers.
12 The remains of a large number of mounds are scattered throughout western North Carolina. Some historians note that in some instances the Cherokee's oral tradition claims that a number of mounds, such as the ancient one located on Governor's Island in Swain County, were not constructed by the Cherokees, but by another race of people.
13 Mooney, 1972:335-336
14 Larson, 1700:219-220
15 Matthiessen, 1986:126-127
16 The witch Spearfinger, like her male counterpart Stone Man, killed Cherokee children for their livers. Despite her magical powers, she was lured into a trap and killed by the Cherokees when a small bird revealed her 'vulnerable spot' to be her hand (where her heart was hidden).
17 Mooney, 1900:
18 Modern Cherokees are still aware of their clan. Many anthropologists feel that the clan concept was a sophisticated way of avoiding inbreeding. The seven clans are: *Ani-waya* (Wolf), *Ani-Kawi* (Deer), *Ani-Tsiskwa* (Bird), *Ani-Wadi* (Paint), *Ani-Shani* (Blue), *Ani-Gatigwi* (Potato), and *Ani-Gilahi* (Long Hair).
19 Speck and Broom, 1951:16
20 When Henry Timberlake witnessed the Black Drink Ceremony at Chota in 1761, he noted that a Cherokee woman, called the *Ghighau* or Blessed Woman, prepared the drink: 'She took out the wing of a swan, and after flourishing it over the pot, stood fixed for near a minute as she mumbled an ancient chant, then reached again into the deer-skin pouch. She withdrew branches of yapon shrub which she cast into the boiling water of the twenty-gallon pot.'
21 The belief system in the southeast often stressed the need to avoid the mixture of opposites. Fire was not meant to mingle with water, nor birds with snakes. Unnatural blendings produced impurity. The tradition of extinguishing fires at the year's end is based on the belief that the fire had become impure through association with mankind and must be born again anew.
22 Hudson, 1976:319.

THE SOUTHWEST

1 Yazzie, 1984.
2 The myths and tales of the Southwestern peoples have many points of similarity running through them, particularly the Western Apache and Navajo who have similar emergence stories, heroes, gods and goddesses. The number four is a broader example: it is the number of directions; the number of Hopi worlds and number of days they use to fast, to think about a problem, or to undergo purification; the number is invariably four whenever anything needs to be counted in a myth (days, events, objects, etc); it is the number of nights taken to tell the Papago origin myth; and so on.
3 Some people believe winter is the only time that it is safe to tell the stories; the time when they are safe from lightning and the snakes are asleep. Such time-of-the-year taboos are not unusual: the Jicarilla Apache, for instance, tell the emergence myth at any time of year, day or night, but stories about bears, snakes, or monsters can only be told during the nights of the winter months when the Dangerous Ones are high up in the mountains.
4 The origins of the Navajo sandpainting ceremonies are related in legend; the Hopi myths describe either how their ceremonies were given by the gods to the clans before they emerged from the underworld or how they were revealed to mythical heroes during the course of their adventures.
5 Opler, 1938:Preface xii
6 An example of 'modern influence' is the inclusion of whites in the myths; that having been said, it is thought that the Hopi myth of the good *bahana*, or white man predicted to come from the east, was pre-contact.
7 Courlander, 1982:14
8 *Kivas* are over 1,000 years old and central to the cultural and ceremonial life of the Southwestern pueblos. The *kiva* is a social gathering place for the men of the village – women are usually excluded – as well as a religious place for the transmission of secret ritual knowledge and practice.
9 To the Hopi the four worlds follow the pre-Earth spirit world of boundless space they call *Topkela*. The first three worlds were destroyed to punish human misbehavior. The Fourth World, or *Tuwagachi*, is the current world we live in. The Navajo recall their story of creation and its multiple worlds in the lengthy Blessing Way ceremonial.
10 The Navajo have seven sacred mountains. Their traditional land is bounded by four of them: Blanco Peak, or *Tsisnaajini*, to the east; Mount Taylor, or *Tsoodzil*, to the south; the San Francisco Peaks, or *Doko'oosliid*, to the west; and Hesperus Peak, or *Dibentsaa*, to the north. These mountains were made from earth brought from similar mountains in the Fourth World.
11 An authority on the North American Indian, Ruth Underhill was associated for 13 years with the United States Indian Service and was Professor Emeritus of Anthropology in the University of Denver.
12 Courlander, 1982:98-99
13 Bahti, 1988:16
14 Letter from Hopi elders to President Truman in 1949, quoted in Matthiessen, 1986:87
15 Navajo belief conceives the universe as being one in which good and evil are maintained in interrelated harmony. Mankind's problem, or duty, is to maintain that harmony, or *hozho*, and ceremonials help to achieve this.
16 Three mesas contain the Hopi villages. First Mesa has Walpi, Sichomovi, and Hano; Second Mesa has Shungopovi, Mishongnovi, and Shipauloi; and Third Mesa has Old Oraibi, New Oraibi, Hotevilla, and Bakabi, with the farming community of Moenkopi nearby.
17 Courlander, 1982: Introduction xxxiii
18 Eagle Walking Turtle, 1991:256.
19 The *hataali* conducts the ceremonial, having memorized the complicated rituals involving word perfect recitation of hundreds of songs. Due to the complexity, singers tend to specialize in just a few ceremonials.

THE PLAINS

1 Dodge, 1877
2 When white contact was first made with the Plains tribes in the 18th and 19th centuries, the region was largely dominated by Siouan and Algonquian linguistic groups, although the Uto-Aztecan and Athapaskan were also represented. On the northern Plains were such tribes as the Blackfeet, Cree, Gros Ventre, and Plains Ojibwa; the central Plains were dominated by the Sioux, Crow, Mandan, Hidatsa, and Arikara; while the southern Plains were occupied by the Comanche, Kiowa, Wichita, Pawnee, and Kiowa Apache. (For a fuller discussion see Sturtevant and Taylor, 1991:62-63.)
3 Linderman, 1930:310
4 These were an otter, duck, badger, and muskrat.
5 This site was referred to by recent Mandan informants as the 'center of the world'. (Paul Ewald interviewed by the author, July 1976.)
6 The ceremonies which were connected with the Bundles evoked two basic ideas – offering or sacrifice.
7 Dooling, 1992:3
8 Patterns worked within the quill or beadwork on these garments were often representations of the Morning Star. Such patterns also occur on the regalia of the linguistically related Cheyenne who, in their ancient *Massaum* Ceremony, used the Morning Star symbol. See, Grinnell, 1923, Vol. II:305; Petersen, 1988:140.
9 The *Tobtob Kin*, four times four, unified the spirit powers as well as the physical aspects of the Sioux cosmos, assigning a definite power quantum and function to a matrix of beings. It embraced all the benevolent gods, each of four classes and four in each class, as one whole.
10 For example, on regalia that was said to have belonged to Crazy Horse, and is now in the Museum of the American Indian and The Smithsonian Institution, are emblems of the Thunderbird, dragonfly and forked lightning that refer to thunder powers – the ability to strike and kill, invulnerability, and direct communication with high powers.
11 'They sang this song above, they have spoken.
They have put new life into the earth.
Paruxti speaks through the clouds.
And the power has entered Mother Earth.
The earth has received the powers from above.'
(First song of the Pawnee Thunder Ceremony – Linton, 1922:10.)
12 Walker, 1917:147
13 Images of Tree Dwellers were made by the Sioux. These were generally man-like figures perhaps no more than 8in (20cm) high. They were placed within a cylindrical tube made of cottonwood which had been split lengthwise so that the contents could be removed easily.
14 Other Star Myths, such as those of the Seven and Bunched Stars, underline the acute observations that the Blackfeet made of the heavens and refer to the North Star, Great Dipper, Ursa Major,

and the Pleiades.

15 Turner, 1977:256

16 The Medicine Wheel is now a National Historic Landmark. It is nearly 10,000ft (3,000m) above sea level. The majority of the stones are limestone and its estimated age is between AD 1200 and AD 1700.

17 Chief Joseph of the Nez Perce was said to have fasted at the Medicine Wheel after his gallant but abortive retreat to Canada in 1877. Chief *Washakie*, a Shoshone, gained his power there to help him guide his people through the torment of reservation life, and an early chief of the Crows, Red Plume, was said to have received eagle feathers and medicine at the Wheel to protect his people from harm.

18 Guthrie, 1947:284

19 Joe Medicine Crow referred to the vision site as *Ala-xabna* or 'where to lay down'. (Joe Medicine Crow interviewed by the author, July 1993.)

20 I am indebted to the late Paul Ewald of New Town, North Dakota, who, following an introduction by the Tribal Headquarters of the Three Affiliated Tribes (Mandan, Hidatsa, and Arikara), took me to the various places sacred to the Mandan in the historic period.

21 Grinnell, 1920:137

22 Plains Indians observed that deer could endure thirst for a long time, the hawk was the surest bird of prey, the elk gallant and brave, the frog watchful, the owl had much night wisdom and gentle ways, the bear fierce and the possessor of many herbs for the good of man, the kit fox active and wily, the crow direct and swift in flight, and the wolf hardy.

23 Sioux flageolets, having five holes, were often carved with the head of a bird or elk while Blackfeet and Ojibwa instruments were generally less elaborate having four and six holes respectively.

24 Fletcher and La Flesche, 1911:147

25 This hide was stolen in 1898 from the elderly keeper, Walking Sacred One (Fletcher and La Flesche, 1911:284). In 1991 it was finally returned back to the tribes (see *Wall Street Journal* August 27, 1991).

26 Special buffalo-calling backrests appear to have been used by these Cree men (Brasser, 1984:56-63).

27 Lakota dream song.

28 It was generally agreed that the more hazardous the quest site and the more that the person fasting was made to suffer by the spirits or by the elements, the more likely he or she 'is to have pity taken on him by the supernatural powers and the greater will be the power that he receives' (Conner, 1982:86).

29 Joe Medicine Crow said that the Crow vision quest site was referred to as *Bi-li-shi-sna*, meaning 'water they do not drink' (Joe Medicine Crow interviewed by the author, July 11, 1993).

30 Catlin, 1841:Vol.I:157

31 Neihardt, 1932:276

PLATEAU AND BASIN

1 McLuhan, 1973:

2 The Eastern and Northern Shoshoni, Ute, Bannock, and Northern Paiute all practiced the Sun Dance ritual but the essential Plains element of self-mortification was rare.

3 The Ghost Dance was a revitalization movement in the 1870-90 period which was influenced by the slightly earlier Dreamer Religion originated by *Smohalla*, chief of the Sahaptin-speaking Wanapum people related to the Nez Perce. *Smohalla* preached that white people's ways were eroding indigenous ones and violating nature, that the people would be led by the dead returned and that whites would go to a different place as a result. The Ghost Dance began in 1869 among the Paiute of Walker Lake, Nevada, who traditionally held an annual Mourning Cry for the dead; it recurred in its largest manifestation during the late 1880s under the influence of the Paiute prophet *Wovoka* or *Kwohitsauq* (Big Rumbling Belly). It culminated in the Wounded Knee massacre of 1890.

4 McLuhan, 1973:10

5 Venderweth, 1971:126

6 In one sense, Peyotism is akin to the Ghost Dance in providing a Pan Native American identity-strengthening movement in the face of the overwhelming white culture.

7 Clark, 1988:23

8 Lopez, 1977:3

9 Gidley, 1981:32

10 Lopez, 1977:2

11 Curtis (1911) quoted in Gidley, 1981:24

12 Among the Nez Perce those who in their youth had visions featuring the Sun, Moon, fish-hawks or pelicans would become a shaman; only these spirits gave the power to cure. Among the Thompson water had this power; elsewhere it varied widely, including night, mist, blue sky, thunder, eagles, crows, wolves, bats, and objects connected with the dead.

CALIFORNIA

1 Densmore, 1958:20

2 Author interview with Henry Azbill in 1969.

3 This story is a compilation from several versions told by Maidu elder Henry Azbill to the author between 1968 and 1973.

4 Author communication with an anonymous Southern Miwok elder in 1973.

5 Author communication with Chief Richard Fuller in 1971.

6 This version of the *Uwulin* story is from LaPena et al, 1993:1-2. This, in turn, was based on a version in Barrett, 1919:2. The word *Uwulin* signifies 'eater'.

7 Latta, 1936:15

8 Author communication with Henry Azbill in 1969.

9 LaPena and Driesbach, 1985:60

THE NORTHWEST COAST

1 A speech delivered by Chief Seattle, or Sealth, at the presentation of treaty proposals in 1845. The Suquamish Museum, 1985:36.

2 Spiritual thought in the region might be viewed as a quest to understand 'power' – the power that drives the universe and human existence within it. In the stories, songs, and rituals there are continual references to the order and chaos of power, the acquisition and loss of power, the taming or control of power, and the alignment of protective or guardian power with human lives. Thus their lives were predicated on the natural cycles of physical and spiritual existence, and in Northwest Coast thought, reincarnation and transformation were the means by which human, natural, and supernatural beings spiraled through cycles of life, death, and renewal.

3 Words borrowed from Northwest Coast languages, such as Naikun, are often spelled differently by different commentators. Here they appear as they did in the text of the authors quoted.

4 Holm and Reid, 1975: Prologue.

5 Boas, 1891:14 and 1898:29-30; Kennedy and Bouchard, 1977:4.

6 de Laguna, 1972:816; Swanton, 1905 (b):108-110 and 1970:454.

7 Kennedy and Bouchard, 1977:4.

8 Swanton, 1905 (a):74.

9 Boas, 1966:42.

10 The Book Builders of 'KSAN, 1977:7.

11 Boas, 1970:584

12 Barnett, 1955:296

13 Swanton, 1970:454

14 Stewart, 1979:65

15 Boas, 1925:269

16 The central roof beam of a Kwakiutl house, for example, was said to represent the Milky Way.

17 The *Gonaquadet* appears to some people as a huge copper house, to others as a great painted house front rising out of the ocean swells, a great bear with sea-lion fins, a giant sea-wolf who carries whales in his curly tail and between his enormous ears, or as a monster several miles in length with many children running along his back. Swanton, 1908:460 and 612-623; Waterman, 1923:450; Sheehan McLaren, 1977:197-229.

18 The potlatch is the major ceremonial on the coast and at it the chief follows *Gonaquadet's* example and distributes his wealth to all who attend.

19 *Sisiutl's* image is prolific in art, song and legend. It may be found not only in Earthly realms but in the sky world and the under world. In one region of the cosmos a *Sisiutl* mask is worn by the Sun; in the opposite, farthest region a *Sisiutl* design is found on a settee in the house of ghosts. Boas, 1935 (b):147-148.

20 The Suquamish Museum, 1985:36.

21 For the Tlingit, placing tobacco, iron, or lead into the mouth counteracted the spirit's influences.

22 Copper Woman and Woman-at-the-Head-of-the-Rivers among the Haida parallel the wealth-giving aspects of *Tsonoqua*, while Frog Woman and Volcano Woman among the Tsimshian share her attributes of great and vengeful power.

23 Curtis, 1916:11:23

24 Swanton, 1905 (a):13

25 Boas, 1935 (b):156

26 Boas, 1930:193

27 Boas, 1895:460

28 Boas, 1966:155

THE SUBARCTIC

1 Nelson, 1983:26

2 Nelson, 1983:18

3 Cooper, 1933:48

4 Jarvpena, 1982:70

5 Jarvpena, 1982:71

6 Nelson, 1983:241

7 Nelson, 1983:23

8 Rossignol, 1938:26-28

THE ARCTIC

1 Rasmussen, 1929:5

2 Rasmussen, 1931:209

3 Rasmussen, 1929:257

4 Rasmussen, 1931:226

5 Rasmussen, 1931:365

6 Rasmussen, 1931:376

7 Rasmussen, 1931:239

8 Rasmussen, 1931:243

9 Rasmussen, 1929:56

10 Rasmussen, 1929:56

11 Rasmussen, 1931:240

THE NORTHEAST

1 Hamilton, 1972:159

2 Hamilton, 1972:32

3 George Copway:147-149

4 The Moon, as the celestial Nocturnal Orb of Light, complements the Sun's diurnal role. As Our Grandmother among the Iroquois and Winnebago, the Moon has various names relating to specific phases and functions. While the Sun oversaw daily life it was the Moon, with her mysterious powers, who regulated the calendric cycle with its attendant ceremonials and seasonality. Strongly associated with women's reproductive powers, the Moon's powers also provided the men with luck in hunting – this last blessing an extrapolation of the notion of reproduction, with the animals' fertility providing an abundance. The Menominee explanation for the Moon's monthly disappearance is based upon the Moon's search for her brother, the Sun, who has gone forth to hunt. For 20 days she follows his trail without success and then dies. Four days pass when nothing is seen of her. At the end of this time, she is given new life to renew her quest once again.

5 Vennum, 1982:107

6 In one legendary version it is only the kind intervention of the West Wind that finally freed the Iroquois by sending these giants to a watery death.

7 Conway and Conway, 1990:43

8 Conway and Conway, 1990:34-35

9 Gooderham, 1969:196

10 Although the actual origins are shrouded with uncertainty, the Drum Dance was given to a woman by the Great Spirit. According to legend, she hid from the white soldiers for several days. In a vision the Great Spirit instructed her to make a large dance drum and taught her the songs and rituals for the ceremony. An organization of members belonged to each drum and the major portion of the ceremony consisted of singing and dancing to the beat of this instrument of peace.

INDEX

Page numbers in **bold** indicate illustrations.

PICTURE CREDITS

The publishers would like to thank the numerous museums, art sources, and individuals in the United States, Canada, and the United Kingdom for their help in the preparation of this book and for granting permission to publish their images. The sources are listed below by page, spelt out in full for their first mention and abbreviated thereafter; artist's names are given where appropriate. Every effort has been made to trace the copyright holders, where known.

Front Endpaper: Jim Winkley; **Page 1:** Seattle Art Museum, ref 85.360, photo Paul Macapia; **2:** Transferring the Medicine Shield by Howard Terpning © 1991, The Greenwich Workshop, Inc.; **5:** Raven Stealing the Moon by Robert Davidson, ref 25/1150, National Museum of the American Indian (NMAI), New York; **6:** Stark Museum of Art (SMA), Orangeville, Texas, ref 82.900/290; **7:** Apache Crown Dance by Allan Houser, Denver Art Museum (DAM), ref 1953.420; **8:** When Omens Turn Bad by Frank McCarthy © 1987, The Greenwich Workshop, Inc.; Edward S. Curtis, Plate 330; **9:** San Diego Museum of Man (SDMM), ref Edward S. Curtis, Plate 330; **10:** Werner Forman Archive (WFA), London, ref 501/ESO354A; **12:** border – Salamander Books Ltd/American Museum of Natural History (AMNH), New York, ref 5821; print – National Anthropological Archives (NAA), Washington D.C., ref 45836-D; **13:** Salamander Books Ltd/Smithsonian Institution (SI), Dept of Anthropology, Washington D.C., ref 133005/133006; **14/15:** Frank H. McClung Museum (FHMM), University of Tennessee, Knoxville; **16:** Peabody Museum of Man, Harvard University (PMHU), Massachusetts, ref T 169; **17/18:** FHMM, Knoxville; **19:** NMAI, ref 2183; **20/21:** North Carolina Travel and Tourism; **22:** (left) Salamander Books Ltd/SI, ref 272972; (right) FHMM, Knoxville; **23:** FHMM, Knoxville; **24:** The Etowah Elite by H. Tom Hall/National Geographic Society (NGS); **25:** NAA, ref 1044-A; **26:** border – Salamander Books Ltd/SI, ref 167429; print – Library of Congress, Washington D.C., ref 262-52476; **27:** Museum of Northern Arizona (MNA), Flagstaff, ref 93C.5a, photo Gene Balzer; **28:** (left) MNA, Flagstaff, ref 93C.4, photo Gene Balzer; (right) MNA, Flagstaff, ref 93C.3, photo Gene Balzer; **29:** (top) The Wheelright Museum (TWM), Santa Fe, ref P1A no 8; (bottom) TWM, Santa Fe, ref P1A no 21; **30:** MNA, Flagstaff, ref 92C.38, photo Gene Balzer; **31:** TWM, Santa Fe, ref P4-4A; **32:** (left) Oklahoma Historical Society, ref 3893; (right) Photo Archives, Denver Museum of Natural History (DMNH), ref 8087 A.B.C.; **33:** (top) TWM, Santa Fe, ref P11-8; (bottom) NAA, ref 1824-

C; **34:** NAA, ref 2267-E; **35:** (top) WFA, London, ref 502/IGO205; (bottom) Jim Winkley; **36:** Mud Owl's Warning by Tom Lovell © 1976, The Greenwich Workshop, Inc.; **37:** (top) Line of Dancers by Awa Tsireh, NMAI, ref 22/8609; (bottom) NAA, ref 2382; **38:** (top) PMHU, Massachusetts, ref T98; (bottom) Milwaukee Public Museum (MPM), ref SWM-1-G-576; **39:** (top) Waldo Mootzka, MNA, Flagstaff, ref C497, photo Owen Lowe; (bottom) PMHU, Massachusetts, ref T98; **40:** border – Salamander Books Ltd/Buffalo Bill Historical Center (BBHC), Cody, Wyoming; print – NAA, ref 233A; **41:** DAM, ref 1959.143; **42:** Collection of Glenbow (CG), Calgary, Alberta, ref AX 70; **43:** (top) NAA, ref 3434-E-4; (bottom) Field Museum of Natural History, Chicago, ref 16231c; **44:** Cheyenne Sun Dance by Richard West, The Philbrook Museum of Art (PMA), Tulsa, Oklahoma, ref 49.20; **45:** Missouri Historical Society, ref 1882.18.46; **46:** (top) Salamander Books Ltd/BBHC; (bottom) Colin Taylor; **47:** Spirit of the Buffalo by Joseph H. Sharp, The Rockwell Museum, Corning, New York, ref 78.63F; **48:** NAA, ref 76-4331; **49:** Jim Winkley; **50:** (top) NAA, ref 1355; (bottom) The Ethnology Program, Provincial Museum of Alberta, Edmonton (EPPMA), ref H65.84.1A; **51:** (left) Richard W. Edwards, Jr/Weyer International, Toledo, Ohio; (right) PMA, Tulsa, ref MI 2681; **52:** Colin Taylor; **53:** The Vision Seeker by Tom Lovell © 1991, Tom Lovell; **54:** border – Salamander Books Ltd/SI; print – Pitt Rivers Museum, Oxford, ref B55 2AA; **55:** Salamander Books Ltd/AMNH, ref 8648; **56:** (left) SMA, Orangeville, ref 82.900/302; (right) University of Exeter Library; **57:** Nevada Commission on Tourism; **58:** Colin Taylor; **59:** (left) NAA, ref 56802; (right) Christie's Images, London, ref KSETH 230692124; **60:** SMA, Orangeville, ref 82.900/193; **61:** Colorado Historical Society (CHS), ref F-8663; **62:** Jim Winkley; **63:** (top) NAA, ref 2987-B-4; (bottom) Oregon Dept of Agriculture, ref HH 79; **64:** Jeff Burn, © Salamander Books Ltd; **65:** NAA, ref 56805; **66:** Hope Springs Eternal – Ghost Dance by Howard Terpning © 1988, The Greenwich Workshop, Inc.; **67:** NAA, ref 2903A; **68:** border – Salamander Books Ltd/SI, ref 19287; print – The Southwest Museum (TSM), Los Angeles, ref N.41008; **69:** DAM, ref 1938.160; **70:** SMA, Orangeville, ref 62.1/1; **71:** (left) TSM, Los Angeles, ref P.21601; (right) NAA, ref 56025; **72:** NAA, ref 76-15807; **72/73:** PMHU, Massachusetts, ref T117; **73:** Craig Bates; **74:** SDMM, ref 10136; **75:** (top) Santa Barbara Museum of Natural History (SBMNH)/Tom Haci; (bottom) PMHU,

Massachusetts, ref T120; **76:** SBMNH; **77:** (top) Jim Winkley; (bottom) Art Directors Photo Library (ADPL), ref WLLL10/21; **78:** (top) SBMNH/Jan Hamber; (bottom, left) TSM, Los Angeles, ref N.19364; (bottom, right) TSM, Los Angeles, ref N.37164; **79:** PMHU, Massachusetts, ref T118; **80:** PMHU, Massachusetts, ref T1220; **81:** (left) NAA, ref 28002-C; (right) DAM, ref 1940.50; **82:** border – Salamander Books Ltd/SI, ref 168292; print – NAA, ref 73-6821; **83:** Salamander Books Ltd/AMNH, ref 8944; **84:** University of British Columbia Museum of Anthropology, Vancouver, photo Bill McLennan; **85:** Thomas Burke Memorial Washington State Museum (TBMWSM), Seattle, ref 117a, photo Eduardo Calderon; **86:** The Seattle Art Museum (TSAM), Gift of John H. Hauberg, ref 91.1.124, photo Paul Macapia; **87:** Thunderbird Lightning Snake and Moon by Tim Paul, DMNH, ref 1545/37; **88:** (left) TSAM, Gift of John H. Hauberg, ref 91.1.82, photo Paul Macapia; (right) TBMWSM, Seattle, ref 1-1451, photo Eduardo Calderon; **89:** Sea *Sisiutl* and Copper by Mark Henderson, DMNH, ref 1545/43; **90:** (left) TSAM, Gift of John H. Hauberg, ref 91.1.30, photo Paul Macapia; MPM, ref 81556B; **91:** Jim Winkley; **92:** (top) TBMWSM, Seattle, ref 2.5E604, photo Eduardo Calderon; (centre) MPM, ref 80937B; (bottom) TBMWSM, Seattle, ref 2452, photo Eduardo Calderon; **93:** (top) CG, Calgary, Alberta, ref R180.219; (bottom) NAA, ref 4117; **94:** TSAM, Gift of John H Hauberg, ref 85.354, photo Paul Macapia; **95:** DAM, ref 1948.229; Edward S. Curtis, Plate 358; **96:** border – Salamander Books Ltd/SI, ref 64279; print – NAA, ref 75-5337; **97:** Salamander Books Ltd/AMNH, ref 7039; Alaska Division of Tourism (ADT); **99:** The Great and Mischievous *Nanabush* by Blake Debassige, McMichael Canadian Art Collection (MCAC), Kleinberg, Ontario, ref 1975.13.2; **100:** (top) Salamander Books Ltd/AMNH, ref 5113; (bottom) Salamander Books Ltd/AMNH, ref 5113; **101:** Salamander Books Ltd/AMNH, ref 5095; **102:** Salamander Books Ltd/AMNH, ref 5118; **103:** (top) Salamander Books Ltd/AMNH, ref 5092A; (bottom) Salamander Books Ltd/AMNH, ref 5091; **104/105:** Art Directors Photo Library; **106:** Salamander Books Ltd/AMNH, ref 5088; **107:** (top – all Salamander Books Ltd/AMNH), refs from top to bottom 7027, 7029, and 7020; (bottom) EPPMA, Edmonton, ref H89.220.233; **108:** (top) Salamander Books Ltd/AMNH; (center) EPPMA, Edmonton, ref H68.159.418; (bottom) EPPMA, Edmonton, ref H76.3.8; **109:** Salamander Books Ltd/AMNH, ref 6996; **110:**

border – Salamander Books Ltd/SI, ref 5772; print – NAA, ref 3862; **111:** Salamander Books Ltd/SI, ref 38717; **112:** Peabody & Essex Museum, Salem, ref E10,529, photo Mark Sexton; **113:** NAA, ref 44,826-B; **114:** Phoebe A. Hearst Museum of Anthropology, The University of California at Berkeley, ref 2-1303; **115:** Shaman Summoning *Sedna* by Abraham Anghik, MCAC, Kleinberg, ref 1984.35; **116:** The University Museum, University of Pennsylvania (TUMUP), Philadelphia, ref T4-34c3; **117:** Legend of the Eagle Who Took the Small Girl to be His Wife by Davidialuk, DMNH, ref 1545/7; **118/119:** Art Directors Photo Library; **120:** TUMUP, Philadelphia, ref T4-367c2; **121:** (left) Glasgow Museums, ref 02-8d; (right) TUMUP, Philadelphia, ref T4-368c3; **122:** A Shaman's Helping Spirits by Jessie Oonark, MCAC, Kleinberg, ref 1984.15.4; **123:** (left) DMNH, ref BA21-090; (right) Royal Scottish Museums, no ref; **124:** border – Salamander Books Ltd/SI, ref 7465; print – NAA, ref 244-3; **125:** Cranbrook Institute of Science (CIS), Bloomfield Hills, Michigan, ref 1131; **126:** Schoharie Museum of the Iroquois Indian (SMII), Howes Cave, New York, ref 4674.0; **127:** Legend of *Atotaroh* by Jack Unruh/National Geographic Society; **128:** Creations Battle by John Fadden, SMII, Howes Cave, ref 2.16; **129:** SMII, Howes Cave, ref 4075.6; **130:** A Man's Vision of the False Face Society by Ernest Smith, NMAI, ref 24/8847; **131:** MPM, ref 24214; **132:** Candace Oberholtzer; **133:** (top) Michigan Travel Bureau, ref 268; (bottom) Minnesota Historical Society (MHS), St Paul, ref E97.37 r48; **134:** (top) Salamander Books Ltd/AMNH, ref 6253; (bottom) MHS, St Paul, ref E97.37 p20; **135:** (top) CIS, Bloomfield Hills, ref 3691; (bottom) MPM, ref 3241; **136:** (left) Salamander Books Ltd/AMNH, ref 5553; (right) MHS, St Paul, ref E97.37 p7; **137:** MHS, St Paul, ref E97.37 r80; **Back Endpaper:** Jim Winkley.

All artwork produced by Howard Terpning, Frank McCarthy, and Tom Lovell has been reproduced with permission by The Greenwich Workshop, Inc. For information on limited edition fine art prints please contact The Greenwich Workshop, Inc. 30 Lindeman Drive, Trumbull, CT 06611, USA.

Editor's note
The selection and captioning of all illustrations in this book have been the responsibility of Salamander Books Ltd and not of the individual contributors.